HELENA
AN ILLUSTRATED HISTORY

VIVIAN PALADIN AND JEAN BAUCUS

HELENA

AN ILLUSTRATED HISTORY

Preceding Page:

Mount Helena, sentinel of an historic gulch

Mount Helena, with a mountain park atop, presides over the town, which has the feeling of a village in the gulch, at the foot of its distinctive profile. Several trails lead to the top of Mount Helena which today has no trace of the shelter constructed by industrious residents of the turn of the century. One of the trails winds past the smoky cave on the right shoulder of the mountain. This cave has been a picnic spot for generations, and the source for spooky stories told by youngsters around many a campfire. Historians say the cave was the hideout of two men who were being stalked by Indians in the 1860s. Photograph by Len Eckel

Cover design by Finstad Visual Design, Helena, Montana

Printed by Walsworth Publishing Company, Marceline, Missouri

Montana Historical Society Press, P.O. Box 201201, Helena, 59620-1201

Printed in the United States of America

97 98 99 00 01 02 03 04 9 8 7 6 5 4 3

Library of Congress Cataloging-in-Publication Data

Paladin, Vivian A.
Helena : an illustrated history / Vivian Paladin and Jean Baucus.
p. cm.
Originally published: Helena, Mont. : Bar-Wineglass Pub. Co., 1983
Includes bibliographical references and index.
ISBN 0-917298-40-3 (alk. paper)
1. Helena (Mont.) —History. 2. Helena (Mont.) —Pictorial works.
I. Baucus, Jean. II. Title.
F739.H4P34 1996
978.6'615—dc20 96-5202
CIP

Contents

FOREWORD 6
PREFACES 7
INTRODUCTION 10
CHAPTER ONE
Discovery and the First Decade 14
CHAPTER TWO
The 1870s: Isolation and Fire 26
CHAPTER THREE
The Surrounding Treasure 36
CHAPTER FOUR
The Stage Gives Way to the Iron Horse 44
CHAPTER FIVE
The Pace Setters 54
CHAPTER SIX
Statehood and the 1890s 78
CHAPTER SEVEN
Dawn of a New Century and
a Capitol for Montana 116
CHAPTER EIGHT
The Decade of World War I 136
CHAPTER NINE
The Decade of Boom and Bust 150
CHAPTER TEN
The Depression Years 160
CHAPTER ELEVEN
The 1940s and World War II 172
CHAPTER TWELVE
The 1950s: Returning Veterans and
a Decaying Inner City 186
CHAPTER THIRTEEN
The Recent Decades:
A Time for Celebration and Renewal 204
BIBLIOGRAPHICAL ESSAY 235
INDEX 236

Foreword

I am proud to have been asked to write a few words about this pictorial history of the town of Helena, Montana. Proud not only because it was written by my mother, Jean Baucus, and her good friend, Vivian Paladin, who for many years was editor of *Montana, The Magazine of Western History*, but proud also because it is a history of my hometown. I grew up in Helena. It was my home until I left for college. My friends were here, my family, my childhood memories.

Helena is a rich town—rich in spirit, civic pride, and neighborliness. I suppose the same could be said for most towns in America, but Helena is truly different. It is a lovely Alpine town, perched on the eastern slopes of the Rocky Mountains. At night, the lights in the Helena Valley sparkle like a mirror of the Milky Way. And Helena is rich in history. Its nineteenth-century buildings stand out as exceptional examples of Victorian architecture. Indeed, Helena was a truly "rich" town in the most literal sense of the word in the 1880s and 1890s. When silver prices were high and gold was still being mined in impressive quantities, my hometown was reputed to have more millionaires per capita than any other city in America. But it is not I who should give you Helena's history. Let this book do it for you.

The words Thomas Jefferson once wrote in a letter to John Adams that "a morsel of genuine history is a thing so rare as to always be valuable" certainly apply to Vivian's chapter openings. The pictures in this book will whet the appetite for anyone interested in history. As recordings of history, they teach us about our past. Photographs of early Helena personalities, places, and events explain and give us a better sense of our heritage. They also bring us closer to Helena. They are photographs of our relatives, of people we have read about and heard about. And, of course, they are photographs of all that is unique to Helena—its mining camps, its large Victorian homes at the base of the mountain named after the town.

The history of Helena is something which has long been needed. I believe that this photographic history of Helena is only a beginning to the recording of the fascinating history of the capital city of Montana. I hope this popular history will encourage the young and old to dig deeper into the history of my hometown and other towns throughout Montana.■

Max Baucus

UNITED STATES SENATE
Washington, D.C.

1996 Preface

In the early 1980s, the Donning Company, a publishing firm specializing in community history books, began looking to the American West for fresh and interesting subjects. Attracted to Montana's capital city after hearing about its colorful gold camp history, the Donning Company sent a representative to Helena to seek out sources of information and find someone to write Helena's history.

One of the people they contacted at once was Jean Baucus, who had published two monographs on Helena's historic homes, as well as *Gold in the Gulch*, a history of Helena's inner city with emphasis on its early mining history. Interested in the project, Jean visited the Donning Company's offices in Norfolk, Virginia, and was impressed with the quality and professionalism of books they had published.

On her return to Helena, Jean talked to me about a collaborative effort in gathering pictures and research material together to produce the large format, illustrated book envisioned by the publishers. We had worked together with mutual enjoyment and respect on other publishing projects, but we realized this was a formidable undertaking indeed. I had recently retired after two decades in the publications division of the Montana Historical Society, and both Jean and I felt we had all the personal and community commitments we could handle.

Meanwhile, the Donning Company arranged for the sponsorship of the Helena Community Chamber of Commerce in producing and distributing the book. After consulting with Mike Weggenman, then Director of the Chamber, Jean and I decided, with some trepidation, to take on the project.

As before, when we began working together, we warmed to the task. Jean spent months gathering pictures, many from her own collection and those of her family and friends. A good number of them had never been published. Combined with photographs from the Montana Historical Society, we soon had a visual treasure with which to work. As Jean continued her photographic research, I concentrated on writing and historical research.

As with all publications, the first task was one of organization. We decided upon a chronological approach, with a chapter devoted to each decade from the gold discoveries in 1864 through the period of Urban Renewal in the 1970s. In addition, chapters emerged that told the story of mining in the surrounding area and the lives and times of the "pace setters," our term for the visionary men and entrepreneurs who were attracted early to

Last Chance Gulch and generally stayed here to insure, not only the permanence of this former gold camp, but its steady growth to become "the Queen City of the Rockies" and eventually the capital of both Montana Territory, in 1875, and the State of Montana, in 1889.

Essays that head up each chapter sought to describe what was happening in Helena and the rest of the Territory and State, and even offered glimpses of national and international events. But by all odds the greatest task, one Jean and I faced with resolution but with the certain knowledge we could not possibly get everything correct or complete, was the writing of picture captions. These lengthy captions, juxtaposed with the hundreds of pictures contained in these pages, constitute a history in themselves.

When it appeared in hardcover in 1983, the book was generally well received, but after two years, it was apparent that a broader readership justified a republication in a less expensive paperback form, using the same format and contents. Jean and I undertook that project in spite of some misgivings on the part of our spouses, and the high gloss maroon paperback, featuring Helena's famed firetower, emerged in the summer of 1985. While neither of us suffered writer's cramp from too much autograph signing, the book remained a steady seller until, in 1995, there were no more, even in our own personal inventories.

Late in 1995, our friends and colleagues at the Montana Historical Society Press suggested a third printing, this time under their publishing imprint. This was especially gratifying to me, for it was possible once again to go to this wonderful place, bounce ideas off the wall with Editor Chuck Rankin and Press Editor Martha Kohl, and get excited once more about making this book available to a still broader audience.

Obviously, a great many things have happened in Helena since we began working on this history. Indeed, the unprecedented growth of the American West in the 1990s has now affected Helena to the point where city and county planners struggle to cope with subdivisions, the most sought-after being on high terrain, amid inadequate streets and infrastructures which still suggest the town's haphazard beginnings.

It is never possible, of course, to write any history and keep it current and free of obsolescence. Fortunately, this book ends at a strategic time, the demolition and Urban Renewal period of the 1970s. It was a time that still inspires nostalgic regret on the part of many, for it changed forever the face of this wonderfully historic town. But the regrets of many more have been replaced by the certainty that the changes were essential to halt an inexorable inner-city decay.

Until there is time for younger heads and hands to take up the task, then, the Historical Society and the authors believe this illustrated history will find a place in the library of anyone, anywhere, who has reason to agree that Montana has, indeed, a wonderfully historic capital city and that in learning more about her beginnings, we learn more about our own beginnings, wherever they may have been. ■

VIVIAN PALADIN
Helena, Montana
January 1996

Preface

The enormity of the task of picturing the history of Helena was continually mitigated by the interest and enthusiasm of old and new friends. Their help not only made completion of the book possible, but added a heartwarming dimension as eager residents searched for pictures or helped identify people in others. There was excitement and a mutually shared pride in what can only be described as Montana's most unique and colorful city.

Over two-thirds of the photographs used in this book were generously shared by private collectors, and that includes both individuals and agencies. Among the individuals were Joan and Jeff Holter, Jane and Tom Tobin, Mrs. A. T. Hibbard, Barbara Kirkland, Clem and Nadine Shafer, Esther Robinson, John and Helen Willard, Blanche Judge, Norman Howard, Eddie Barbeau, John Marshall, Joe Reber, Mrs. George Huber, Lee Sweeney, and Nelson Seeley.

Public agencies and institutions which were generous of both time and photos included Carroll College, Helena Catholic Diocese, Blue Shield, Montana Club, Bureau of Reclamation, Bray Foundation, Helena Chamber of Commerce, Helena Water Department, Montana Power, Helena Symphony Society, Second Store Cinema, Morrison Flying Service, *Helena Independent-Record,* Title Trust and Insurance Company, Helena Valley Irrigation District, and Helena High School.

Because the book is as much about people as we could make it, we relied on countless memories to help us identify individuals in group pictures. The fact that we have been as successful as we have in this regard is due to the efforts of such friends as Kay Satre, Peter and Harriett Meloy, Connie Flaherty, Avis Ann and Betty Tobin, Kay Wandler, Arnie Malina, Leah Brickett, Barbara O'Connor, Clem and Nadine Shafer, and Bill Bausch.

Photographer Mark McBride of Third Eye Gallery, who has a special reverence for history, shared his own collection of photographs and carefully processed countless rolls of film and enlarged several hundred photographs from other collections.

For more recent Helena pictures, we are grateful to Gene Fischer, Gordon Warren, George Lane, and Dave Shore of the *Independent-Record,* and to such contemporary Helena photographers and collectors as Clarence DeWalt, John Wheeler, Garry Wunderwald, Len Eckel, Barbara Welter, Mark Meloy, Ellen Detzler, Bill Schneider, John Marcinek, and Don Smith. Great Falls photographer Denny McCall made up prints of his fine pre-urban renewal photographs and allowed their use as contrasts between the very old and the very new.

About one-third of the photographs used are from the holdings of the Montana Historical Society. They were professionally copied by John Stuart of the Photographic Archives, and we relied heavily on the expert and graciously given help of the society's research staff, notably David Walters, Bob Clark, and David Girshick.

With the usual nod of appreciation to our patient and sometimes neglected spouses, we extend thanks, in a broad sense, to all who gave encouragement and expressed the belief that our efforts were worthy and the final goal attainable.■

Vivian Paladin
Jean Baucus

Introduction

Montana is the fourth largest state in the Union, its more than 93 million acres of greatly varying terrain stretching 550 miles across plains and foothills on the east, to and through the rugged spine of the Rocky Mountains in the western third, which formed a historic barrier to those who sought passage to the Northwest and Pacific Ocean. The great waterway, the Missouri, was the highway for exploration and penetration by early fur traders and the redoubtable Lewis and Clark, whose expedition in 1805 and 1806 spent more time and covered more mileage exploring in what is now Montana than in any other state.

The first white people who came here were either on their way elsewhere or they stayed only long enough to extract the natural wealth they encountered in woodlands and streams. The bonanza they first sought was in furs, not in the mineral wealth whose abundance was to lead to settlement, permanence, and, in 1889, to admittance of Montana—the Treasure State—to the Union.

The first permanent settlement, aside from a few isolated pockets of civilization established by Catholic Jesuit missionaries, came in the early 1860s, and they were in the western mountains. The bonanza this time was in minerals—specifically, gold. In July 1862 a party of men found quantities of "colors" on Grasshopper Creek, a tributary of the Beaverhead River in extreme southwestern Montana. By late fall, the richness of the strike was so apparent that a wagon train was sent to Salt Lake City for supplies, and the town of Bannack was laid out. By spring, over 1,000 people jammed the area.

Montana was still a part of Idaho Territory, whose capital was Lewiston, far to the west. In 1863 President Lincoln appointed Sidney Edgerton of Ohio to become chief justice of Idaho Territory; ignorant about the nature of conditions in the far-off Western territories, the federal government designated Bannack as Edgerton's official place of residence.

During his first winter in the rough mining camp, Edgerton realized the enormity of the country he was expected to administer, and with the help of his nephew, lawyer Wilbur F. Sanders, petitioned Congress for separate territorial status for Montana. Edgerton left his wife and family to face the rigors of an 1863-64 Montana winter in a rough log "mansion" in Bannack and journeyed to Washington, D.C., where he succeeded in getting the bill through Congress. He was in Salt Lake City, en route back to Bannack, when he heard that President Lincoln had named him Montana Territory's first governor.

Meanwhile, a new and even more promising gold strike was made in Alder Gulch, some fifty miles to the east. Much of the restless populace of Bannack began changing residence, and they were joined by countless others as the town of Virginia City quickly sprang up in Alder Gulch, along with a number of satellite camps now only dimly remembered. By late 1863 an estimated 6,000 people, most of them men, lived and worked and caroused along the course of this historic gulch, and Virginia City soon superseded Bannack as territorial capital.

As was always the case in these temporary gold camps, rumors of new strikes continually swirled around the bars and hostels. Miners in Alder Gulch began hearing tales of rich finds on the Kootenai River, far to the northwest, and by spring 1864 the familiar exodus began.

Among the restless horde were four men: John Cowan, D. J. Miller, Reginald Stanley, and John Crabb. They got as far as Hell Gate (near present-day Missoula) on the Clark Fork of the Columbia, when they met discouraged prospectors returning from the Kootenai. The four men (subsequently known as the Four Georgians, although it was only partially an accurate appellation) turned back and did some prospecting along the Little Blackfoot River with the intention of eventually trying their luck on the Marias River, to the north and east.

En route, the four encountered a beautiful valley populated with hundreds of pronghorn antelope, and in a stream called Prickly Pear Creek, they found a few "colors" in their gold pans. Not sufficiently interested to forego their original objective, they pressed on to the Marias. But when bad luck continued to plague them and they were almost out of food and supplies, they decided to try once more the vicinity of what they came to call Last Chance Gulch.

On July 14, 1864, near where the Colwell Building now stands, the party found enough gold to warrant sending Cowan and Crabb to Alder Gulch for supplies. Wary by now, the two were quiet about the discovery, and remarkably few gold-seekers followed them back, new arrivals coming in trickles during the first few months before winter set in.

When new arrivals did come, the discoverers were ready for them. They had already drawn up a code of "laws" protecting their own locations and providing a primitive but effective system for locating new claims. For those who protested too loudly, the stay in Last Chance Gulch was brief. For those who sought to have their way forcibly, the famed Hanging Tree in Dry Gulch was utilized very early in Helena's history.

In the fall of 1864, a general meeting was held, the new community was named Helena, streets were laid out, the size of lots determined, and a kind of government based on traditional mining law was established. Montana's future capital city was born.

Such erstwhile lively places as Bannack, Nevada City, Diamond City, and many others are today visible only in small, faint letters on Montana maps. Such cities as Billings and Great Falls are in large bold-face type now, but during the heyday of the others they were nonexistent. An exception has been Helena. Since 1864 it has been on every regional map, and in reasonably prominent letters.

A number of factors has made this possible, among them the obvious fact that the city is surrounded by a virtual ring of mineral treasure. It was strategically located for overland transport from the head of the Missouri River navigation to settlements to the south and west, but of equal importance to the growth and development of this once-rough mining camp to solidity and permanence was the fact that a group of pragmatic businessmen and visionary entrepreneurs were early attracted to Last Chance Gulch.

By 1876, when the country was celebrating its centennial, Helena so dominated the Montana scene that the town was sometimes called, derisively, "the Territory of Helena." The year before, after a desperate battle, Helena had wrested territorial capital status from Virginia City.

An even more desperate battle was to come in 1894, five years after statehood was finally achieved. Now one of the most notorious political battles in any state's history was waged over the capital issue. Helena, with the backing of William A. Clark, won over Anaconda, which had been supported by Clark's arch-rival, Marcus Daly. Regardless of the merits of the outcome, this was one more bizarre chapter in what has become known as "the war of the Copper Kings."

Moreover, regardless of the shabby political machinations of these men, both of whom had made their fortunes in Butte, Helena by 1889 was unquestionably the Queen City of the Northwest, her storied Last Chance Gulch (Main Street) filled with imposing business blocks built of solid stone and brick, many of them reflecting the tastes of nationally known architects. Her entrepreneurs, men who made their fortunes in mining, banking, ranching, railroading, and utilities, had built mansions in which their wives and families entertained with a Victorian grace equal to any community in the country. These elegant residences, built to last, are still a major reason why Helena is a uniquely interesting and historic place to live in and visit.

Helena has, of course, had its ups and downs since the Four Georgians changed their luck in 1864. The natural chimney effects of the narrow gold-bearing gulch from which it sprang led to a series of disastrous fires from which the town had not yet entirely recovered in the glorious centennial year. It struggled for years to overcome the isolation so familiar to the Western territories until the railroads and statehood finally brought a measure of viable transport to and communication with "the states."

As the seat of government, Helena was host to a series of badly qualified political appointees who sought and usually failed to bring order from political chaos and confusion. There were long and agonizing attempts to incorporate the city and ensure police and fire protection, and to fend off the effects of financial panic in the early 1870s. There was political scandal surrounding the capital fight, another when the capitol building itself was built early in the century and greedy men sought to profit by using inferior materials.

There have been the fear and realities of earthquake, culminating in a series of grave tremors in October 1935, when many buildings and homes were destroyed and high school students attended classes in railroad coaches as their new building stood in ruins.

Finally, there was the unsettling but necessary process of inner-city renewal in the 1970s, when many of Helena's venerable buildings along its historic gulch disappeared in a demolition program and were replaced by new buildings, parking lots, and ramps. A pedestrian mall was in place through a large segment of the old main street, now officially known as Last Chance Gulch, which once rang with miners' picks, fire, and streetcar bells.

Many highlights of this colorful Montana city are illuminated in pictures in this book, arranged in chronological sequence, and headed by a series of essays which seek to give a broadly scoped historical setting for the people and events depicted. Helena's famous buildings and imposing private residences have been well represented in many publications. In-depth studies have been made of the political machinations which plagued

Montana's early years, when the action was in the smoke-filled hotel rooms of Helena.

Thus the emphasis in this book as much as possible has been on the people of the city, its first residents, the mighty and the lowly, their business affairs and activities, their social gatherings, the tragedies of fire and earthquake, flood and hail.

As with all efforts of this magnitude, there are necessarily some gaps, and indeed not all aspects of Helena life and by no means all of its people can be covered. A careful search, as broad as time strictures have allowed, has uncovered hundreds and hundreds of pictures, not only in such obvious archival repositories as the Montana Historical Society, but in the collections of private citizens whose family albums were explored in an effort to visually tell the story of Helena and its people.

A careful selection has been made to fit size and format which the compilers hope will reflect the broadest possible panorama of a city which many say does not yet possess enough sophistication and culture and shopping opportunities to serve the 1980s and beyond, but whose citizens generally love her—as much for her colorful past as for her renewed present and promising future.■

Helena

An Illustrated History

Looking North on Main Street

Chapter One

Discovery and the First Decade

Commercial structures of brick built side by side have replaced the burned-out log buildings first erected down the gulch. Later cross streets were cut through, and irregular blocks were formed. The merchants dressed up their brick fronts with arched windows and ornamental brick facade trim. The South Pedestrian Mall is approximately at this site today. Courtesy of the Mark McBride Collection

Reginald Stanley, one of the four discoverers of Last Chance Gulch, made a return visit to the scene in 1883, after an absence of sixteen years. The memory of how he and John Crabb, John Cowan, and D. J. Miller had found their "last chance" bonanza was still fresh, however, and he granted a memorable interview to the *Helena Herald* which gave an intimate, on-the-scene look at the momentous events of 1864 which led to the establishment of Helena.

Stanley, a native Britisher who had first come to Montana in 1863 with one of the first Fisk expeditions, apparently returned to his country not long after reaping his share of the initial proceeds of the strike at Last Chance Gulch and seeing the town laid out and named. By 1883 he was operating a manufacturing and colliery (coal mining) business at Nuneaton, England, and the pressures of it did not allow him to linger long on his return visit to the city he had helped establish. But he remembered many things no one had recorded and talked about them in somewhat flowery but interesting detail:

> The appearance of the gulch gave no intimation above hundreds of others of its auriferous [gold-bearing] character. There was no 'mother rock' in sight from the banks of the purling brook chanting a low melody in its hurried course down the pebbled channel to the valley. From its shallow, gravelly beds . . . gold could be panned wherever tried. Ascending the gulch, the stream was fringed with a growth of underbrush, with occasional clumps of chokecherry bushes. Near what is now Bridge [State] Street, the undergrowth became denser and continued so to above the canyon, where the cherry bushes, laden with fruit, grew in profusion.

Stanley described how a huge grizzly bear made nightly visits to feast on the berries, thus lending the name Grizzly Gulch to the upper part of the original diggings. Rattlesnakes, which the discoverers killed in unbelievable numbers throughout July and August, inspired the naming of the lower portion of the gulch, Stanley recalling that a snake of "monster proportions" with a ten-button tail had been killed and nailed to a post to act as a marker for the Rattlesnake district.

Wolves and coyotes "made the nights hideous with their howling and barking," and the discoverers sometimes fired rifle volleys in a vain effort to quiet them down. The miners pitched their first sleeping place, Stanley recalled, on bar ground back of the 1883 site of the first First National Bank, then on the corner of South Main and Wall streets. "It was," he said, "a bower of bushes on forked uprights, with cross poles." A horsehair lariat was drawn around it in the hope that it would keep out rattlesnakes.

"This bush bower was utilized till we were warned of the approach of cold weather, when the construction of log cabins was commenced," Stanley reported.

Meanwhile, the four prospectors, wise in the ways of other gold finds, took their time in prospecting the gulch, testing prospects, making sure their claims would be adequate and on select ground. When Crabb and Cowan went to Alder Gulch for supplies, Stanley and Miller stayed behind. Among other chores they dug a ditch to the bar to secure water rights.

Reginald Stanley's word picture of what Helena was like during those first few months stands as perhaps the best that can be found:

> The camp on Sundays was the scene of intense animation and activity. The streets were crowded with gaily shirted miners. Mexicans with bands of broncos careened through the main business thoroughfares. The shouting oratory of auctioneers was heard above the din of tramping horses and the noisy explosions of bibulous throngs day and night. In the afternoon, a general stampede of horsemen

Panorama of Helena, 1866

In May 1866 an enterprising photographer climbed surrounding hills and produced this panorama of what had become, in less than two years, a lively, sprawling settlement named Helena, Montana's future capital city. The panorama, ironically given circulation by the Fireman's Fund Insurance Company, is remarkable, not so much because of the architecture it reveals, for virtually every building was made of rough planed lumber or logs, but because it shows how the first two cabins built by the discoverers had burgeoned into a bustling town whose growth in the first few years was nothing short of phenomenal. The irony of sponsorship by an insurance company lies in what was to come in only a few years: a series of devastating fires which destroyed the hastily constructed wooden buildings and led to the permanence of brick, stone, and mortar. Courtesy of the N. J. Holter Collection

took place toward Ten Mile, where racing was indulged, if there was not a prize fight or other attraction at the Fighting Corral. Among all this, when violence threatened, or bloodshed occurred, the Committee of Safety had some occasional work to do, and Hangman's Tree became a well known rendezvous.

Stanley ended his reminiscences with the statement that during part of 1865 and 1866, the discovery party had as many as seventy men on its payroll, wages averaging from $6 to $10 a day. The ground during the time they worked it yielded nearly $250,000, with the discoverers netting some $170,000 in gold dust which was "securely boxed," according to Stanley, and sent to Philadelphia via Fort Benton and the Missouri River.

Helena, which was to wait nearly two decades for incorporation as a city, held its first town meeting on October 30, 1864, in the cabin of Captain George Wood, whose log residence was the third, built after those of Stanley and Cowan. By secret ballot, the name "Helena" was given to the camp, and three commissioners, including Wood, H. Brown, and C. L. Cutler, were named to survey the streets. It was Wood's particular job to lay out the streets, number the thirty-by-sixty-foot lots, and record them.

In spite of the Four Georgians' care in securing their own claims and those of the first arrivals, there was some violence in early Helena, with some disgruntled prospectors threatening to reduce the size of the original claims and jumping and rejumping choice locations. The original claim holders, however, met in secret, pledging to uphold their own rights and those of others—with their lives if necessary.

Things, indeed, were happening very fast along the gulch as spring broke in 1865. The Masons, whose influence on early Montana history was very considerable, got together for the first time. The occasion was the death, in March 1865, of Dr. S. Rodney Peacocke, whose last wish was for a Masonic funeral and burial. Establishment of Helena's first Masonic Lodge soon followed.

Later that same month, the first religious sermon was preached by the Reverend E. T. McLaughlin in an open area on Cutler Street, and a month later he became superintendent of the first Sunday school even as Professor A. B. Patch opened Helena's first day school. The first wedding was performed in May, and in June the first recorded murder, that of a gambler named Harry Slater, took place at the hands of John Keene, who was hanged from Dry Gulch's famous Hanging Tree. In July the Methodist Episcopal Church, Helena's first religious edifice, was completed and dedicated by the Reverend A. M. Hough. The first baptism he performed was at the request of another malefactor who had been condemned to vigilante death on the Hanging Tree.

In December 1865 Helena saw its first hometown newspaper, the *Radiator,* which was published until October 1866. By then, however, the town had three other newspapers, the *Weekly Herald,* the *Montana Post,* and the *Rocky Mountain Gazette,* all of them extolling the future prospects of Last Chance Gulch. "As a centre of population and trade in the future settlement and development of the Territory, Helena must far outrival every other, from her commanding geographical position, and many other natural advantages which surround her," editorialized the *Herald.*

Where there had been only five cabins in Helena that first winter, in less than two years there were hundreds, built side by side, rows branching out in all directions. Many residents added rectangular false fronts and devoted themselves to operating such businesses as stores, saloons, gambling houses, and hotels. In 1866 Helena boasted 188 retail and wholesale businesses, a surprising 45 engaged in selling groceries and produce.

As with all mining camps, water was an ever-present need, and supplies in discovery gulch were notably scant. Thus, when operations closed down for the winter, the Yaw Yaw Ditch was built from Ten Mile Creek, following the base of Mount Helena, to the west of the gulch. The first sawmill was set up on West Main (near where the Tatem House is now located), relieving miners of the hard task of hand-sawing lumber for sluice boxes. Later that same year, Anton M. Holter located his sawmill, forerunner of one of Helena's oldest business firms, near the mouth of Colorado Gulch, west of town.

A little more than a decade later, Robert Fisk, editor of this same newspaper, was writing on a more plaintive note, for by the 1870s things did not look quite so rosy. "Whom are we to blame," he asked "that Montana has been decreasing in population and shrinking in its assessment lists for the past few years? Before Montana is steadily and permanently prosperous again, we who live here must change our habits acquired in the flush times of 1863-1869, come down to habits of steady, patient, persevering industry, wise economy and courageous enterprise."

This clarion editorial call for solidity and industry was to be answered, in large part by the organization of the Helena Board of Trade, whose members were both pragmatic and visionary. It was time for a change, from gold camp to city.■

Bridge Street, 1865

This view of bustling Bridge Street (now State Street) is believed to be the first photograph ever taken of Helena's inner city. Less than a year after the gold discoveries of 1864, the camp first known as Last Chance Gulch had obviously grown to house not only itinerant miners, seeking shelter in their log cabins, but a sizable array of business houses ready to dispense groceries, tools, dry goods, clothing, medicines—and, of course, whiskey and beer. The ox-drawn freight wagon winding its way among wood piles, buggies, and hitched horses suggests an important reason why Helena early developed a permanence not usually found in gold camps after the initial strikes played out: its strategic location between the head of Missouri River navigation at Fort Benton and centers of population westward. Reinig photo; Montana Historical Society Collection

The Assay Office and Samuel T. Hauser's First National Bank were both housed in this brick building on the corner of Wall Street and Main, which featured stone arches, heavy security doors, and a sod roof. The Colwell Building is on this site today, and during demolition, the mortar from one of the original stone walls was tested and found to contain traces of gold. King and Gillette, builders of the toll road north of Helena which punched its way through the imposing Prickly Pear Canyon, had their offices next door. The two builders acquired the toll road charter originally held by Malcolm Clarke and E. Lewis and in 1866 began the arduous work of building a road through this awesome canyon, more familiarly known today as Wolf Creek Canyon. Because all traffic from Fort Benton to Helena went over this route, King and Gillette recovered their $60,000 investment in a short time and well before the road was taken over by Lewis and Clark County and eventually by the interstate highway system. Montana Historical Society Collection

First National Bank and Assay Office

John Potter, Helena's first postmaster, is seen holding a mailbag which has just arrived by stage at the town's first post office, located on Broadway. Since the date of the photograph has been confirmed as late in the season, the sack may have contained cherished Christmas mail and packages. This log building with the tidy, wood false front was one of the early structures on Broadway. Note the sign designating this as the office of a notary public, indicating that there was legal business to tend to this early in the city's history. Montana Historical Society Collection

Post Office, 1866

Men who avoided the risky future of gold prospecting and instead went into business to supply the miners often fared better and sometimes went on to establish fortunes. No better example can be found than the Highland City Meat Market, operated by Conrad Kohrs on lower Bridge Street. Kohrs, who went on to establish one of Montana's largest ranch operations, sold meat in the form of game animals as well as domestic cattle which were soon grazing on the grasses of the Helena Valley. Kohrs brought the sign for his market from a similar establishment he had operated at Highland City, a transitory camp which had gone into a decline. It is interesting to note that the meat market as well as the bakery and confectionery next door already boasted large glass windows which had to be shipped by riverboat and overland freight wagon from "the states." Montana Historical Society Collection

Early Cabins, circa 1865

These early Helena residences were located at the corner of present-day Jackson and Lawrence streets, with the two to the left suggesting solidity with the look of stucco and solidly-built chimneys. The building in the background also suggests progress at this early date in Helena's history: it is believed to be the Sheridan School, located just south of Reeder's Alley. Montana Historical Society Collection

This very early Helena home, still standing at 540 West Main, is one of the few buildings left in the United States designed in the Renaissance style, using crossed timbers and brick on the upper story and chinked logs below. The logs are reputed to have come from the timbers used in the construction of the first water flume across the gulch. Jeff Thompson, a black man who claimed to be the first of his race to work as a stonemason west of the Mississippi, lived in this house longer than any of its residents. Now on the National Register of Historic Places, the building has been restored as offices of Helena architects Taylor and Holtz. Denny McCall photo

Kluge Home

Uncle Johnny Thornburn's Place of Business, 1865

One of Helena's first entrepreneurs was colorful Uncle Johnny Thornburn, whose log cabin emporium and residence was located in Chinatown, on the south end of Last Chance Gulch. A later city directory listing credited Thornburn with dealing in flowers, canaries, and other birds. The sign above his door in this picture suggests the same kind of merchandise, which no doubt fascinated the kids in the neighborhood. Montana Historical Society Collection

Vigilantes and Early Law in Helena

Wilbur F. Sanders as a Young Man

Courtesy of Great Falls Public Library

Like all early mining camps, Helena had only two kinds of law in its early years: rough and ill-defined mining laws whose purpose generally was to protect rights to claims and water, and the swift, extra-legal mechanism known as vigilantism.

Early and effective use was made of Helena's Hanging Tree in Dry Gulch, although vigilante justice here was far outshadowed by that in Virginia City, where a vigilance committee organized late in 1863 eventually brought summary justice to every known member of the infamous Plummer gang.

Interestingly, Helena became the residence of two men who had been active in the Virginia City vigilante movement. They were Wilbur F. Sanders, nephew of Montana's first territorial governor, Sidney Edgerton; and a somewhat mysterious man named John X. Beidler.

Wilbur Sanders became, quite literally, the prosecuting attorney for the Vigilantes, a group of citizens who banded together to round up and mete out justice to a growing number of outlaws and highwaymen who were terrorizing such gold camps as Virginia City and Bannack.

The first outlaw arrested was one George Ives, who had shot a German-born settler in the back and stolen his valuable mules. A panel of twenty-four jurists found him guilty, but Ives, a lieutenant of the notorious Henry Plummer, who was sheriff at Bannack but a leader of the outlaws, believed his chief and others in the gang would come to his rescue. Pleading that he wanted time to write his mother, Ives asked Sanders to stay carrying out any sentence on him. Beidler, watching the proceedings from a rooftop, called out to Sanders, "Ask him how much time he gave the Dutchman!"

Sanders, knowing there were outlaw guns upon him during the outdoor proceedings, coolly sentenced Ives to immediate hanging, a sentence which was carried out on the exposed beam of an unfinished house. Within a few days, Sanders went to Bannack and recruited additional Vigilantes, all of which contributed to the eventual hanging of the most vicious of the outlaws, including Plummer, and the permanent banishment from the territory of many others.

By 1870 both Sanders and the shadowy Beidler were Helena residents, and neither was engaged in making vigilante use of the Hanging Tree. On a cold morning in January of that year, however, a Chinese named Ah Chow was hanged on the Dry Gulch pine tree, charged with the murder of three people. The body carried a grisly placard which said that Ah Chow was a murderer, adding the chilling words, "Beware! The Vigilantes still live!" Subsequent issues of Helena papers, however, made it clear that this was probably the work of a mob and not of the Vigilantes, whose work was by now well over with the coming of law and order.

In 1876 a well-meaning Methodist minister named Reverend Shippen chopped down the historic tree, and a short time later, fire destroyed even the stump he had left.■

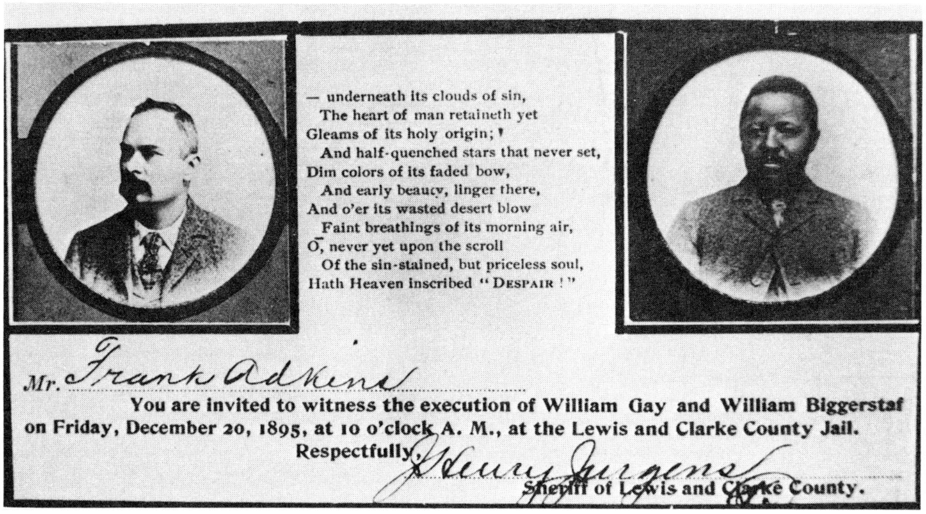

— underneath its clouds of sin,
The heart of man retaineth yet
Gleams of its holy origin;
And half-quenched stars that never set,
Dim colors of its faded bow,
And early beauty, linger there,
And o'er its wasted desert blow
Faint breathings of its morning air,
O, never yet upon the scroll
Of the sin-stained, but priceless soul,
Hath Heaven inscribed "DESPAIR!"

Mr. Frank Adkins

You are invited to witness the execution of William Gay and William Biggerstaf on Friday, December 20, 1895, at 10 o'clock A. M., at the Lewis and Clarke County Jail.

Respectfully,
J. Henry Jurgens
Sheriff of Lewis and Clarke County.

Invitation to a Hanging

This was an accepted practice at the time, and often the invitations were eagerly sought. Courtesy of the Norman Howard Collection

Hanging Tree

Helena citizens, many of them youngsters, gathered under the Hanging Tree early in 1870 to witness the hanging of two alleged murderers, Joseph Wilson and Arthur L. Compton, said to have been tried by the Vigilante court. The lad in the foreground with hands in pockets is said to be David Hilger, member of a pioneer family, who was to become librarian of the Montana Historical Society. Courtesy of the Mark McBride Collection

John X. Beidler

Although his personal life was always somewhat mysterious, John Xavier Beidler was early Montana's most famous law enforcer, a tireless tracker of malefactors from his earliest days in Alder Gulch in 1862, through the famed vigilante period which followed, and later as a deputy sheriff and deputy U.S. marshal. Born near Harrisburg, Pennsylvania, in about 1835, Beidler was so successful at staying alive that he was thought to lead a charmed life. After leaving his boyhood home, he stayed for a time in Illinois and then went to Kansas, where he was crippled for life in an altercation as one of John Brown's followers. He later went to Colorado to follow the gold strikes, ending up in 1862 in Alder Gulch, where he began his famed exploits as a law enforcement officer.

He was as close to the Sanders family as he was to anyone, and an amusing journal kept by a young son of Wilbur F. Sanders related how Beidler brought a young Indian girl he had found at Fort Peck on the Missouri to serve Mrs. Sanders as a maid. The lonesome girl tried to run away, but as he had done to so many others, Beidler tracked her down and brought her back. When she was invited to a church Christmas party, however, and got a doll for a present, the young girl finally found happiness in the Sanders home. Beidler died of pneumonia on January 22, 1890, and one of his obituaries praised him in these words: "He died poor, having served his territory much better than himself. Peace to his ashes!" Courtesy of the Mark McBride Collection

A Muddy Parade, Late 1870s

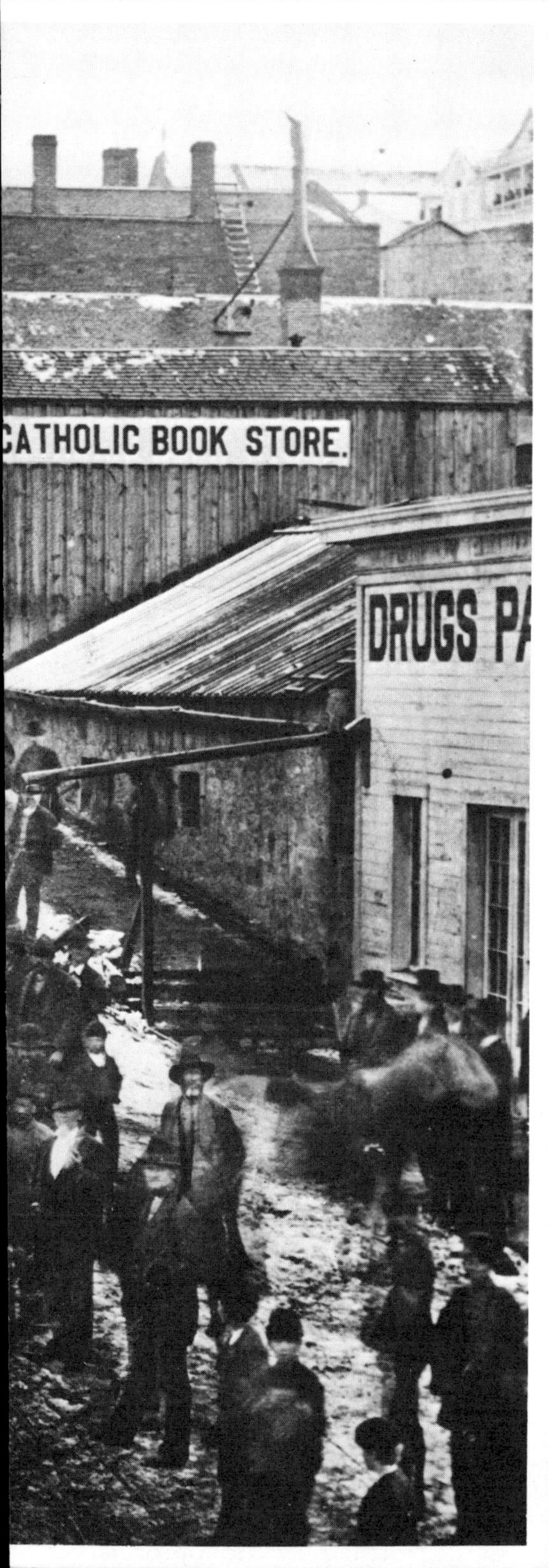

Chapter Two

The 1870s: Isolation and Fire

Wagon-rutted and muddy streets failed to dampen this parade in the late 1870s. The large building looming in the background at the left is the 1875 U.S. Assay Office, still standing at the corner of Broadway and Warren. The tower of St. Paul's Methodist Episcopal Church is seen in the center background. This historic church was destroyed in the 1935 earthquakes. The two brick buildings on the right side of the street are the Helena Herald *building with white letters on the second story, and the Blake Block immediately west of it, which served as Montana's capitol building when the territorial seat of government was moved from Virginia City to Helena in 1875. Jorud photo; courtesy of Helena Catholic Diocese*

According to a federal census taken in 1870, Montana Territory had in its entirety only 20,599 residents. Helena, with a population of 3,106, was its largest city. By some standards, this growth in the dozen years since the Four Georgians made their "last chance" discoveries, would seem modest indeed. But it must be remembered that growth in an immense and unsettled country such as Montana in the 1870s could not be measured by standards common to the eastern United States.

The vitality and the impact of population centers such as Helena were far out of proportion to the actual number of people counted by the census-takers. Moreover, Helena was surrounded by many other settlements, where mining was going on at a lively pace, and in 1870 a monthly average of $500,000 in gold was being shipped from the district. On September 6 of that year, Wells-Fargo carried out a single-day's shipment worth $80,000, putting on extra security guards; a sudden outbreak of stagecoach robberies had begun plaguing overland freighting lines.

As the decade of the 1870s began, however, it was clear that the days of placer gold mining were over, and that new and substantial capital was needed to exploit the real mineral wealth, which was in quartz and other hard rock. Years of federal mismanagement had left Montana Territory in grave financial straits, and even when the new, pragmatic territorial governor, Benjamin Potts, arrived from Ohio and began inaugurating austere measures, the territorial debt stood at $150,000, a staggering figure for the times.

The continuing isolation of Montana from the rest of the country, the expense of trying to maintain wagon roads, a deepening national depression, all combined to make the decade of the 1870s frustrating, a "season of trial" for Helena. The panic of 1873 combined with Helena's worst fire, in 1874, brought the city to near ruin.

On January 2, 1875, it was announced in the press that "the seat of government of the Territory of Montana has been, in due form of law, removed from the City of Virginia to the Town of Helena, in said Territory." It was the first of two bitter capital city contentions in which Helena figured; the second, for state capital, was to occur a little less than two decades later.

As the country as a whole made proud observance of the nation's 100th birthday in 1876, Helena was without question the leading city in Montana Territory. In January it got ready to welcome its first legislative session; a newspaper announced that "the House of Representatives will meet in the hall on the corner of Main and Wood Street, and the Council in the hall on Broadway."

On the morning of July 2, 1876, as most of Helena's citizens prepared to join the nation in centennial celebration, the staff of the *Herald* was busy putting out a special edition. "A TERRIBLE FIGHT!" screamed the headlines of Robert Fisk that day as he reported the death of General George Custer and his entire Seventh Cavalry command at the Little Big Horn River. The festivities in Helena, and the nation, came to a halt.

Meanwhile, although it basked in the glory of being Montana's center of population, Helena continued to battle financial and transportation problems. Even as he encouraged his readers to return to old habits of thrift and hard work, editor Robert Fisk argued for organization. At his urging, late in November 1877, a group of businessmen met at the International Hotel and formed the Helena Board of Trade. Comparable in some ways to today's chambers of commerce, this historic organization proved to be infinitely more pervasive in its effects on Helena's business climate. The answers to Helena's woes were not immediately found, but this group, a list of which reads like a "Who's Who" of Helena, were soon doing some very practical and visionary things to assure future solidity. By January 1878 they had raised $5,000 to begin construction of a wagon road between Butte and Helena, and ten months later the road was open, by way of Boulder, as is today's interstate route.

The overriding goal of the board of trade, however, was to achieve railway service, and although three railroad subsidy bills were passed by the territorial legislature in 1876, it was not until 1882 that the Northern Pacific reached the city. Meanwhile, the city continued struggling to transport its products out and receive merchandise in, many a merchant finding his "supplies . . . strung out, mud-bound and flood-bound" on the road between the railhead at Corinne, Utah, and Montana's new territorial capital.

Any number of attempts were made during this time to incorporate the city, but most of them were opposed by such civic leaders as Robert Fisk of the *Herald*, who maintained that politicians seeking incorporation were engaging in a "wolf-like scheme for robbery, clothed in lamb skins of plausibility." Eventually Fisk agreed that orderly growth required incorporation, and it finally came in 1881.

In 1877 Fisk wrote: "We've suffered much already for want of organization. With proper regulations about the character of buildings, care of flues and water supplies, we might have avoided the fires that have so often devastated our centers of trade and broke up so many of our old citizens."

Thus, as the decade of the 1880s approached, Helena was looking at city incorporation even as she watched the lines of the Northern Pacific approach ever closer to end for all time the isolation that had kept her from realizing the promise engendered by the exciting beginnings of the 1860s.■

Helena and the Scourge of Fire

"These baptisms by fire have occurred with too painful frequency to allow hope to be very buoyant," agonized the editor of the *Helena Herald* on January 10, 1874, the day after the city suffered its ninth, and worst, fire in less than five years. "It will, undoubtedly, change the future of our city in many material respects, yet we love the place, its very name—and we love it even more for its many and oft-repeated disasters."

The disasters had indeed been repeating themselves, largely due to the narrow, chimney-like qualities of the city's main street, a lack of water, and an early preponderance of fragile wooden buildings. "In such a broad land as this," the *Herald* editor went on to say, "it is a shame that a city should ever have been laid out in such mean, narrow streets and lots. The idea that men can so huddle their houses together, and then think them safe in such hurricanes of flame is preposterous."

Editor Robert Fisk had reasons for venting his spleen. In a destructive fire on Broadway on October 1, 1871, his own newspaper office had been a victim. Moreover, some insurance companies which carried policies on destroyed Helena buildings were unable to pay claims when the great Chicago fire, which occurred only a week later, brought them to bankruptcy.

Overall, Helena suffered a total of nine fires, three of them "great fires," between 1869 and 1874. There were three fires in 1869 alone, one of them, in April, a major conflagration which started in a Chinese gambling house at the corner of West Main and Bridge (now State) streets. The holocaust of 1874, Helena's worst, had its beginnings in the same location.

It was on a bitterly cold January 9, 1874, that this destructive fire almost brought the city to her knees, occurred. The raging flames, again carried along by near-hurricane winds, did not stop until they reached North Rodney Street and Fifth Avenue. Along with most of her business houses, many of them rebuilt after the 1871 and 1872 fires, Helena lost 150 homes in this blaze, started, according to a bitter newspaper reporter, by a "Celestial" cook who mistook a bucket of oil for water when he tried to put out a fire in his stovepipe.

This time, all the records of the Montana Historical Society, stored in the law offices of Wilbur Sanders, were destroyed. And again the International Hotel, which had been leveled before and rebuilt, was a victim, along with a hotel employee named Konrad Knipper, who tried and failed to escape from the second floor.

Helena was proud of its new fire department and its fire tower, where nightly vigil was kept, but after the 1874 disaster, the *Herald* was moved to say that "five hundred engines, with as many companies to manage them, would have been utterly impotent after the fire had gained such headway." The editor advocated building solid fireproof buildings and also advised insuring with "reliable companies."

"Our Legislature is now in session," the *Herald* continued, "and our citizens ought to meet, consult, organize and act forthwith to procure the passage of some general law for protection against fire. . . . Let us heed the numerous and terrible warnings we have had, and try to learn something from the costly tuition."

There were other fires to come, of course, including a destructive blaze in 1928 which again struck the gulch itself and thus the center of the business district. There were earthquakes to come as well, notably the tremors of 1935, which destroyed or damaged countless buildings and because of their frightening recurrences left the city on the verge of the same kind of terror which had seized it after the great fires.

But as the 1870s came to a close, Helena hoped its newer, more substantial buildings, its improved fire department and water sources and its increased vigilance would save it from fire disasters of the proportions it had suffered since 1869.■

The International Hotel is the most prominent structure on the east (right) side of Main Street as it curves north on the left side of the photograph. The bare hill in the center is Catholic Hill, and it is crested with the Catholic Church and Catholic Hospital. Bridge Street (State Street) is the principal street running at the foot of Catholic Hill and horizontal in the center of the photograph. At the far left, Clore Street (Park Avenue) curves around the hill with the Helena Athletic Club building the principal structure on that street. From the Jean Baucus Collection

After the Fire of 1872

On August 23, 1872, fire broke out in the rear of the North Pacific Hotel on the east side of Main Street, the flames whipped by high west winds. Before it could be contained, it swept across Jackson Street and destroyed virtually every building from Broadway to Grand, Jackson to Warren and Ewing streets, stopping only when it reached Courthouse Square. Montana Historical Society Collection

Broadway Rebuilt after the 1872 Fire

Broadway became a more important street after rebuilding following the 1872 fire. In this picture, the Helena Daily and Weekly Herald *was doing business in an imposing brick building which stood for many years. In the brick adjunct to the right, with the Ladies Bazaar sign on the front, was the place where the territorial legislature met after the capital was moved from Virginia City to Helena in 1875. Note many of the buildings on Main Street, seen in the after-the-fire picture were still standing and doing business when this mid-1870s picture was taken. Courtesy of the Mark McBride Collection*

Fire Department Parade, July 4, 1873

Helena's new fire department, organized on December 29, 1872, paraded down Main Street as a part of the Independence Day celebrations in 1873, preceded by a brass band. Chief Seth Bullock, wearing a white helmet, led the ranks of his men. Marching at his right is Wilbur Sanders, prosecutor of the Vigilantes in Virginia City and later a prominent lawyer and politician in Helena. Only six months later, these men were powerless to stop Helena's most destructive fire, which destroyed Sanders's law office, his library, and all the records of the Montana Historical Society, of which he was president. Montana Historical Society Collection

Fire Tower

The disastrous fires of the 1860s and 1870s led to the construction of a tower on Catholic Hill which lies between Bridge (State) Street and Broadway. In 1874 a larger fire tower was built with a room on top for the watchman. A 2,200-pound bell was installed to replace the huge triangle the fire wardens had used up to that time to sound alarms. In 1982 the Helena City Council officially proclaimed the fire tower as the city emblem. Denny McCall photo

International Hotel

If ever a place of business could be said to have survived in the face of diversity it was the International Hotel, first built in 1865 on the corner of Main and Bridge (State) streets by Marcus Lissner, an energetic man who was one of the early developers of water and suppliers of ice. Lissner's hotel was known from the start for its excellent cuisine, "commodious baths," and pleasant rooms. His first hotel burned down in the 1869 fire, and he promptly rebuilt. Indeed, because the International had been destroyed so many times by fire with the owner holding no insurance, the historic lodging place became known as the Phoenix of Helena. The disastrous 1874 blaze not only destroyed the International once more but claimed one life. In 1884 the hotel had constructed an annex across the street, and this was connected to the main structure with a covered walkway over the street. This "bridge" is also associated with Bridge street. Reproduced from Helena City Directory, 1877

Magnolia Hotel

The Magnolia Hotel, built in 1865 by E. M. Dunphy, was destroyed in the October fire of 1871. The Central Brewery, located next door, is said to have hauled beer to the roof in an attempt to stem the blaze. Edwards Street was cut through about where the North Pacific Stable is shown in this photograph. The brick, two-story structure next to it was Helena's second Masonic Temple, which was later razed when the Merchants Bank was built on the northwest corner of Main and Edwards.

Today this is the location of the Park Plaza Hotel, and Edwards Street no longer exists. In 1885 the buildings seen here, with the exception of the Masonic Temple, were razed for the contruction of the Union Block. The contractor for the excavation, it is said, made several hundred dollars over his expected profit by working the excavated dirt for gold. Montana Historical Society Collection

Paynes Hotel

Three ladies grace the balcony of the Paynes Hotel, built in 1870 on the site of what is today the City-County Building at the head of Sixth Avenue. Ice cream, soda water, fruit, and tobacco were available next door, and an early Helena entrepreneur held forth in a tent. A traveler of the time wrote that all Helena hotels were thronged with people during this period, and in the lobbies were "big cabinets full of specimens of gold and silver ores" taken from nearby mines.

This hotel, then on the extreme north edge of Helena, was a logical stopping place for overland freighters coming in on the Benton Road. The Paynes Hotel accommodated the drivers, and the Paynes Stables, located in the lower block to the east, took care of the oxen, mules, and horses. Montana Historical Society Collection

Last Chance Gulch in Flood

A heavy cloudburst in 1878 brought a deluge of water down the narrow gulch, despite attempts of workers to divert the waters, which reached depths of from six to seven feet between Clore (Park) and West Main. The gulch itself was submerged to three and four feet, with everything floatable or loose washed away. This flood proved that the flume in the center of the city was incapable of handling such unusual runoffs, which led to completion of the "great flume" in 1884. A total of 139 feet of stone culverts were laid underground, starting at Bridge (State) Street, with lumber and plank flumes installed to carry water as far as present Sixth Avenue. Courtesy of the John Wheeler Collection

Territorial Council, November 1, 1878

This group of distinguished men, some of them Helena residents, met late in 1878 after their election as members of the Territorial Council. Population figures for that year showed that Montana had a population of 50,000, with 4,000 of them living in Helena. There were 1,039 children enrolled in the grade schools, and newspapers boasted that the city had had no business failures during 1877, suggesting recovery from the economic woes of the early 1870s. Council members pictured as they met in Helena are identified as follows. Top row: Martin Barrett, R. J. Kennon, W. G. Conrad, and Oscar A. Sedman. Bottom row: William Padberry, F. C. Ives, R. O. Hickman, W. O. P. Hayes, A. H. Mitchell, J. G. Sanders, A. M. Holter, W. C. Gillette, and J. A. Hyde. Courtesy of the Holter Collection

Freighting through Little Prickly Pear Canyon

This canyon, now known as Wolf Creek Canyon, was the most difficult part of the journey from Fort Benton to Helena. Little Prickly Pear Stream had to be crossed numerous times, and the narrow, rocky canyon and fast-flowing stream made tough going. In times of high water, travelers quite often resorted to the old Mullan Trail, which avoided this canyon and went up and down the steep mountains to the west. From the Jean Baucus Collection

Overland Freight by Wagon

Kirkendall's freight outfit is seen about to leave Prickly Pear Canyon (Wolf Creek Canyon). The road seen here, improved as a toll road by James C. King and Warren C. Gillette, was a decided improvement over the old Mullan Trail which went over Medicine Rock Mountain on the west.

Robert Vaughn, an early bullwhacker who later became a citizen of Great Falls and in 1900 wrote his reminiscences in Then and Now or 36 Years in the Rockies, *remembered that this was a dim Indian trail when he first saw it in 1865. That year he and Malcolm Clarke obtained a charter to build a toll road through the canyon, a charter they later sold to King and Gillette. Clarke, a West Pointer who was an early Montana settler and married into a Piegan Indian family, established a ranch at the south end of the canyon, now the site of the Sieben Ranch.*

"Think of it! Goods from Corinne to Helena—a distance of 480 miles—in eight days!" exulted the Helena Herald *in February 1871, when it was announced that the Diamond R Company would soon begin a "fast freight" service from the railhead in Utah to Helena. In spite of such optimism, the overland freight wagons were slow, frequently the victims of weather, and residents of Helena clamored for faster and more certain railroad service. Indeed, in its first winter of service, the Diamond R, in spite of heroic efforts, got so bogged down that Helena was without mail service for several weeks. From the Jean Baucus Collection*

Marysville

M*arysville around the turn of the century claimed 2,000 residents, along with four general merchandise stores, six hotels, two churches, and a public school. Like most residents of mining camps, including Helena, those who settled in Marysville hurriedly laid out three principal streets with cross streets, but after that built houses in helter-skelter array against the mountainside. Courtesy of the Mark McBride Collection*

Chapter Three

The Surrounding Treasure

As suggested earlier in this book, one of the factors which led to Helena's permanence as a financial and transportation center was its surrounding ring of mineral wealth. After the rich discovery in Last Chance Gulch, miners poured into every adjacent gulch, about 150 of them, searching for gold and usually finding small quantities. Lump Gulch, Snowshoe Gulch, Blackfoot City, and others yielded large nuggets to fire further interest. Most of these had small, "instant" settlements which have since vanished, but at the time Helena was the hub of all this activity.

Visitors to Montana today are intrigued with many of these once-rich gold camps, especially those that are now ghost towns, their buildings decaying, their mine shafts and mills falling into ruin.

Montana's most famous gold camp was Virginia City, located 120 miles to the south, once territorial capital and site of Alder Gulch, where the greatest gold production of all was recorded. From its discovery in 1863 until just before the turn of the century, Alder Gulch had produced over $60 million in gold. But today Virginia City is far from a ghost town. It is the county seat of Madison County and, thanks to restoration by the Bovey family, it is one of Montana's important tourist attractions.

Another "ghost town" is Marysville (with 100 or so live inhabitants), which nestles in the mountains some twenty miles northwest of Helena. This is where Irish immigrant Thomas Cruse found gold in quartz rock in 1868, stubbornly holding to his theory that the mother lode was here, imbedded in rock. In January 1876 he filed on the mine which he named the Drum Lummon for a parish in his native Ireland.

For six years, Cruse worked the mine with its shallow prospect holes, its tunnel only 200 feet long. Yet he recovered an estimated $144,539 in bullion and slowly developed the property, knowing by this time that financial backing and sophisticated equipment would ultimately be the keys in unlocking the mineral wealth. In 1880 he constructed a five-stamp mill and two years later he sold out to an English syndicate for $1.5 million plus an interest in the company.

Another "ghost town" of renown is Elkhorn (with only a dozen or so live inhabitants), which is situated in the mountains about fifteen miles east of Boulder, Montana. The old Opera House has been the subject for many artists, and the lovely little graveyard over the hill gives mute testimony to the many children who died of diphtheria in this remote mining camp of the 1880s.

Even closer to Helena was the Whitlatch-Union mine which yielded $3 million. Unionville was another principal mining district at this time.

A number of other nearby gold camps are pictured in this section, but in most cases, barely a trace remains. They include Diamond City, the town that sprang up at Confederate Gulch, famous for its concentration of gold in a small area. In the summer of 1866, a party of men took out one-and-a-half tons of ore, then worth $1.5 million. Located some thirty miles east of Helena, this fabulous gulch reveals in its name the potent Southern sympathies of many early Montana residents. Diamond City itself became such an important town that it was once seriously considered for territorial capital honors. Also included here is Wickes, located on a dirt road some eighteen miles west of Helena, which boasted Montana's first lead and silver smelter.

Mining and its importance to the development of Montana, and certainly of Helena, is a complex topic. But it is important to remember the progression from the days of free placer gold, available to prospectors with no more sophisticated equipment than a pick, shovel, gold pan, and a few carpenter's tools with which to build crude sluice boxes.

By 1876, when the nation's centennial was being celebrated and Helena was known as the Queen City of the Northwest, mining had become a matter of technology. The fact that she was at the center of mineral wealth, of transportation and politics, as well as the home of a sizable number of men who knew the realities of a new era, accounts in large measure for the fact that Helena is still a major Montana city and her surrounding camps, in most cases, small settlements or merely interesting ruins.■

Photographer F. Jay Haynes took this panoramic view of the town of Wickes, south of Helena, late in 1886, showing the territory's first silver-lead smelter in full operation. Three years later, it was reported in the Helena Herald *that the Helena Mining and Reduction Company, which was then operating the Wickes smelter, decided to lease the property to the East Helena smelter "without limitation of time on the lease." This resulted, according to the* Herald, *in the closing down of the Wickes smelter, its future use limited to "auxiliary to the one at East Helena." In practical terms, the heyday of Wickes and its historic smelter was over. F. Jay Haynes photo; courtesy of the Haynes Foundation Collection, Montana Historical Society*

Thomas Cruse had built a five-stamp mill to process the rich quartz rock gold he discovered in 1876. When this picture was taken by F. Jay Haynes in 1886, the Drum Lummon was at the height of its activity, with a British-owned company called Montana Company, Ltd. building a twenty-stamp mill and a sophisticated cyanide gold processing plant. The trestle of the Montana Central Railroad line can be seen in the foreground. Eventually, the British company failed and was once bailed out by Cruse, who by now was a successful Helena banker and rancher. F. Jay Haynes photo; courtesy of the Haynes Foundation Collection, Montana Historical Society

Charcoal Kilns, Wickes

The remains of many roundbrick kilns may be seen throughout the region. This battery of the kilns, used for the reduction of ores, was photographed at Wickes in 1886. F. Jay Haynes photo; courtesy of the Haynes Foundation Collection, Montana Historical Society

Hydraulic Mining at Diamond City

The use of hydraulic pressure to expose gold deposits was common in Western mining after the easily accessible stream gold played out. This picture, taken in about 1888, shows the flumes built at Diamond City at work in Confederate Gulch. From the Jean Baucus Collection

Mine Shaft and Winch

This very early photograph, taken near Canyon Ferry, shows a group of miners by their mine shaft. The horse walked in a circle, winding up line to pull the ore car out of the shaft. Courtesy of the Court Sheriff Collection

Once-Glorious Elkhorn

Although there are a few inhabitants left today, the charm of Elkhorn, located south of Helena, lies in the old buildings of mining camp days. The principal attraction is the elaborate Fraternity Hall, popularly known as the Opera House. It is a particular favorite of artists who seek to portray buildings of the past. The facade of the hall is seen in the right background of this photograph. Elkhorn, acquired by A. M. Holter from a Swiss, Peter Wys, who had discovered the rich quartz deposits prior to 1870, once had a monthly payroll of over $15,000 and a production of more than $14 million in silver and gold. During the first ten months of operation, the silver-bearing calcite ore shot produced over $188,000 in silver alone. The Elkhorn was sold to an English syndicate in about 1889 for a reported half million dollars. Lambert Florin photo; courtesy of Montana Historical Society

Canyon Ferry

The old settlement of Canyon Ferry was established by John Oaks early in 1865. Miners of Confederate, Magpie, and Cave gulches had to come to this point to cross the Missouri, and rowing across the river was hard work. In 1866 Captain J. V. Stafford bought out the ferryboat interest and built a hotel and store here. He soon sold out to Court Sheriff, who operated a general merchandise business in Cavetown at that time. After the purchase from Captain Stafford, Sheriff opened a livery stable and hotel, and this then became known as Canyon Ferry.

Mr. Sheriff is shown at the right with his racehorse. Mrs. Sheriff is in the buggy with their children, Court, Jr., and Mary. At the left is the stage which the Sheriff family operated for nearly fifty years, carrying mail and passengers to and from White Sulphur Springs and Helena over the rough mountain roads. This stage was a Concord Coach, locally called the Mud Wagon, for its trips on muddy, rutted roads. Canyon Ferry was a meal station midway along the trip. From the Jean Baucus Collection

Across the Wide Missouri

This shot of the original ferry shows the Sheriff stagecoach with a party of early Canyon Ferry residents. The old ferry was strung across the river at the spot where the first Canyon Ferry Dam was built in 1898. Court Sheriff, Jr., ran the ferry when he was about twelve years old. The toll was twenty-five cents for a horse and fifty cents for a team. The heavy barge, anchored by cables, was carried across the Missouri by river current. After the dam was built, the river below it was too rough for the ferry, and it was abandoned. Canyon Ferry residents had to cross the river in rowboats until the first county bridge was built in 1899. From the Jean Baucus Collection

Last Stage in Little Prickly Pear Canyon

Chapter Four

The Stage Gives Way to the Iron Horse

Mindful that an era was passing, nostalgic passengers rode the stage from Fort Benton to Helena on its last trip in 1883. Montana Historical Society Collection

No more appropriate way to introduce the decade of the 1880s can be found than to point out the transition in transportation from stage stations, stagecoaches, and freight wagons to boxcars, parlor cars, and depots of the railroad era. The completion of the Northern Pacific (NP) to Helena in June 1883 at last ended the isolation territorial capital citizens had for so long deplored. It was the end of an era, and the early years of the decade saw the last of the stagecoaches and freight wagons whose colorful but uncertain services had plagued businessmen and travelers alike.

No longer was it necessary for Helena newspapers to announce that beginning on February 8, 1877, it was possible to take a coach from Helena to White Sulphur Springs and make the trip in one day, or proclaim somewhat pridefully that in August 1879 Gilmer and Salisbury began three-times-a-week service between Helena and Butte, via the Boulder Road, at a fare of two dollars each way.

Instead, in 1883, the papers were jubilantly reporting the last trips of many of these same lines. "The last coach of the Gilmer & Salisbury mail line on the Bozeman route came in today," the *Herald* reported in June, "decorated with evergreens and red, white and blue bunting, with a flag on each horse . . . . The horses and the coach were viewed by many citizens who gathered 'round the old and welcome institution in the time that tried men's souls, some with sorrowful hearts and recollections, but all impressed with the dissolving view of the driver, horses, and coach."

Then in the issue of June 12, an enthusiastic *Herald* reporter wrote:

> The first whistle from a locomotive that ever awakened the echoes in the canyons of Last Chance and Grizzly Gulches, and cheered the hopes of the people of Helena, sounded at precisely 11 o'clock this morning as the construction train of Winston Brothers pulled into place where the depot will soon be erected. A great concourse of people on foot, on horseback, and in all sorts of vehicles, was at the depot to welcome and cheer the iron horses . . . . The morning was delightful, the weather warm and inviting, and no lovelier day ever dawned upon a mightier work than the completion of the Northern Pacific thus far into the Rocky Mountains.

On a bid of $150, Samuel T. Hauser, president of the First National Bank, bought the No. 1 ticket over the NP lines from Helena to St. Paul and return. The ticket, elaborately printed on ribbon, was then presented by Hauser to Mayor Kleinschmidt, who had been a "responsible employee" at Hauser's bank for some eighteen years.

The first through train from St. Paul arrived in Helena on June 15, and one of the passengers was a man named T. G. Merrill who twenty years earlier had been a passenger on a bull train which made the trip from St. Paul to Prickly Pear Valley, not far from where the Four Georgians had made the gold strike in 1864. The trip which Merrill took in 1863, the *Herald* pointed out, took two-and-a-half months. On the new Northern Pacific Railroad, Merrill, along with some forty other comfortable passengers, made it in two-and-a-half days.

As the decade of the 1880s began, Montana Territory had 38,998 citizens, as compared to 20,580 in 1870. Helena still had a little less than 4,000 residents, and Butte, spurred on by the development of its copper riches, was rapidly catching up. But on March 7, 1881, Helena at last found itself incorporated as a city after thirteen years of striving and countless elections for which turnouts were poor.

By 1881 Robert Fisk, along with his fellow Helena editors, had come around to supporting incorporation after years of opposition, and in his issue on the day after the election, Fisk rejoiced: "The old days of idle and thoughtless waiting for something to turn up or for somebody else to come and deliver us without the cost of an effort on our own part we hope and trust have gone forever . . . . There's a tide in the affairs of men, we are told, and we believe that turn in the tide took place in Helena yesterday. Let us mount and ride to the safe and solid shore of victory and prosperity."

Fisk's predictions for a new business and economic climate in Helena after incorporation and after the end of isolation came true in spite of the silver panic of the 1890s, the coming of World War I, the Great Depression of the 1930s, the frightening earthquakes of the same decade, and many other events and crises yet to come.

But in 1882, as an incorporated city, Helena looked bright indeed. On August 28, she became Montana's first city to have electric lighting. Miss Stella Knight, daughter of the man who was not only Helena's mayor but president of the Brush Electric Light and Power Company which installed the lighting, had, according to the *Helena Herald*, "the honor of setting free, by the delicate touch of her little hand upon the lever of the dynamo machine, the mighty electric current which in a moment flashed along the wire and blazed forth in brilliant light from every lamp on the uptown current."■

Montana Central Railroad in Little Prickly Pear Canyon

Colonel C. A. Broadwater, in association with James J. Hill, built the Montana Central Railroad from Butte through Helena to Great Falls. In this view, taken in Little Prickly Pear Canyon (Wolf Creek Canyon), the viewer can see the hand-hewn railroad ties as well as the carefully constructed drywall stonework along the road bed and mountainside. One hundred years later this rock work is firm as ever. Montana Historical Society Collection

Mullan Tunnel

The Northern Pacific Railroad line leaving Helena for the West had a long climb to the Continental Divide and the Mullan Tunnel on top. This tunnel was named for Captain John Mullan, who built a primitive wagon road from Fort Benton to Walla Walla, Washington, in the 1860s. Courtesy of the Norman Howard Collection

Corner of Cutler and Water Streets, 1885

Mrs. O. C. Bundy (right) posed with a friend for photographer E. H. Train on Cutler Street, located a block south of Bridge Street (State) which terminates in Reeder's Alley. Little Last Chance Stream, in which the four discoverers made their historic find six years earlier, can be seen passing under a small footbridge at the bottom of the incline. This street was West Main, which ran in front of the new city hall and fire station, the imposing, two-story brick structure seen in the right background. E. H. Train photo; Montana Historical Society Collection

Helena Brewery

In 1865 John Horsky, Ignatius Miller, and Herman Richter built this pioneer brewery at the south end of Last Chance Gulch, taking advantage of cold spring water which issued from the limestone canyon wall. This picture, taken in 1885, may well have been the occasion on which the name of the brewery was changed to Capital Brewery, with four huge beer casks arriving and Helena male guests seated to taste the brew. Many years later, this building was the site of one of the country's leading summer theatre groups, known as the Brewery Theatre. Today the building is gone, replaced by modern condominiums. Courtesy of the N. J. Holter Collection

1866 ESTABLISHED 1866

GANS & KLEIN,

MANUFACTURERS, IMPORTERS AND DEALERS IN

CLOTHING

Gents' Furnishing Goods,

THE

OLDEST AND LARGEST CLOTHING HOUSE

IN MONTANA.

BOOTS, SHOES, HATS, CAPS,

HYDRAULIC HOSE,

Rubber Coats, Boots and Caps,

OIL CLOTHING, BLANKETS, QUILTS, TRUNKS, VALISES,

AND A

Full Line of Notions.

HELENA, MONTANA.

We have at all seasons a full assortment of everything in our line, and sell at the lowest prices. All orders from abroad attended the same as if selected in person.
Our motto: "The Best Goods for the Least Money."
ONE PRICE ONLY.

FACTORY: 184 AND 186 CHURCH ST., NEW YORK.

Gans and Klein Clothing Store

This pioneer Helena store for men and boys, established in 1866, leased this brick building on the corner of Broadway and Main in May 1877, and it was the site of their store until the early 1920s. At the time, a Helena newspaper announced that the firm's former location on South Main would be used as a warehouse and for their wholesale business. Since electric power poles are clearly visible, it is probable that this picture of the store, with patrons and employees lined up in front, was taken in the 1880s before the third story was added. Montana Historical Society Collection

J. R. Drew and Company, Boots and Shoes

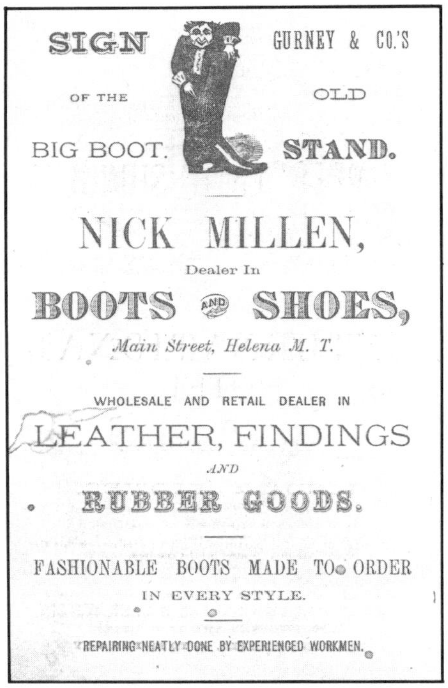

A number of male Helena residents lined up in front of the J. R. Drew and Company emporium, which had dealt for many years in men's boots and shoes. Notice that the sign of Nick Millen, also a pioneer dealer in this same line, is affixed to the right of Drew's sign. The crate in the right foreground, obviously containing merchandise, was sent to the store via the Northern Pacific from St. Paul. That and the presence of the "street railroad" tracks in the foreground means that this picture was taken sometime after 1886, when the new "hoss cars," built by the Pullman Company, began operating from the Northern Pacific depot to Bridge Street in 1886. Montana Historical Society Collection

East Side Market

Proprietor T. L. Matthews and his wife were off for a sleigh ride in front of their East Side Meat Market, located at 203 Rodney Street, an area of Helena just beginning to burgeon as a business district in the 1880s. Meat and poultry, oysters and game were prominently advertised in the windows, along with sides of beef tied to the outside windows and awning. A son of Mr. and Mrs. Matthews became a well-known judge, and their granddaughter is Mrs. George Huber of Helena, from whose collection this picture comes. Courtesy of Mrs. George Huber

Shorty Huber Blacksmith Shop

A good blacksmith was a busy man from the first gold rush days. The rush of miners to the gold fields brought many who purchased horses at fancy prices and in a few months would sell them at low prices after the strike had played out. In the early days of the city no single rigs could be rented. All were doubles, and the standard charge was fifteen dollars a day. Holding the horse is Philip Henry "Shorty" Huber, who opened his blacksmith shop on Fuller in about 1909. Courtesy of the Mark McBride Collection

Lissner School

As the residential area was pushed up Bridge Street to Rodney, this two-story brick building, the city's first solidly-built elementary school, was constructed on the hillside south of Bridge (State) Street on the corner of South Warren and Pine streets. In 1888 it became the First Ward school building. Bundy/Train photo; courtesy of Montana Historical Society

Helena Churches, circa 1880

The eminence known as Catholic Hill is clearly seen in this picture with the brick Cathedral of the Sacred Hearts of Jesus and Mary, completed in 1876, seen in the right background. The white frame building to the left of the cathedral housed St. Vincent's Academy, established in 1870 as a boarding school for grade and high school students. The building was replaced soon after this picture was taken with a new brick building, which was used by St. Vincent's Academy high school until its destruction in the earthquakes of 1935. The Cathedral of the Sacred Hearts of Jesus and Mary, no longer standing, was replaced in 1914 by St. Helena Cathedral.

On the corner of Broadway and Ewing in this picture is the imposing brick St. Paul's Methodist-Episcopal Church, also no longer standing. Across the street, the steep-roofed home is the Cannon residence, built as one of Helena's first large homes in 1868. This picture was apparently taken from the roof of the U.S. Assay Office in Broadway, since the iron cresting of that building is clearly visible in the right foreground. Courtesy of Helena Catholic Diocese

For over thirty years, this colorful, little, red brick school in the Helena Valley was the place where children of the North Valley attended school. Land for the building was acquired in 1888, and after its completion the school was called the Silver Creek School for a time and later was known as College Place School, a reference to the presence of nearby Wesleyan College. Classes were held here until 1921, and for many years later it was used only as an election polling place until completion of the Rossiter School in the area. When the little brick school began to fall into disuse and decay, a group of concerned citizens whose ancestors had once been students there, gathered together and, led by Mrs. Floy Peterson, began restoration which led to its designation on the National Register of Historic Places. Courtesy of Floy Peterson

KESSLE
BR'W'G. C

Chapter Five

The Pace Setters

Every community in America has its builders, its pace setters, its entrepreneurs—men who were the leaders of development and economic stability. Because it was a gold camp, Helena might well have gone the way of most settlements which sprang up at the capricious bidding of the yellow metal which made its presence known in the early placer diggings.

As William C. Campbell said in the concluding chapter of his first volume of *From the Quarries of Last Chance Gulch:* "Outside of Helena, the many civic leaders here for whom we have so much admiration and respect were sometimes referred to as the 'Helena Hogs.' But it must be remembered that Helena had few if any natural advantages to warrant its existence after Last Chance Gulch had been relieved of its glittering gold. Had it not been for the grim determination and uncompromising attitude, even selfishness, of Helena's old timers, it is probable that cattle would be grazing on Main Street today, and this city would be a 'ghost' similar to Bannack."

Campbell, who gleaned the columns of Helena's newspapers, especially the *Herald,* to give us a portrait in two volumes of what this city was like from 1865 through 1900, was well aware, as are the compilers of this book, that not every person who made a contribution to Helena's growth can be discussed. Indeed, it is regrettable that there is no record of the countless personalities and deeds which have made up the fabric of this colorful community.

In 1887 the *Boulder Sentinel* published a lighthearted summation of what many of Helena's leaders had been doing twenty years earlier. Excerpts about some of those dealt with in this section are both revealing and entertaining:

> Twenty years ago Sam Hauser was a modest banker on a small scale, and occasionally dabbled in politics. He was bashful and diffident then. C. A. Broadwater was a slim, energetic youth, stuck the bottom of his pants in his boots, and whooped up the great trains of the Diamond R Company, of which he was the leading spirit. "Broad" was a dandy among the boys then, and made a ten strike wherever he hit, from a horse race to packing a political convention for a favorite candidate.
>
> Tom Cruse was an unknown prospector, frying his flapjacks in a dirt-roofed cabin, little dreaming of the fortune in store for him. Charley Cannon had a little bakery about where the *Herald* building now stands, and sold pies and peanuts at 500 percent profit, all on account of 'the freight, you know.' Dicky Lockey was his clerk and did up the goods of the plain little establishment with the grace and politeness of a Chesterfield. . . .
>
> Colonel Wilbur F. Sanders was a busy, hard-working lawyer, with a large practice, a healthy political ambition, but with less money and experience in defeat than he now possesses. . . . The Holter Brothers owned a small hardware store on Main Street, and ran a sawmill on Ten Mile Creek.

In 1936, James E. Stuart, who first saw Helena in the summer of 1883, wrote some of his impressions, which were published in newspapers of the day: "It was then reputed the wealthiest city of its size in the world," Stuart wrote, "and there seems to have been some excuse for that vanity. Every newly made millionaire of the place seemed to be striving to outdo all others, of whom there were many. On all sides my bulging youthful eyes viewed widely varied grandiose profusion."

As a clerk for the old First National Bank, Stuart said that it seemed to him everyone except bank clerks was "ponderously rich," and he pointed out that some of the newly affluent would lose their wealth with the panic of the early 1890s and the disaster visited upon the silver market. But he had praise for the likes of Thomas Cruse, who husbanded the wealth he had garnered from his Drum Lummon mine in Marysville, and was now "bailing out" some less fortunate colleagues, but not, according to Stuart, "the high fliers of this amazingly extravagant town, toward some of whom he held a lasting grudge."

This chapter deals, not with the "high fliers," but with Cruse and others who left lasting monuments to the town they helped develop and enhance. In some instances, pictures have been made available from the collections of their descendants who still live here. And while they represent only a slice of life in the Helena of their time, they form a portrait, in microcosm, of the former gold camp's development from the days of log cabins, tawdry honky-tonks, and extra-legal justice which characterized the first years into a center of Victorian grandeur.■

Charles A. Broadwater

Although he claimed no profession, Charles Arthur Broadwater was one of the canniest businessmen who ever lived in Montana. Born in St. Charles, Missouri, in 1840, he arrived at the gold diggings at Bannack in 1862 and made a name for himself in a variety of enterprises, including supplying the frontier military, before he elected to live in Helena. He was a man of enormous energy and accomplishment, his capacity, according to one writer, "too broad to limit to the boundaries of a simple life."

He initiated and nurtured the famed Diamond R Company whose mule trains supplied the growing territory with goods before the coming of the railroads. It is interesting to note that when A. H. Wilder of St. Paul got the contract for U.S. Army transportation in the mid-1870s, he turned the major part of the work over to the Diamond R, and because of his admiration for Broadwater, Wilder backed him when he established the Montana National Bank in Helena a decade later. Broadwater named his daughter Antoinette Wilder Broadwater after this man, and the name persists today in Helena's Wilder Avenue.

Canny as he was, when the railroads approached Montana in the 1880s, Broadwater allied himself with James J. Hill, who was rapidly building the lines of the Great Northern from St. Paul to the West Coast. Broadwater, who was president of the Montana Central at the time of his death, invested heavily in bringing the lines from Great Falls to Helena and Butte.

Broadwater was never an office-seeker, but his behind-the-scenes influence on politics was immensely important. A devoted Democrat, he is often referred to as one of the Big Four of influence, the others being Marcus Daly and William A. Clark of Butte and Samuel T. Hauser of Helena.

The brightest jewel in Broadwater's string of accomplishments came in 1889, when he opened his Broadwater Hotel and Natatorium on Helena's western edge. Surrounded by broad verandas and set in lavishly landscaped grounds, the hotel was finished in the great Victorian tradition of antique oak, velvet carpets, stained-glass windows, and cut-crystal decorations.

At the opening on Monday, August 26, Broadwater himself was in Anaconda attending a Democratic convention, but his wife, the former Julia Chumasero, and her mother were present to do the official greeting. Dinner was served by waiters in full dress, the ten-course meal ranging from breast of veal to fresh oysters, fine wines, fruits, and desserts. The Capital City Band played and the absent Broadwater was praised in talks by Mayor Fuller, Tom Carter, Wilbur F. Sanders, and R. C. Walker, secretary of the board of trade.

Charles A. Broadwater

Schelten photo; Montana Historical Society Collection

Less than a week later the equally imposing natatorium, built along Moorish lines, was opened to the public which was to enjoy it for over four decades. Heated by natural hot water, the indoor pool was 300 feet long and 100 feet wide, its precise temperature maintained by hot and cold water which issued from a fountain of boulders at one end.

Broadwater realized a good deal of publicity in brochures issued about his hotel and pool by the Montana Central Railroad. It was, the brochures proclaimed, "the place to effectually and completely recover lost nerve force and to rebuild a debilitated system." Nevertheless, Broadwater's dream that the railroad's lines would actually serve the hotel and thus deliver patrons from faraway places in sufficient numbers to keep it open and flourishing beyond his lifetime did not materialize.

Broadwater's health began deteriorating in 1891, when his doctors advised he take a trip to Italy to regain his strength. On his way home, he spent some time in Washington, D.C., using his considerable influence in urging a military post be built for Helena, which later became a reality with the establishment of Fort Harrison, not far from the Broadwater Hotel.

In the spring of 1892, weakened by influenza, Broadwater sat on the veranda of the hotel with his friend, Sam Hauser, and greeted guests as the hotel and pool opened for a third season. On May 24 he died in his suite at the Broadwater, and his funeral, held five days later, was the largest ever seen in Montana to that time. He was four months away from his fifty-second birthday.

Broadwater's disappointment that his railroad never served his hotel would have been minor compared to the sadness he would have felt at the ultimate fate of his dream. Following his death, his nephew, Thomas A. Marlow, took charge of his banking interests with long and notable success. The hotel and natatorium did not fare so well.

The complex was operated through the years by seven different entities, the longest, from 1920 to 1939, by the Broadwater Hotel Company. The natatorium and plunge were weakened by the earthquakes of 1935 and today, the bare outlines of the pool are the only visible reminders of a once-glorious plunge.

The Broadwater itself changed from a luxury hotel to a place for dancing and gambling during the 1930s, the soft lighting replaced by garish neon. With a statewide crackdown on gambling in 1941, it closed its doors forever. There was a chance during World War II to utilize federal funding and renovate the hotel as a "rest and recuperation" center for servicemen, but the opportunity passed.

In recent years, demolition of the stately old building has continued apace, with a public auction of artifacts erasing the last of the stained-glass windows and graceful cupolas which once graced Charles A. Broadwater's place of Victorian grace and hospitality. ■

When the Broadwater Was New

Inside the Broadwater

The lobby and front parlor of the Broa water Hotel are seen in these photograph taken in 1890 by F. Jay Haynes, a ye after the facility was opened. F. Jay Hayn photo; the Haynes Foundation Collectio Montana Historical Society

It is possible that this is Colonel Broadwater in front of his imposing Broadwater Hotel, completed and opened in 1889 on Helena's western edge. Young trees graced the carefully landscaped grounds. In 1983, as the old trees are gnarled with age and the grounds no longer manicured, the hotel itself lies almost entirely dismantled, many of its historic accoutrements, including stained-glass windows and the steepled tower, removed to other places. Courtesy of the Mark McBride Collection

Broadwater Natatorium

Water from natural hot springs served this great covered swimming pool, built on the Broadwater Hotel grounds by Colonel Broadwater. The building, described at the time of its opening as "a lofty and picturesque structure of Moorish architecture," is seen here, with snow on the slopes of Mount Helena in the background. The fountain at the entrance featured the statue of Boy with the Leaky Boot, a memento which is now in the First National Bank's north lobby. The grounds, like those of the hotel, were carefully landscaped and featured a bandstand for evening concerts and an oval pond for boating in the summer and skating in the winter. Montana Historical Society Collection

Inside the Broadwater

Natatorium Pool

The gigantic indoor pool, 300 feet long and 100 feet wide, featured a twin waterfall made from boulders, which poured natural hot mineral water and cold mountain water. All the dressing rooms had large round stained-glass windows which cast an eerie darkness as bathers dressed and entered the pool with its high vaulted ceiling. The earthquakes of 1935 weakened the pipes and loosened the boulders of the waterfall to the point where the pool was never reopened and eventually fell into total ruin. Montana Historical Society Collection

Broadwater Funeral

Colonel Broadwater's funeral was held at his hotel on Sunday afternoon, May 29, 1892, with William A. Chessman in charge of the Masonic ritual. With thousands of people from all over Montana attending, it was said to be the largest funeral thus far held in the territory and state. Pallbearers were Joseph K. Toole, who was serving his term as Montana's first state governor; Samuel T. Hauser, Broadwater's political and financial colleague and a former territorial governor; Nick Kessler, Helena brewer and brick manufacturer; Henry M. Parchen, pioneer druggist; W. A. Chessman, developer of Helena's water system; and C. K. Cole, physician and financier. In this picture, as the American flag hangs at half-staff, the long horse-drawn funeral cortege is about to leave the grounds for Forestvale Cemetery, where Broadwater was buried with full Masonic rites. Montana Historical Society Collection

Thomas Cruse

Although not out of the same mold as Montana Territory's typical "pace setter," Thomas Cruse, born in Ireland and a miner whose experience ranged from the early strikes in California and Nevada, left a mark on Helena which remains to this day. Devoted to his Roman Catholic faith and to those causes he believed just, Cruse was more philanthropist than he was entrepreneur once he made his fortune at his famed Drum Lummon mine at Marysville, some fourteen miles northwest of Helena.

Thomas Cruse lived from his birth in County Craven, Ireland, in 1836 until his death at his Helena residence in 1914, when he was just short of his seventy-ninth birthday. Yet his personal life, his philanthropies, the sources of his wealth all remain in a kind of mysterious limbo, even though many of them are on the public record. It is said he was illiterate; yet his schooling in Ireland, while sparse, was solid enough. It is said he somewhat accidentally "struck it rich" in the quartz rock in the Marysville area; yet he was never unsuccessful or a typical down-at-the-heels prospector. He prospered in mining to some degree long before he came to Montana Territory in 1866, although he did not find his real bonanza until 1876, when he discovered rich, gold-bearing quartz rock at Marysville and established the Drum Lummon mine.

In spite of the apocryphal stories about his illiteracy and his "mad Irishman" propensities for looking for gold in unlikely places, Thomas Cruse was a canny miner, and turned out to be a skilled businessman once he found his fortunes at Marysville. He sold out to an English syndicate in 1884 for over a million dollars, and went on to more successful mining ventures and to delve into such lucrative sidelines as extensive cattle raising and establishing Montana Territory's first savings bank, the Thomas Cruse Savings Bank of Helena.

Cruse's personal life has also long held overtones of some mystery and certainly sadness. In 1886, when he was fifty years old, Cruse married Miss Margaret Carter, sister of Thomas H. Carter, who became one of the territory's early U.S. senators. In less than a year Mrs. Cruse died, after giving birth to Tom Cruse's only child, a daughter, Mary, who throughout her short life was called Mamie.

Without his wife, he continued to maintain his house at the corner of Park and Benton avenues which had been a home of T. C. Power until that Montana "pace setter" moved into an even more spacious mansion on Harrison Avenue. Cruse's home, which gave way to a modern apartment building in 1963, was quite imposing. It was said that Cruse purchased it from the owner because he harbored an Irish superstition that it was unlucky to live in a house you built yourself.

Thomas Cruse

Engraving from Progressive Men of Montana

Installing his niece, Miss Mary Cruse, to manage the home, Thomas entertained his Helena friends with open-handed hospitality, especially on New Year's Day, meanwhile taking pride in his young daughter and in his successful business ventures. The tragedy of this Irish-born miner climaxed with the early scandal-ridden death of his daughter in 1912, which marked the decline of his own health and his death only two years later.

The philanthropy of Thomas Cruse is also surrounded in some misapprehension and exaggeration, although the record shows he picked up the bonds for Montana's capitol building when they were refused by Eastern financial circles around the turn of the century. It is also true that his donations to the Catholic Diocese of Helena included both land and building funds for St. Helena Cathedral, which remains one of the Northwest's finest examples of ecclesiastical architecture. At his death, the great twin-towered edifice was nearing completion and dedication. Thomas Cruse did not live to witness either. He was buried in an imposing mausoleum in Helena's Resurrection Cemetery which he had had erected to receive his wife, his daughter, and finally himself.

Thomas Cruse Residence, 1886

Thomas Cruse and his bride, Margaret Carter Cruse, the sister of Senator Thomas H. Carter, stood in front of their new home on the corner of Benton Avenue and Lawrence Street. Mrs. Cruse died at the birth of her child, Mary, in 1887. Courtesy of Helena Catholic Diocese

Thomas Cruse was noted for philanthropy towards people and causes in which he believed. There is a story, probably true, which reveals another side of him: he did not support those who were imprudent or who sought to profit by wild speculation. When silver was demonetized and the country as a whole and Helena in particular was teetering on ruin during the panic of the early 1890s, a group of Helena bankers met and "earnestly pleaded" with Cruse to tide them over. After a long meeting, the Irish miner, whose fortunes were still secure, is said to have rose from his seat and thundered in Irish brogue: "When I was a-diggin' me head off in Marysville tryin' to develop me moin, knowin' dom well it was a bonanzer, I was always ragged an' manny toimes hungry. One fall in partic'lar I needed a grubstake to see me through the comin' winter. I went to you an' you an' you (pointing a gnarled forefinger at the bankers in turn) and begged ye fer a little help, jest a little help. An' what did ye do fer me? Nawthin; not a dom one of ye's lent me a doim. All roight, me dandies, it's me turn now: as fer as I'm concerned, ye may all go t'hell!" ■

Miss Mary Cruse

The only child of Thomas Cruse was his daughter, Mary, who was known as Mamie. Cruse feared she would be kidnapped so she was closely watched throughout her childhood. She had beautiful toys, including a pony cart, a few selected friends, and was part of a cast of children who put on Shakespeare's Midsummer Night's Dream *for her father's miners at Marysville. Mamie became betrothed to a man from San Francisco, and Thomas Cruse chartered a train to bring the wedding guests to Helena from San Francisco. A lavish wedding was held at the Cathedral of the Sacred Hearts of Jesus and Mary on Catholic Hill, but the marriage was soon dissolved and from then on Mamie led a rather scandalous life, became very ill, and after a desperate search for good health, died in 1912 in Helena at the age of twenty-six. The Sisters at the House of the Good Shepherd took care of Mamie at the end of her short life.*

In her memory broken-hearted Thomas Cruse gave $100,000 toward the finishing of the interior of St. Helena Cathedral, which was under construction. Also in Mamie's memory $15,000 was given for the purchase of the splendid pipe organ, a gift from Mrs. H. M. Rae, who was a niece of Mr. Cruse. Montana Historical Society Collection

Dinner Table at Cruse Residence

Twenty guests were expected to sit at this dinner table set with a damask cloth, cut crystal goblets, and stemmed wine glasses banded with gold. At each place were five forks, and the knives were under the napkins. At each lady's chair was a solid gold vase with eight roses tied with a satin ribbon. Each gentleman received a solid gold cigar box with a rose for his lapel. The sterling silver candelabra stood at either side of the sterling silver bowl filled with roses. Wide panels of handmade lace banded the curtains covering the window shutters. Courtesy of Mrs. Lee Sweeney

Cruse Mausoleum

Thomas Cruse and his family rest in this mausoleum in Resurrection Cemetery, north of Helena. The domed structure is the largest in any of the city's historic cemeteries. Jean Baucus photo

Samuel T. Hauser

The financial and political influence of no single Montanan was more pervasive during the 1860s and 1870s and well into the 1880s than that of Samuel T. Hauser, a canny and pragmatic Kentuckyian who arrived in what was to become Montana Territory in 1862 after a career as a railroad civil engineer in Missouri. Not quite thirty years old, Hauser tried gold prospecting for a time at Bannack and was a member of the civil/military Yellowstone Expedition of 1863, a perilous undertaking which helped open up the Yellowstone country for white settlement.

Hauser began building his banking empire in 1865, when he and N. P. Langford organized the S. T. Hauser and Company Bank in Virginia City. His introduction into corporate mining came at almost the same time, when he launched a mining company and built the first metallurgical furnace in Montana Territory at Argenta. In rapid succession, in 1866, he organized the First National Bank in Helena, and the St. Louis Mining Company in Philipsburg which, under the corporate name Hope Mining Company, built Montana's first silver processing mill. His mining interests also spurred development of the town of Wickes, which at one time was a prime producer of silver, gold, and lead.

Eventually, Hauser controlled banks in Butte, Fort Benton, and Missoula, and was associated with other capitalists in building a number of short but vital railroad lines throughout the territory. As if all this were not enough, he entered into a partnership with A. J. Davis and Granville Stuart to form the gigantic DHS Cattle Company which in 1883 was reorganized as the Pioneer Cattle Company.

Perhaps more important than all his financial dealings was Sam Hauser's political influence. An earlier friendship with the powerful Senator George C. Vest of Missouri led to an inordinate capacity to pull wires in Washington, D.C., as well as in Montana. So great was his political power that one writer was moved to say that Hauser "not only had a voice in selecting a majority of governors sent out to his territory, but he did more to direct territorial policy for Montana under Republican and Democratic administrations alike than any official in Washington." While this may be an exaggeration, it is nonetheless true that for over two decades Hauser, a staunch Democrat, was the man to see if one wanted something done politically.

In 1885 Montanans generally rejoiced when President Cleveland appointed Hauser as the territory's first resident governor. Oddly enough, however, the duties of political office did not greatly interest him. He was away on business much of the time and resigned after only sixteen months in office, pleading pressure of business interests.

Samuel T. Hauser
From Progressive Men of Montana

It was about this time that Hauser built the twenty-nine-room mansion at 720 Madison Avenue over which his wife, Ellen, graciously presided. Mrs. Hauser, daughter of a prominent St. Louis physician, married Hauser in 1871, and they had two children, Samuel T. Hauser, Jr., and Ellen, who later married A. P. Thatcher and lived in Eugene, Oregon.

This lovely home, notable for extensive use of stained glass, was the home of Catholic bishops for many years and later was used as a residence for the Teaching Sisters of Charity of Leavenworth, Kansas. It is the home today of another former Montana governor, Tim Babcock, and his wife, Betty.

In 1893, when he was sixty years old, Sam Hauser's fortunes and influence began fading. His First National Bank failed during the silver panic, and although he managed to reopen it, its doors were closed for good in 1896. An even more crippling blow came in 1908: his steel-plated Hauser Dam collapsed when water began seeping between the plates and the bedrock. The dam, rebuilt at enormous cost, had been completed in 1907 and thus withstood the pressures of the Missouri River for only a year.

In his later years, this once powerful man was said to have been somewhat pathetic. But he lived to be nearly eighty-two years old, dying at the home of his son on November 10, 1914.■

Montana Historical Society Collection

Hauser Residence at 720 Madison Avenue

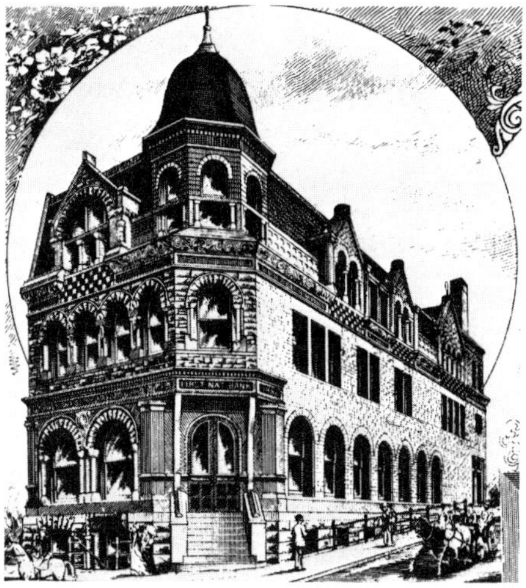

Hauser's First National Bank

This bank, built by Sam Hauser in 1886, was the epitome of the Richardson Romanesque style, which expressed the grand manner the bankers wished. The tower had to be removed after the earthquakes of 1935, but Hauser's thumbprint, carved in granite, still remains in the circle between the two first-story arched windows on the Main Street side. Today this structure, known as the Securities Building, is one of the finest examples of the 1880s architecture remaining in the city of Helena. Montana Historical Society Collection

Cornelius Hedges

The contributions of this educated, cultured New Englander to the development of Montana generally and Helena in particular had little to do with wealth or indeed of politics but rather with education and a passion for learning and an informed, law-abiding citizenry. Cornelius Hedges was born in Massachusetts in 1831 and began his education at the Westfield Academy, followed by his graduation from Yale in 1852 with an A.B. degree and an A.M. degree two years later. After a year of studying law with a firm in Westfield, he entered the law department of Harvard and was admitted to the Massachusetts bar.

In 1865 Hedges went to Independence, Iowa, where he began a law practice and edited and published a newspaper as well. The young lawyer/editor had been in somewhat delicate health since a youthful bout with food poisoning, and in 1864 he decided to go west. Leaving his wife, Edna, whom he had married in 1856, and a family of young children, Hedges literally walked all the way to Virginia City, Montana Territory, a story which sounds apocryphal but has been established as the truth.

Hedges moved to Helena soon after his arrival and in 1866 returned to Iowa for his family. He was by then serving as U.S. district attorney for the territory. In 1872, following adoption of the territorial school law which he had helped formulate, he was named Montana's first superintendent of public instruction, a post he occupied for six years. He traveled tirelessly throughout the territory in all kinds of weather, and the mark he left on Montana education remains today.

Hedges continued to follow his interest in journalism as well, writing columns and doing editorial chores for the *Helena Herald.* It was in these columns that he wrote extensively about the wonders of Yellowstone, which he saw first-hand in 1870 as a member of the Washburn exploration party. Hedges is generally credited with being one of the first to urge the establishment of Yellowstone as the country's first national park, which became a reality in 1872.

Deploring the lack of reading material in early Helena, Hedges was a leader in establishing the city's library. He was also active in building the collections of the Montana Historical Society and was one of the leading spokesmen and officials of the Masonic Lodge.

Cornelius Hedges died at his home on the corner of Broadway and Rodney streets on April 29, 1907, surrounded by his wife and their surviving children. He was seventy-six years old and beloved by many, but his great contributions to Montana's cultural growth had been obscured by more dramatic events which took place during his long career. ■

Cornelius Hedges
From Progressive Men of Montana

Hedges and Scottish Rite Masons

The literate, education-minded Cornelius Hedges contributed to many areas of Helena life and indeed that of Montana. His Masonic commitment included numerous offices held and reports written to serve the order through the years. Here he is pictured in 1881 as the Scottish Rite was introduced in Helena by Robert Carrell Jordan, grand inspector general for Nebraska (seated, center), present for the occasion. Seated, front row: Hedges, Harry R. Comly, Daniel M. Dellinger, Jordan, John C. Major, A. J. Davidson, and Henry Cowden. Standing in the background: Richard Lockey, William N. Baldwin, and James H. Moe. All were Thirty-second Degree Masons at the time. Montana Historical Society Collection

Anton M. Holter

An innovative, industrious man named Anton M. Holter left his mark on not only Helena, which was his home until his death in 1921 at the age of ninety years, but on all of Montana and the Northwest. Learning the carpentry trade in Iowa soon after his arrival from his native Norway in 1854, Holter used his manual as well as his creative gifts to accomplish a number of "firsts"—including Montana's first planing mill, its first sash and door factory, and one of its first fully-stocked hardware stores.

Born in 1831 on the eastern shore of Christiana Fjord in Norway, Holter left his native land when he was twenty-three years old, migrating to this country via Quebec. After learning the craft of carpentry in Iowa, near Dubuque, he went to St. Louis in 1860 and was joined by his brother Martin. Together they went to Colorado where, in 1863, Anton acquired a sawmill, which he brought up to Ram's Horn Gulch near Virginia City, then Montana's leading gold-producing camp.

With the know-how and energy which characterized his long life, Holter organized lumberyards at both Virginia City and Nevada City and built a municipal waterworks system for Virginia City as well. In 1865 he purchased a second-hand portable steam engine and boiler and set it up on Ten Mile Creek, just west of Helena. This became Montana Territory's first planing mill. A trip to Chicago in 1866 resulted in the purchase of more sophisticated equipment for the sawmill, along with machinery for a sash and door factory, equipment for a distillery, and a stock of hardware goods.

It was on the Chicago trip that he met Miss Mary P. Loberg, also of Norwegian descent, and they were married on April 6, 1867. Soon after, the Holter brothers, Anton and Martin, built a hardware store on Last Chance Gulch, and the next year they opened their sash and door factory and a distillery as well. Disastrous fires in 1869 all but wiped them out, but stubborn and industrious, they not only survived but flourished.

Diversity marked the career of A. M. Holter as it did most of the "pace setters" in early Montana. In 1871 he became interested in the Rumley mine, and it was here he installed a German-patented concentrating jig, the first of its kind in the American West. Finding the jig too frail for the work in the mine, he upgraded and strengthened it and thus had a hand in devising sophisticated means for extracting precious metals from Montana's rich native ore. Eventually, he was involved in both gold and copper mining interests throughout the region, including the Coeur d'Alenes of Idaho, Oregon, and eventually, Alaska.

As he and his brother Martin continued to live in Helena and operate their pioneer hardware business on Last Chance Gulch, Anton sought other outlets for his energy and inventiveness. In 1890 he, with others, made application for the use of the waters of the Missouri River near Helena for power generation. This project, which pioneered hydroelectric development in Montana, included a dam across the Missouri some thirty-five miles north of Helena which raised the waters through the spectacular Gates of the Montains canyon an average of forty feet above where Meriwether Lewis first navigated and described it in 1805 and created Holter Lake as one of the area's leading recreational sites.

Anton M. Holter
From Progressive Men of Montana

The contributions of A. M. Holter are difficult to overstate. His inventiveness included one of Montana's first waterworks systems, at Virginia City, which included a two-mile flume made of logs fitted together, an auger fashioned by Holter boring the three-inch opening through which the water flowed. In his obituary, published in the *Helena Independent,* the editor commented on this period of his life: "Mr. Holter's natural mechanical genius came into effective play many times when the problem of construction and service seemed impossible of practical solution."

It is interesting to note that this same inventive genius was unquestionably passed down to A. M. Holter's grandson, Norman "Jeff" Jefferies Holter, whose scientific attainments have included an EKG heart monitor now in international use. His contributions to Helena in recent years have included the granite arch from the burned-out Denver Block, recently installed as a gateway to Women's Park on Neill Avenue, thus saving another distinctive feature from Helena's past. ■

Holter Sawmill

O*ne of A. M. Holter's many sawmills was located on Wegner Creek, a drainage area which empties into the Missouri from the west and near the site of the present Holter Dam. This wonderful 1885 photograph shows oxen bringing in the logs and the neatly stacked wood shingles by the mill.*

Holter logged along the banks of the Missouri and floated logs to Great Falls. His big lumberyard was near the mouth of the Sun River. Men and teams rode the rafts down the river. Usually they managed without too much difficulty, but once during high water they were unable to guide the log raft to the Sun River lumberyard, and they had to push the horses overboard, jump in and swim themselves, and let the logs go over the Great Falls of the Missouri. Courtesy of the N. J. Holter Collection

B*y 1891 Mr. Holter's store offered garden tools, including a lawn mower, all manner of hardware, and an amazing contraption seen in the show window. Courtesy of the N. J. Holter Collection*

A. M. Holter Hardware Company

Interior of Holter Hardware Store

Saws, gauges, hinges, wire rope, and valves are arranged in a decorative display on the wall of the store. A barrel of sauerkraut was kept at the front door for customers to dip into. Courtesy of the N. J. Holter Collection

A. M. Holter Residence on Jackson Street

This home, built about 1868, was one of the largest and most comfortable homes in the early mining camp. While the residence was being constructed, the Holters, including baby Norman, lived in the back of the store across the street. In the 1880s the Holters built a new home on Park Avenue and gave this structure to be converted into St. Peter's Hospital's new facilities. Courtesy of the N. J. Holter Collection

A. M. Holter with Grandson

This 1916 photograph shows A. M. admiring one of his grandsons, N. J. "Jeff" Holter, who still lives in Helena. Courtesy of the N. J. Holter Collection

Holter Family

This 1905 family photograph has all the family together in front of A. M. Holter's home on North Benton (where the Park Avenue apartments stand today). From left to right: Norman B. Holter, born 1868; Baby Richard, born 1904; Florence Jeffries Holter, born 1880; Holter Kennett, born 1889; Edwin O. Holter, born 1871, with two-year-old Marion, born 1905, standing at their feet. Next is Clara H. Kennett, born 1869, and her son, Hauser Kennett, born 1893, in the front row. Behind her son is Holter Kennett, born 1889; and Aubrey Holter, born 1883. The last three are Mrs. A. M. (Mary) Holter, born 1841; A. M. Holter, born 1831; and his son, Aubrey Holter, born 1883. Courtesy of the Barbara Kirkland Collection

Nicholas Kessler

Although his influence may not have been as sweeping as some of Montana's "pace setters" who lived in Helena, Nicholas Kessler was one of the most beloved. Born in Germany in 1833, Kessler came to this country in 1854 and subsequently made his way westward during the Pike's Peak gold rush. He spent some time prospecting in Colorado before arriving at Virginia City late in 1863. Kessler gave up his dreams of striking it rich through gold, and established a bakery, restaurant, and liquor business. In 1864 he went back to Germany to visit his family and on his return went to Blackfoot City, near Helena, with the intention of constructing a brewery for Charles Beeher, a Navadan who already was operating a brewery in Helena.

Beeher sold out his interests to Kessler in 1868, and the energetic young German soon added to the Helena brewery to the point where it became one of the leading establishments of its kind in the region. He also established a brickyard in connection with the brewery on the city's west side. For many years, Kessler's beer and bricks were familiar adjuncts to life in Helena, even as his affable personality brought him so many friends that at his death in 1905 eulogies came from countless friends—among them fellow businessman A. M. Holter, who said of him, "a truer and more honest man never lived."

Kessler was married in New York in 1873 to Miss Louise Ebert, and they became the parents of three children, who were still youngsters when Mrs. Kessler died in 1880 after exposure to flood waters when Chessman Reservoir on Ten Mile Creek west of the city collapsed. Kessler was a kindly father to his children, whom he raised in the family's brick mansion, still standing near the old brewery building. ■

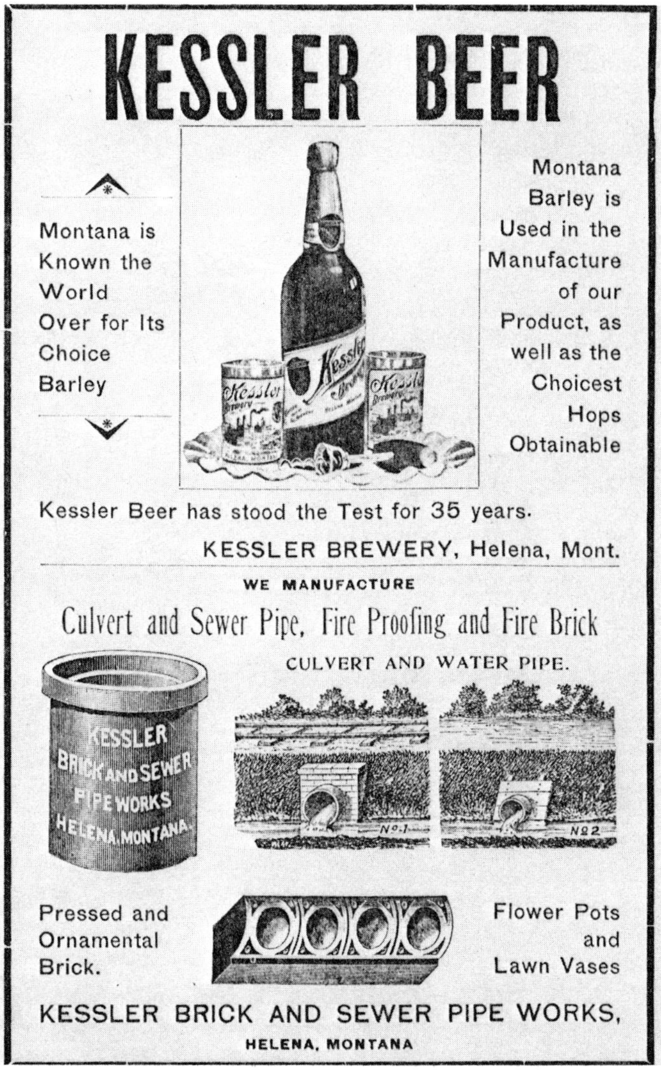

The massive brick brewery which Nick Kessler developed on Helena's western edge, is seen in this early picture, with beer kegs stacked in front and cows grazing in the foreground. Courtesy of Helena Water Department

Nicholas Kessler
Taylor photo; from the Jean Baucus Collection

Kessler Beer Wagon

Courtesy of the Mark McBride Collection

Nick Kessler and His Family

After the death of his wife in 1880, Nick Kessler raised his three children alone. Here he poses with Charles, Frederick, and baby Matilda. Montana Historical Society Collection

Thomas C. Power

No Montanan better fits the "merchant prince" or "pace setter" mold than Thomas C. Power, born in Dubuque, Iowa, in 1849 of Irish parentage. He was a resident of Montana from his arrival in 1867 until his death at his palatial home in Helena in March 1923 at the age of just under eighty-four. Tom Power was the oldest in a family of four children. They included a brother, John W. Power, who was to join him in Montana and establish his own home and family. One of his two sisters was Miss Sarah E. Power, who, following the death of his wife, became chatelaine of the Power mansion at 600 Harrison Avenue.

Raised on a hard-working farm near Dubuque, Tom Power gleaned enough education to qualify for a youthful teaching career. But in 1860, when he was twenty-one years old, he found his real destiny when he joined a surveying party in the Dakotas. He became a government surveyor, and in the early 1860s was a member of an expedition which ascended the Missouri River to the head of navigation at Fort Benton. Here he saw the potential for developing Montana Territory.

In 1867 Power opened a general merchandise store at Fort Benton and quickly sensed the need for faster transportation of goods. In 1874, in association with I. G. and George Baker, he built the steamer *Benton*, which eventually made forty-four trips laden with merchandise from "the states" and returned with furs, precious metals, and other raw materials produced in the new Montana Territory. Eventually, the *Benton* was joined by the *Helena*, the *Butte*, and the *Black Hills*, all carrying the famous Block P insignia which is still associated with the Power interests.

Thomas Power was notably diverse in his interests. He moved to Helena in 1873, correctly predicting the emergence of the city as a center of transportation and politics and the fading of Fort Benton as the railroads approached to replace steamboating. In 1879 he established a stage line between Fort Benton and Helena and was soon building solid business blocks in Helena, starting with the Steamboat Block, still standing on the wedge-shaped lot where Helena Avenue meets Main Street. T. C. had his office in the "prow" (now removed), and his many other ventures were managed from the offices behind.

On the corner of Sixth and Main he built the imposing Power Block which today still dominates the business district. Next to it, Senator Power built the five-story Gold Block which lasted until the fire of 1928, at which time his firm rebuilt a new two-story Gold Block still standing. Aside from the Power Block annex on Sixth, Senator Power, with a partner, Charles Belden, constructed the handsome Diamond Block with tiny diamond-shaped mirrors on the facade. Today this restored building greatly enhances the corner of Park and Sixth avenues.

Thomas C. Power
From Progressive Men of Montana

Power's wide-ranging interests extended to banking, with the establishment of the American National Bank of Montana in the Power Block, to extensive livestock operations, and a deep involvement in Helena's waterworks. He served several terms in the Montana legislature and was a delegate to two major constitutional conventions. In 1888 he was narrowly defeated in his campaign for governor, and two years later joined Wilbur F. Sanders as one of two U.S. senators from Montana Territory.

Senator and Mrs. Power lived in a number of Helena homes, but the one for which they are best known still stands at 600 Harrison Avenue, its distinctive rose porphyry rock coming from Power's own quarry near Helena. This mansion, which includes a massive carriage house, was built with minute attention to detail in the cherry and oak interiors and for many years was the scene of formal but gracious entertainment. Mrs. Power, the former Mary Flannagen, whom Power had married in Dubuque in 1867, died a few years after the mansion was completed, and the senator's sister, Sarah, came to preside over its entertainments in later years.

Power's only son, Charles Benton Power, joined the family's business operations after his education at Georgetown and Columbia universities. Some years after Senator Power's death in 1923, the mansion was given over to the Helena Catholic Diocese, and it was used until recent years as a bishopric residence and diocese headquarters. T. C. Power's granddaughter, Jane, was married to Thomas Tobin in the chapel when the residence served the diocese. The Tobins are still Helena residents.■

Steamboat *Helena*

This was the second boat built for T. C. Power and Brother at Pittsburgh in about 1879. The large number of passengers included a crew of men coming from St. Paul to build Fort Assiniboine, a military post near Havre. On the upper deck (right side) marked A, is Mrs. Martin Maginnis, whose husband was Major Maginnis, the fort commander and a man who served many years in Congress as Montana's delegate. Mrs. T. C. Power and her young son, Charles B. Power, are marked B and C. The mountain boat had been developed especially for rocky, shallow, snag-strewn and sandbar-infested Western rivers. Piled on deck was wood the riverboat burned for fuel. The crew stopped along the way to refuel at points where cutters had been hired to keep woodyards supplied. Courtesy of the Jane Power Tobin Collection

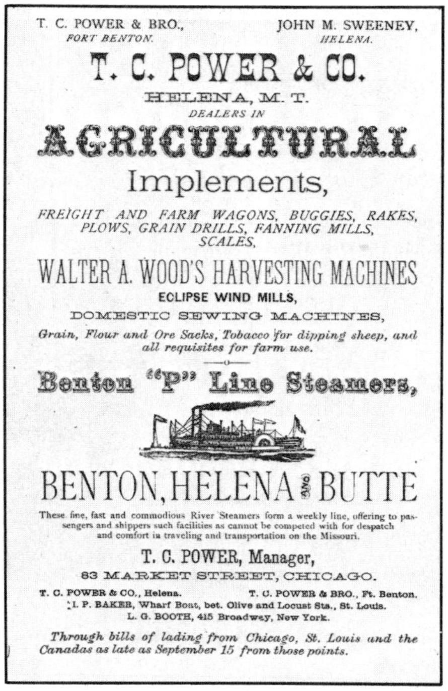

Senator T. C. Power and Son

Charles Benton Power, born in 1869, was the only child of the senator. He is pictured here with his father in about 1876. Courtesy of the Jane Power Tobin Collection

Senator Power and His Grandson, circa 1910

Senator Power had one grandson, Benton, who died while still a young man, leaving two sisters, Margaret and Jane. Courtesy of the Jane Power Tobin Collection

Senator Power Residence on Harrison Avenue

This handsome mansion, which took two years to build, was constructed of rose granite, mined from Power's own quarry. Senator and Mrs. Power had a gala opening of the new home the evening of Friday, November 22, 1891. Mrs. Power lived only a few years more, and at her death the senator invited his sister, Sarah, to take care of young Charles and to manage the household. After the senator's death the home was unoccupied for several years, and Charles Power then gave it to the Catholic Diocese. Bishop Hunthausen remodeled the carriage house to serve as a chancery, and the main house was a residence of Sisters serving the diocese. Today the main house is a private residence, and the chancery building houses the offices of the architectural firm, Crossman, Whitney, and Griffin. Montana Historical Society Collection

Power Block

Dominating the gulch is the massive, six-story Power Block, which was built in 1889 on the corner of Sixth and Main. Senator Power was the leading builder in Helena at the time, having built the Gold Block joining the Power Block on the south, the Power Block annex joining the same structure on the west, and the wedge-shaped Diamond Block at the top of Sixth Avenue. Previously he had constructed the Steamboat Block where Helena Avenue joins Main Street. Denny McCall photo

Wilbur Fisk Sanders

One of Montana's first and most influential citizens, Wilbur Fisk Sanders, was born in New York state in 1834 and died at his home in Helena in July 1905 at the age of seventy-one. A staunch and outspoken Republican, Sanders moved in 1854 to Ohio, where he taught school and studied law in the offices of his uncle, Sidney Edgerton, who in 1863 was named chief justice of Idaho Territory, of which Montana was then a part.

Although he was not in robust health as a young man, Sanders served in the Civil War as commander of a company of infantry which he had recruited in Ohio. Throughout the remainder of his life, he was known as Colonel Sanders.

After the war, in an effort to regain his health, he accompanied his uncle to Idaho Territory and was with Edgerton in Bannack when the decision was made to seek separate territorial status for Montana Territory. Sanders became a permanent resident of the territory, making his first notable contribution to public life while he still lived in Virginia City. He became the prosecutor for the Vigilantes, formed to rid the territory of a band of infamous criminals whose reign of terror and lawlessness had plagued the early gold camps.

Sanders's courageous stand against the outlaws who were summarily hanged at Bannack and Virginia City was a forerunner of the legal and political career which was to follow after he moved his family to Helena in the early 1870s. He had a sharp tongue, but even those who felt its sting credited him with the courage of his convictions. He served a number of terms in the Montana legislature and conducted a busy law practice which included among its clients the Northern Pacific Railroad.

One of Sanders's deep concerns was for preserving Montana history, and he was a leader in the formation and continuation of the Montana Historical Society's collection of newspapers, manuscripts, and maps. Although a major part of the collection was destroyed when Helena's worst fire consumed his law office in 1874, Sanders led a crusade to begin collecting material again, and today the society's collections still contain much of that material.

In 1889, after a bitter fight with contending Democrats, Sanders became one of Montana's two U.S. senators, and once more his caustic tongue and wit were heard, this time in the halls of Congress. He was one of the few westerners who opposed the free coinage of silver in the early 1890s, and he all but lost his political influence in Montana when he spoke up against it at the state Republican convention.

Wilbur Fisk Sanders
From Progressive Men of Montana

Colonel Sanders continued to voice strong opinions until death approached in 1905. With him at the time of his death at his home on Ewing Street were his wife Harriet, whom he had married in Ohio in 1856, his sons, James U., Wilbur E., and Louis P., his brother, Junius G., and his sister, Miss Sarepta Sanders, a pioneer Montana teacher. ■

W. F. Sanders and Grandchildren, circa 1897

Mr. Sanders was photographed here with the children of his son, James U. Sanders. They were Margaret and Harriet. Montana Historical Society Collection

Sanders Residence on Ewing

The new Lewis and Clark Courthouse building was at the head of Ewing, which was still an unpaved street in 1894. At the far right is Sanders's home, and beyond it are the tower and gables of the Chessman home, now the old Governor's Mansion. F. Jay Haynes photo; courtesy of the Haynes Foundation Collection, Montana Historical Society

Panorama of Helena, 1890

Photographer F. Jay Haynes climbed the hill on the south side, where the Hale Reservoir is now located, in August 1890 and took this panoramic view of the city, which in that year claimed 13,834 residents and a substantial number of well-established business blocks. Last Chance Gulch starts at the lower left of the photograph and runs diagonally towards the north. The first four-story brick building in the center foreground was the Bristol Hotel, and next door was the International Hotel, located at the juncture of State (formerly Bridge) and Main streets. Clearly seen at the extreme right is the Bluestone House, now restored, and the famed fire tower above it on the hill at the extreme right. Further down Main Street is a large building with two horizontal white bands across the top. This is the Gans and Klein building on the corner of Broadway and Main. To the right, up Broadway, is the top of the facade of the Masonic Temple and the Parchen Block, and immediately behind the twin gables of the Parchen Block is the full facade of the Helena Hotel on Sixth Avenue.

On West Sixth, in the center of the picture, can be seen the Electric Block with its tall smokestack. In the left background a row of telephone poles marks Dearborn Avenue on the city's west side, with the old Hawthorne School, its flagpole dome vis-

ible, to the left of these. The very large residence to the left of the school, minus the trees of today, is the great T. C. Power mansion with arched veranda and tall chimneys. Far left and center can be seen Reeder's Alley. The present-day Stone House restaurant is the long, low building at extreme left center. F. Jay Haynes photo; courtesy of the Haynes Foundation Collection, Montana Historical Society

Chapter Six

Statehood and the 1890s

It was a crisply beautiful Friday, November 8, 1889, when J. Swan, manager of Helena's Western Union office, hurried up Broadway to the courthouse office of Joseph Kemp Toole to deliver in person a telegram which announced that President Benjamin Harrison had just signed the document proclaiming Montana as the nation's forty-first state.

This piece of news, awaited and strived for from the very beginning of territorial days a quarter of a century earlier, came shortly before Helena entered the 1890s, the decade which was to see opulence but financial panic, political upheaval and graft, two more fights with rival cities for capital city honors, a peak of population which would not be seen again for forty years, and finally a surge of patriotism as young men marched off to fight the Spaniards in Cuba and the Philippines.

There was rejoicing in the streets of Helena on November 8, 1889, however, as Joseph K. Toole, Montana's new thirty-nine-year-old bachelor governor, took the reins of office only three hours after Swan delivered his telegram. There was rejoicing in the press as well. "The 8th day of November, A.D., 1889, will forever be a red-letter day in the history of Montana," trumpeted the *Helena Herald* in its issue of the same afternoon. "It marks the termination of our Territorial vassalage, the beginning of our grand career as a sovereign state, the peer of the oldest and most powerful of all the sisterhood. . . . Today the people of Montana become endowed with the fullest measure of the rights of citizenship, the right and power to choose our own rulers, make our own laws, subject only to the limitations of the Constitution."

Much of the euphoria of that day ended only three weeks later, when Governor Toole convened the first state legislature on Saturday, November 23. Eight Republican senators met at noon at the courthouse, with Lieutenant Governor John E. Rickards presiding. Eight Democratic senators refused to sit with them, and the first session of the Montana Senate adjourned without a quorum.

The same thing happened to the House of Representatives. Thirty Republican members responded to rollcall at the new Iron Front Block on North Main and were sworn into office by Judge Henry Blake. At the courthouse, meanwhile, twenty-eight Democrats organized their own "House" with C. P. Blakely of Gallatin County, who claimed he was the oldest member present, presiding and eventually assuming the speakership.

This incredible state of affairs, which persisted for the first two years of statehood, had its roots in the political battles of opposing Clark/Daly forces, a matter so complex that it is not possible to deal with it here in depth. Suffice to say that as Montana entered its first year of statehood, the seats of power in the U.S. Congress and in Montana's temporary state capital in the Lewis and Clark County Courthouse were all occupied by Helena men. W. F. Sanders and T. C. Power were duly seated in the U.S. Senate by the Senate Committee on Privileges and Elections, which rejected the claims of W. A. Clark and Martin Maginnis. Thomas H. Carter took his seat as Montana's sole congressman, and Joseph K. Toole, former congressman who had led the final battle for statehood, was the first governor-elect of the state.

On January 1, 1890, there was plenty to celebrate in spite of the divided condition of governmental affairs. Helena was marking its twenty-fifth anniversary, and although it was eighteen degrees below zero outside, Helena's prominent hostesses threw their homes open for guests. They included Governor Toole, who was preparing to go to Washington, D.C., shortly to marry Miss Lilly Rosengrans and bring her back as the state's first First Lady. "Callers were surfeited of the most delicious edibles consisting of cakes, jellies, ices and all things delightful to the palate but conducive of dyspepsia," said the *Herald* of the New Year's Day celebrations in 1890.

While T. C. Power was in Washington as one of Montana's U.S. senators, he announced that the first floor of his new Power Block on the corner of Sixth and Main was being fitted up to house his American National Bank. A few months later, yet another bank, the Helena National, with John T. Murphy as president, opened up right next door. Helena now claimed six national banks, four daily newspapers, and a population of just under 14,000, an incredible growth of over 10,000 since 1880.

In 1892 the first hint that a military establishment was planned for Helena came when the U.S. Senate appropriated funds for what was to become Fort Harrison. The Montana Club paid $45,000 for the lot at the corner of Sixth and Fuller, which is the site of its building today, and on May 24, Colonel Charles A. Broadwater died in his quarters at the Broadwater Hotel.

At the November election in 1892, Grover Cleveland was elected president, and although Helena garnered 14,032 votes to retain the capital, she failed to receive the required majority of all votes cast. Anaconda, with which Helena had to compete again in 1894, came in with 10,172, while lesser totals were garnered by Butte, Bozeman, Great Falls, Deer Lodge, and Boulder.

In 1893, as John E. Rickards became Montana's second state governor and the last spike was driven on the western slope of the Cascades to complete the Great Northern Railroad from coast to coast, the demonetization of silver began affecting Montana, as it was the entire country. In March it was announced that over a million dollars in gold was held in the vaults of Helena banks, half of which was exchanged for treasury notes at the direction of the new Helena Clearing House.

Montana saw its first bank closure in June, when the Higgins Western Bank of Missoula could not keep up with demands for withdrawal. The next month, when the price of silver dropped to sixty-two cents, the gigantic Bi-Metallic and Granite mines tied down their whistles and closed operations. Almost immediately the First National Bank of Philipsburg closed its doors, and on the twenty-seventh, Helena depositors were greeted with closed doors at Sam Hauser's First National Bank and at the late Colonel Broadwater's Montana National. The panic had spread, from Wall Street and London to Last Chance Gulch.

Although Hauser was able to reopen his bank, its days were numbered; consolidations and the solidity of men like T. C. Power and Thomas Cruse saw their banks through the crisis. They joined other members of the Helena Board of Trade in "exchanging views" on the financial climate and suggesting ways to reduce municipal and school expenses.

In 1894 nationwide railroad strikes caught up with Montana when an estimated 1,700 Great Northern employees walked off the job. As of old, the wagon road between Helena and Fort Benton was put to use, with all manner of carriages and wagons carrying goods, including six wagonloads of Kessler Beer, which went in a single shipment to Great Falls.

Captain George S. Hoyt, who arrived to take charge of building Fort Harrison, announced bid openings for some of the buildings, and Mrs. T. C. Power gave an afternoon entertainment in honor of Mrs. Hoyt.

At the general election on November 7, 1894, the *Helena Herald* headlines screamed, "HELENA WINS! The Capital Stays Here! Boodle and Bossism Rebuked at the Polls by Our Patriotic People!" One of the longest parades ever assembled in Montana followed. William A. Clark, the Butte Copper King who still yearned for a Senate seat but was a hero in Helena because he had vigorously supported her against his archrival, Marcus Daly, led the procession in a buggy trimmed with garlands of flowers. A gigantic anaconda snake, fashioned of canvas and with a bleeding wound in its side, was taken through town to the strains of a funeral march.

"It was the only sight of its kind in Montana," said the *Herald*, "and will remain for a lifetime indelibly stamped on the memories of those who were fortunate enough to witness it."

In 1895, for the first time, both houses of the legislature met in a single building, the Merchants Hotel. Since the first two "rump" sessions of a divided legislature, the lawmakers had met at such diverse places as the Electric Block, the Power Block, and the courthouse.

As the 1890s came to a close, sites for Montana's capitol building were considered and architect's plans submitted. At a meeting of the Capitol Commission in April 1898, Thomas Cruse appeared and offered to take the entire issue of $350,000 in bonds bearing 6 percent interest, thus assuring that building could proceed. The cornerstone was laid on July 4, 1899, and in spite of predictions, the domed building had to wait exactly three years for dedication. Thus for the sessions of 1895, 1897, 1899, and 1901, the Merchants Hotel was, literally, Montana's statehouse.

Patriotic fervor filled the Helena air in 1898, when the First Montana Regiment, billeted in tents on Peosta Avenue, trained in the shadow of Mount Helena. In mid-July the regiment sailed for the Philippines, where two of its popular officers, Lieutenant Colonel Robert Bruce Wallace and Major James W. Drennan, were wounded and eventually died of complications. Their funerals in Helena were the largest seen here since the death of Colonel Broadwater six years earlier.

As the new century began, the Fisk brothers retired from the newspaper business after publishing the *Helena Herald* for an uninterrupted period of over three decades, and in Ohio, Sidney Edgerton, who had been Montana's first territorial governor, died at his home in Akron at the age of eighty-two.■

Governor J. K. Toole

Joseph Kemp Toole, born in Missouri in 1851, was Montana's territorial delegate in Congress when statehood finally became a reality in 1889. On January 15 of that year, he formally presented Montana's case to Congress, pointing out that the territorial treasury had a surplus of $130,192.70, that four-fifths of the residents were American born, and that over $13 million had been taken from Montana mines in 1888. A handsome man and an eloquent speaker, Toole, a Democrat, defeated Republican T. C. Power by a scant 1,000 votes to become Montana's first state governor, but he served in the post longer than any other man. Completing his first term in 1893, he returned to private law practice until 1900, when he again was elected. He was reelected in 1905 for a third term but resigned on April 1, 1908, with another year yet to serve. Reasons of ill health were given for the resignation, but J. K. Toole lived another twenty-one years, dying in Helena in 1929 at the age of seventy-eight years. Montana Historical Society Collection

Lewis and Clark County Courthouse

On July 5, 1887, Lewis and Clark County's Romanesque courthouse was dedicated, designed to house all territorial, county and, later, state offices until Montana's capitol building was completed in 1902. In 1887 this was an imposing building. Contracts for construction were let in 1886, and in December of that year, the county commissioners purchased the town clock from a Boston firm for $2,400. This included a 3,000-pound bell "tuned in the key of a, b or c natural, upon which the hours and half hours will be struck." At the time of its dedication, at which Chief Justice Decius Wade was the main speaker, the new courthouse superseded the second Lewis and Clark County Courthouse, a square, brick structure next door, which had been demolished by the time this picture was taken.

Today this building, minus the clock tower, which was destroyed in the earthquakes of 1935, serves as headquarters for a limited number of legal and judicial county offices. Most county offices are now in the City-County Building at the head of Sixth Avenue, the former Federal Building which has been replaced by a new edifice at the head of Main Street, built as part of Helena's renewal program of the 1970s. State offices have long since moved to the capitol complex. Montana Historical Society Collection

Assay Office and Merchants Hotel

Helena's solid and historic U.S. Assay Office, established in 1875, is in the right foreground of this picture, looking down Broadway. At the turn of the century, it was reported that the Helena office, once presided over by Russell Harrison, son of the president, had processed an average of $2 million worth of gold bullion per year. At the time this picture was taken, the Merchants Hotel down the street was still one of Helena's grander hotels, but by 1889, the year of statehood, it had long since been upstaged by more elegant stopping places. This building was, however, Montana's statehouse, the place where the legislature met for the sessions of 1895, 1897, 1899, and 1901. As work on the new capitol building was under way, it was hoped the old Merchants Hotel could be replaced for the 1901 session. But it was not to be: managers of the Merchants scurried about for yet a fourth time, getting its rooms ready for the lawmakers. Later the old hotel was converted to an apartment house called the Monticello, but today it is no more. It was one of the few prominent buildings on Broadway to be demolished during the urban renewal period. The historic Assay Office still stands. Montana Historical Society Collection

Iron Front Building

This building, still standing in the 400 block of North Last Chance Gulch, boasted a spacious assembly hall on the third floor, where thirty Republicans met in 1889 to form their version of the first state House of Representatives. The cast-iron components of the building's facade were manufactured by the John Stedman Foundry, west of Helena. This type of prefabricated construction, using repetitive cast-iron elements, was a forerunner of modern steel and glass curtain wall construction. This historic building was completed in 1887 at a cost of $100,000. Courtesy of the Nelson Seeley Collection

Last Chance Gulch, 1894

Photographer F. Jay Haynes took this picture of Helena's main thoroughfare, looking south, in 1894, the year the fight was finally won against Anaconda for capital city honors. Streetcar tracks are visible along the street, paved with bricks from Nick Kessler's brickyard on the city's western edge. Power and telephone poles and wire clutter the view, but in 1894 these were evidences of industrial progress.

T. C. Power's massive Power Block, built in 1889 at the corner of Sixth and Main, dominates the right side of the picture; across the street is the Goodkind Building. Across Sixth Avenue to the north, with horse and buggy parked in front, is the Broadwater-Ashby Block, which was sold in 1894 to the Weinstein brothers for $45,000, considered the largest single real estate deal in Helena history to that time. This building was demolished in 1930 and is now the site of the First National Bank. F. Jay Haynes photo; courtesy of the Haynes Foundation Collection, Montana Historical Society

Telephone Exchange

Telephone service began in Helena in the summer of 1882, when poles with as many as fourteen crossbars were in place. Gradually, service expanded in the city and outside, and in July 1888 the exchange was moved to the third floor of the First National Bank Building, now known as the Securities Building, overlooking Jackson Street. It is probable that this picture, with a watchful supervisor overseeing the operators, was taken after this move, when a total of 240 telephones were keeping the boards flashing. Telephone operators, employed at the boards for almost a century, were replaced in 1982 by the automatic dial system. Montana Historical Society Collection

Electric Block

Electricity for Helena, Montana's first city with such luxury, was steam-generated for many years in this building with minaret-like smokestack which once dominated the corner of Sixth and Park. The plant was established in 1894 by the Helena Electric Railway to power its street railway system. The first Canyon Ferry Dam, started in 1896 and completed in 1898, soon furnished plenty of electric power, not only for Helena but for much of central Montana. By the end of 1898, the Helena Herald *exulted that "very soon, the people of Helena will read at night by the aid of electricity generated by water!" Now demolished and replaced by a parking ramp, the Electric Block was once used for many purposes other than electric generation, including some sessions of the legislature.* Montana Historical Society *Collection*

Montana Historical Society Collection

Helena's Street Railway

Courtesy of the Mark McBride Collection

In March 1886 the Helena Street Railway Company, organized by C. A. Broadwater, T. C. Power, Charles W. Cannon, H. M. Parchen, A. M. Holter, D. A. G. Flowerree, and John B. Wilson, was authorized by the city council to build and maintain street cars in Helena and its vicinity. At first, the motive power was horses, and according to the Helena Herald, *the fourteen-foot cars, built by the Pullman Company, had "cushioned seats and backs, and large plate glass windows." They were painted a pleasing buff color, and each car bore the inscription, "Bridge Street to Depot—Helena Street Railway Company."*

Later, as can be seen in the wintry scene above, steam engine power was used, filling the air with black smoke. Still later, as seen in the upper picture of a Lower Broadway car parked at Broadwater's natatorium on Helena's western edge, quiet and sophisticated electricity powered these popular conveyances. It was in 1927 that the last vestiges of the street railway days were removed, replaced by modern buses.

First Canyon Ferry Dam

This fine panoramic view of the first Canyon Ferry Dam, completed in 1898 by private investors in the Missouri River Power Company, shows the barrier nearly complete. The location was at the mouth of Black Rock Canyon, just above the old Canyon Ferry village. Lake Sewell, created by the dam, which generated 3,200 horsepower of current, submerged a few ranches and sections of the old stage lines, but the modern Canyon Ferry Dam, built a half-century later, would submerge a great deal more.

The press of the 1890s was filled with references to this pioneer Missouri River hydroelectric project. Surveys began in 1894, and by October 1896, 150 men were at work, living in quarters on the west side of the river and taking their meals at the Canyon House, seen at the left side of this picture. The dam was forty feet wide, resting on piles driven to bedrock. While the work went on, a crew of men under Hugh Kirkendall was busy building a road which would carry heavy machinery from the railroad at Clasoil and over the divide to the damsite.

Early in 1898 it was announced that a large casting, which weighed 40,000 pounds, was unloaded at Clasoil and carried over Kirkendall's road for installation. In February, when the wheels began to turn and the Missouri "went dry" at French Bar, gold seekers descended on the site and, according to the Herald, *"panned out enough gold to give them all the fever." Canyon Ferry pioneer Court Sheriff purchased about $300 worth of the dust and brought it to Helena for processing. The dam began supplying electricity to Helena in September 1898, after the project had been completed at a total cost of $450,000.*
From the Jean Baucus Collection

Helena's Tenderloin District

The International and the Bristol hotels which faced Main Street are at the very bottom of this picture and partially cropped. Between them is the covered bridge with Gifford's HHH Medicine sign affixed. The bridge linked the International and its annex, which adjoined the Bristol. State Street, first named Bridge Street for the first bridge across Last Chance Stream, winds upward and to the left. At the top of the hill can be seen the Italianate home with tower, built by China Clarke and later occupied by Henry Parchen. At the far right in the background can be seen the two-story Lissner School.

Along State Street at the left side may be seen many of the city's famous early-day houses of ill fame, notably the Coliseum Theatre, a vaudevillian variety theater owned by Chicago Joe (Josephine Hensley). Towards Main Street from here, next to the International Hotel, can be seen Chicago Joe's Red Star Saloon. The square, brick building with two chimneys and two dormer windows was the Grand, also owned by the notorious Helena businesswoman.

The large, two-storied, red brick structure behind it with white cupola with sunburst design and round, turreted tower on the extreme left corner is the Castle, the most fashionable house of easy entertainment known in Helena, constructed and managed by Belle Crafton who later sold out to Lillie Ashton. The Castle, now gone, is often confused with the Blue Stone House to the south of this picture, originally a private residence, which was restored during urban renewal days. The low, brick house with the twin towers directly behind the Castle, still standing on State Street, was for many years the private residence of Belle Crafton, who later changed her name to the more respectable Molly Byrnes. Courtesy of the Mark McBride Collection

Helena's Finest, 1891

Plainclothes detectives posed with uniformed members of the Helena police force in 1891, in front of the brick city hall building at the corner of West Main and State streets, which had been completed in 1885. Seated in front at the left is Chief of Police William Sims, and seated next to him is Sergeant Sam Mickelson. Second row, left to right: William F. Bossler, Milton Whitten, Quill Lawrence, Con Reiss, Nils P. Walters, and John Gibson. Third row, left to right: Tom Finnegan, John Flynn, Mose Quinten, William Lloyd, William Treacy, and Ed Wanesse. Fourth row, left to right: John Grogan, John Back, Gee Baker, Joe Callaghan, William McKenzie, Peter Scharrenbroich, and William Bushnell.

It is possible that many descendants of these men still live in Helena. It is known that Patrolman Bossler was the granduncle of Dr. David W. Bossler, while Detective Walters, who later became the Pinkerton detective agent in Helena, was the maternal grandfather of Dr. Clem L. (Bud) Shafer. It is interesting to note that Scharrenbroich, who later became a deputy sheriff, led a raid on the venerable Montana Club on March 15, 1903, when Helena law officers were cracking down on wide-open gambling in the city. An embarrassed Henry A. Meyer, steward at the club and a city alderman at the time, paid a small fine for the offense. A month later, the Montana Club, which claimed it had allowed gambling only for drinks, was destroyed by fire. Courtesy of Clem L. Shafer

Helena City Hall and Fire Department, 1891

The horse-drawn equipment of the Helena Fire Department posed in front of the new city hall completed in 1885 at the corner of West Main and State streets. Montana Historical Society Collection

Dance Hall Girls

State (formerly Bridge) Street, Wood and Clore streets, as well as South Main, were crowded with bars and dance halls. Hurdy-gurdy houses which first appeared in every mining camp were soon replaced by more elaborate bars with dance hall girls to entertain the local and visiting gentry. The identity of this early Helena bar and dance emporium cannot be established, but certainly it was similar to such places as Chicago Joe's Coliseum or Belle Crafton's Castle. The numbered call box to the left of the bar has two of its arrows pointing downward, suggesting that there have been calls from rooms for drinks to be brought up. The mirrored sign in back of the man at the right partially reads that no minors were allowed at performances, which suggests that this, like Chicago Joe's, was a place for bawdy vaudeville entertainment. Reinig photo; courtesy of Blanche Judge

Josephine Hensley (Chicago Joe)

By 1871 this pragmatic businesswoman was queen of Helena's red-light district. She had learned the ways of city nightlife in Chicago as a fourteen-year-old girl, and at that time changed her name from Mary Welch to Josephine Airey. By 1883 enterprising Josephine had become Helena's largest landowner on Wood Street. She married a gambler known as "Black Hawk" Hensley, and from then on she was known as "Chicago Joe" Hensley. Most of the girls in her establishment were from her former town of operation, Chicago. C. W. Carter photo; Montana Historical Society Collection

Saloon Action in Helena

It is difficult to say whether a fight is brewing between the small man in the foreground who has thrown down his coat and hat or whether there is a bet on as to how long the horse and rider will be allowed inside. This typical Helena saloon, complete with spattered spittoons, was selling chances on a ten-pound turkey at a dime a chance, as well as drinks at two for a quarter. The rule was that when a man put twenty-five cents on the bar, he received a copper chip good for a second drink, hence twenty-five cents was referred to as two bits. Courtesy of the Mark McBride Collection

Waiting to Be Served

It was February 1909 when some fairly well-dressed customers lined up at this Helena bar, with white-jacketed bartenders waiting to serve them. Notable on the back wall, aside from the calendar which dates the picture and proclaims the wines, liquor, and cigar wares of Goodkind Brothers, are some family pictures, including a fanciful cutout picture of three young ladies in an automobile and a clock which indicates it is eight-fifteen, probably in the evening. Courtesy of the Mark McBride Collection

Broadway Fish Market

Proprietors of this popular early Helena store, located at 122 Broadway, were ready for the Thanksgiving trade of 1889, offering a free can of oysters with every turkey "bought at retail." It was time for giving thanks in Montana, and particularly Helena, which had just become the capital of the new state. Montana Historical Society Collection

Cosmopolitan Hotel

In its day this was a first-class hotel noted for excellent cuisine; rooms were offered at fifty cents and seventy-five cents. Mail Pouch tobacco was advertised on the side of the building. The facade of this four-story building was quite handsome, with nicely designed brick verticals and three lovely wrought-iron balconies across the front. The lower, more modest structure on the right apparently was the hotel's coffee shop with rented rooms above. This building, at 43-45 South Main, was demolished many years ago. Montana Historical Society Collection

Novelty Block

This fanciful structure was built at 13-15 South Main in 1888 by Auerbach and Purcell as "one of the handsomest buildings, one that would be a credit to the city." A seven-and-one-half ounce gold nugget, one of the largest ever to come out of the gulch, was found on the site at the time of excavation. Imposing though it once was, the Novelty Block did not survive the urban renewal period. The two picturesque towers were preserved, however, and today stand as the tops of kiosks on either end of the pedestrian mall.

Cutting through Lawrence Street

Rough preliminary work had been completed in the early 1890s on the extension of Lawrence Street east of Main when this picture was taken. In the spring of 1891, the Helena Herald *complained bitterly that ground for the street extension could have been had four years before for $1,500. "Now," the paper said, "the owners want $34,000." J. B. Blakeslee sits in apparent defiance in front of his rough stone photo gallery, perhaps waiting for a court order for its removal to make room for the streeet. In the background and in sharp contrast to Blakeslee's modest little establishment are the soaring turrets of the new Helena High School, the cornerstone of which was laid in October 1890 and which was finished in 1893. Courtesy of the N. J. Holter Collection*

William G. Conrad and His Helena Bank

The Conrad brothers, William G. and Charles, came to Fort Benton in 1868 to work as clerks in the I. G. Baker mercantile firm and eventually built up major trading and merchandising interests which in 1880 led them into banking as well, Charles in Kalispell and William in Helena. Just before the turn of the century, W. G. Conrad established the Conrad Trust and Savings Bank in Helena, in which he is here pictured in 1910 with his assistant cashier, China Clarke, standing by his side. Conrad died in Helena in 1914 at the age of sixty-six years. From the William Clarke Collection; courtesy of Helena Abstract and Title Company

Sands Brothers Store

Morris and Julius Sands were among Helena's earliest merchants, establishing their first dry goods emporium in a frame building at 32 South Main in the 1870s. This first building burned in the fire of 1874 and was replaced by this two-story, Romanesque granite structure, which still stands. This enterprising firm dealt in a variety of merchandise for milady and the home. Montana Historical Society Collection

West Lawrence and North Main Street

This photograph, taken after 1883, is one of the few early views of Last Chance Stream, which can be seen flowing through the center of the picture toward mine dumps in the background. The Sanford maps of 1884 and 1888 indicate that A. M. Holter operated lumbering yards on both sides of the stream. Far back across the railroad tracks was the C. T. Perry Factory where candles and soap were manufactured. The three-story brick structure beyond the Windsor House is the Steamboat Block, which T. C. Power built to house offices of his various enterprises. His office was in the front "prow" of the building, a part which was removed many years ago. Lawrence Street crosses the bottom of the photograph, and at the very bottom right is a white screen with folding chairs erected in Haymarket Square, perhaps for a Chautauqua or other performance open to the public. Courtesy of the N. J. Holter Collection

Helena's West Side, circa 1890

Historic Paynes Hotel stands in the lower right foreground of this picture, which shows Lawrence Street cutting diagonally from right to left and up towards the original Hawthorne School with bell tower which dominates the center background. Many of the large homes on the west side had already been built, but yard trees had not yet grown large enough to obscure them. Discernible in the right background is the great T. C. Power mansion with towering chimneys. The Paynes Hotel and adjacent small wooden buildings were torn down in 1904 to make room for the Federal Building, which is today the City-County Building. Courtesy of the N. J. Holter Collection

Medical Staff, Fort Harrison

This group of medical officers and staff was photographed in front of the Fort Harrison administration building soon after the turn of the century. Montana Historical Society Collection

Fort William Henry Harrison

This is a panoramic view of Fort William Henry Harrison, which began building in 1894, two years after Congress authorized a military post in Helena provided the city donated 1,000 acres as a building site. Carrying a $200,000 appropriation, the project got under way in June 1894, with the arrival of Captain George S. Hoyt. By 1895 everything was completed except the original hospital. The facility had cost about $214,000 up to that time, and two infantry companies arrived late in September for billeting and training.

Fort Harrison was used as a regular army base until 1912, and in 1917 the Montana National Guard trained here off and on until 1919, when the facility was taken over by the U.S. Public Health Service for hospital services. During World War II, the First Special Service Force, a joint American/Canadian commando force, received intensive training and was billeted here. No regular army troops have been stationed at the fort since that time, but its facilities are regularly used for Montana National Guard equipment storage and maintenance and weekly training. Dominating the grounds today is the Veterans Administration Hospital, which, with modern enlargement, is one of the country's leading medical centers for veterans. Reinig photo; Montana Historical Society Collection

A Helena Beauty

Sarah Hewitt Kessler, wife of Charles N. Kessler, Sr., epitomized feminine beauty at the turn of the century, the Gibson Girl era. Montana Historical Society Collection

Thanksgiving Dinner at the Chessman Home, circa 1890

This group of Thanksgiving dinner guests was photographed by W. A. Taylor at the W. A. Chessman home, at the corner of Sixth and Ewing, which some thirteen years later became the home of Montana chief executives. Seated in the foreground are Martin B. Hirschfield, who taught piano in Helena for many years, and Frank N. Chessman, who became a distinguished Los Angeles physician. Seated behind them are David Owen, a clerk at the William Weinstein store; Penelope Cuthbert, a cousin of the Chessmans who later lived in Los Angeles and died in 1932; George Dana Linn, a bookkeeper for realtors Steele and Clements; Clare Wade (Safford), who had just graduated from Wellesley College; George H. Tilley, who served as a captain in the Spanish-American War and was killed in action in the Philippines; and Phil G. Schroeder of the real estate firm of Schroeder and Osborne.

Standing in the back row are Edgar Howell, a brother of Mrs. Chessman and at this time a teller at the Montana National Bank; Mrs. W. A. Chessman; John R. Barrows, who practiced in the law firm of Judge Decius Wade, and later moved to the small cattle town of Ubet and wrote a book about the town; May Cuthbert, a niece of Mrs. Chessman and daughter of Helena's first druggist, and later the wife of David Herron, mining engineer in charge of operations at the Drum Lummon mine at Marysville; James Shoemaker, at the time cashier of the Helena Water Works with offices on Fuller Avenue; Susan B. Chessman, daughter of Mr. and Mrs. W. A. Chessman; and a man who is believed to be Reverend Streater, a missionary who lived at this time in the 300 block of North Ewing. Montana Historical Society Collection

Fourth of July on Haymarket Square

Ladies in long skirts and many carrying umbrellas, men in their best suits, and children with pets and bicycles all gathered for a July Fourth celebration, probably to hear a patriotic speech, in this favorite early Helena assembly place. Across the top of the hill can be seen Helena's soaring new high school, the old Central School, and the city auditorium and library. F. J. Nye's saddle and harness shop, seen at the left, is now the site of the Northwestern Bank. Montana Historical Society Collection

Peter Larson Family on Vacation

Railroad contractor Peter Larson, second from the right, took his fashionably-dressed family on a mule ride in about 1890. All the ladies are riding sidesaddle. The two young ladies at the left are nieces of the Larsons, and the young lad on the right, Gordon Lamey, is a nephew. Mrs. Larson is in the center. Larson's daughter, Mabel, seen third from the right, later married Charles Power, son of the renowned Fort Benton and Helena businessman and political leader, Thomas C. Power. The man third from the left is unidentified. Courtesy of the Jane Power Tobin Collection

Helena Tennis Club

Eight ladies and eight men made up the Helena Tennis Club which gathered for this picture, taken in the 1890s. Jane Freeman is the young lady seated on the first step. Second row: Mr. Paris, Will Jones, Emily Hedges Woodbridge, E. C. Russell, Harry Brendegell, Mrs. May Cuthbert Herrin (holding baby), and behind her, Sue Chessman, daughter of William A. Chessman. Third row: Mrs. Will Jones, Lallah Brooke, sister of a pioneer Helena physician and a piano teacher throughout her life, unknown lady, Bill Barbour Turner, and Mrs. Edna Hedges Palmer. Men in the back row: Mr. Sackett, P. C. Schroeder, and Ed Brendegell. Montana Historical Society Collection

Fergus Family Gathering

The family of the venerable Montana pioneer, James A. Fergus, held a reunion, probably a short time before his death in 1902 at the age of eighty-nine. Fergus, for whom the central Montana county is named, came to the territory in 1862 with the Fisk Expedition, went on to become the first judge of the miners' court in Virginia City, the first recorder at Alder Gulch, and county commissioner for Madison and, later, Lewis and Clark counties. He ranched at the site of the present Sieben ranch before he went on to develop large holdings on Armells Creek in central Montana. This wise and canny pioneer, a member of the 1884 Constitutional Convention, was one of the few open range cattlemen who warned against policies which brought disaster to the cattle industry during the historic winter of 1886-87. Montana Historical Society Collection

Young Scions of Old Families

A group of Helena young people posed for this photograph in the summer of 1891. The occasion is not known. From left to right: B. Ferguson, Ella Blaine, Frances Murphy, E. W. Presser, L. P. Sanders, Bella Sharp, E. O. Holter, May Franklin, and C. F. Word. Montana Historical Society Collection

Picnic at the Gates

A stagecoach cab such as this often brought groups from Helena to take a boat trip through the Gates of the Mountains on one of Judge Hilger's crafts. This picture, taken by artist/photographer Ralph DeCamp, who married Judge Hilger's daughter, is apparently of one of those occasions. In 1884 the Helena Herald *published a story headed DOWN THE MISSOURI, which read, in part: "Excursionists who want to visit the grandest scenery in the Rocky Mountains will be glad to know that Judge Hilger is prepared with two boats to carry parties from 10 to 24 miles down through the Gates of the Mountains, over the loveliest waterway in the world. Persons or parties of not less than 10 can leave Helena at an early hour, drive to Judge Hilger's house by 10 o'clock, take boats through the canyon and be landed under the shadow of the great Bear Tooth, where they will take the trail and join their wagons on top of the hill, and home to Helena before dark." Today, two modern excursion boats, named the* Sacajawea *and the* Pirogue, *take eager passengers over the same route and from approximately the same landing spot as Judge Hilger used a century ago. DeCamp photo; Montana Historical Society Collection*

Rose of Helena

Judge Nicholas Hilger, who established his ranch close to the Gates of the Mountains north of Helena in 1867, was a longtime Missouri River navigation enthusiast. In May 1886 his new steam launch, Rose of Helena, *arrived in Townsend via the Northern Pacific. He launched it there and took it on its maiden voyage to Hilger's Landing, thence through the spectacular canyon with a group of Helena citizens, headed by Governor Sam Hauser, on board. Courtesy of the N. J. Holter Collection*

Sacajawea at the Gates

Ever since the Rose of Helena *and other riverboats operated by Judge Hilger took visitors through the spectacular Missouri River limestone canyon north of Helena, thousands of sightseers have made the trip. Today, two large launches, operated by the Gates of the Mountains Boat Club, continuously cruise these waters throughout the summer. Here the* Sacajawea *is making a sweeping turn at the upper end of the canyon so passengers get the illusion of the opening of the two cliffs on either side of the river. This is the sight Meriwether Lewis noted in his journals in August 1805, as he and his party, sailing and often cordelling their boats after leaving the Great Falls of the Missouri, approached the canyon which at first looked to be impenetrable. When the gates seemed to open and admit them to the canyon, Lewis named it Gates of the Mountains in his journal. Present-day visitors are impressed in much the same way as they see the gates open and their boat proceed back through the canyon to the marina and docking area close to where Judge Hilger once launched his pleasure crafts. Thanks in large measure to the efforts of Bob Tubbs, longtime manager of the boat club, a visitor's center now contains museum displays of pictures and memorabilia about this historic and beautiful place. Garry Wunderwald photo*

Cows and Mansions

With Mount Helena as a backdrop, cows grazed peacefully in this picture, taken at the corner of Floweree and Dearborn on Helena's fashionable west side at the turn of the century. The home at the extreme left was built in 1886 by S. C. Ashby, pioneer Helena businessman, who later sold it to Thomas H. Carter, one of Montana's early U.S. senators. Today it is the home of Mr. and Mrs. Tom Tobin. Mrs. Tobin, a granddaughter of T. C. Power, is the daughter of Mr. and Mrs. Charles Power, who lived here after it was purchased in 1910.

In the center background are the Swett-Bickett residence and the Tatem-Young home, both new at the time of this photograph, as evidenced by the small trees in the yards. Both of these homes are still standing, owned, respectively, by the Catholic Diocese of Helena and Mr. and Mrs. Richard Remington.

The three-story mansion with a mansard roof at the right is no longer standing. It was built for the pioneer cattleman D. A. G. Floweree for the handsome sum of $12,000. Many more imposing mansions were built in this favored section of the city, while others sprang up in other additions, such as Lenox and Kenwood, interspersed today with more modern and usually less palatial dwellings. Courtesy of the N. J. Holter Collection

Helena is still famous for its many imposing residences, built throughout the city by the merchants and entrepreneurs of the 1880s and 1890s who vied with each other for sites and grandeur. Seen here are three great homes which are no longer standing, reminders of the versatility of design and location and that the march of time caught up with even the most solidly built.

Above right is the Ming mansion, built in 1883 at the head of Edwards Street, where Olive Street now intersects. Designed by Paulsen and McConnell, the mansion was the scene of a gala housewarming on February 5, 1884, when over 300 invited guests were seated for a banquet, 100 at a time, as younger guests danced to the music of a string band. Included among the guests were members of the 1884 Constitutional Convention, who had adjourned their meeting early in order to attend.

Right center is the great, brick, Italianate mansion built by A. G. "China" Clarke at the top of the State Street hill. Clarke, who came to Helena from Virginia City in 1865, was for many years associated with the firm of Clarke, Conrad and Curtin, which sold a variety of hardware and household goods at the store on Grand Street, also now gone. This pioneer merchant formally named his son China Clarke; hence this unusual name has long been remembered in Helena, along with this palatial home, which was later the residence of pioneer druggist Henry Parchen, whose Parchen Block on Broadway still stands next to the Masonic Temple.

At right is the massive Word-Conrad mansion on Madison Avenue, considered by many to have been the finest residence ever built in Montana. The mansion was built in 1887 by Samuel Word, canny pioneer lawyer who got his start in Virginia City and eventually became counsel for the Union Pacific Railroad and is said to have made his greatest wealth when he directed floating of stock in Thomas Cruse's Drum Lummon mine in Marysville. The home was purchased in 1893 by John H. Conrad of the famed pioneer Montana merchandising and banking family, but after a well-publicized divorce from his wife, he is said to have left Helena, abandoning the home with all its contents. When the first Montana Club burned in 1903, members moved into this house, old-timers recalling that Julian, the bartender, "never missed serving a drink!" Hatfield Conrad, president of the Conrad Trust and Savings Bank, lived here from 1906 to 1910, but gradually the great house fell into decay and became a favorite place for children to explore and vandals to destroy. After its final demolition, it was replaced by four houses, which occupy the grounds today.

From the Jean Baucus Collection

Courtesy of the Mark McBride Collection

From the Jean Baucus Collection

Central Hall, Ashby-Power Home

The open staircase, with a portrait of Theodore Roosevelt prominently displayed, greeted guests when it was the home of U.S. Senator and Mrs. Thomas H. Carter. Built in 1886 by S. C. Ashby and occupying an entire block on Dearborn, the house was sold first to the Carters and in 1910 to Charles Power, only son of T. C. Power, who hired Marshall Field of Chicago to completely redecorate the rooms and the pioneer State Nursery west of Helena to landscape the grounds. Today it is the residence of the Power's daughter, Jane, and her husband, Tom Tobin. Montana Historical Society Collection

Kleinschmidt Home

This nineteen-room "gingerbread" residence at 1823 Highland in the Lennox Addition is now on the National Register of Historic Places. Built in 1892, it features imported cherry, oak, and birch woods from Germany, a forty-two-foot ballroom on the third floor, and elaborate fireplace mantels. Its builder was Theodore H. Kleinschmidt, a native of Prussia, who arrived in Virginia City in 1864 and soon made his way to Helena, where he worked as a cashier in S. T. Hauser's First National Bank for over forty years. He was twice mayor of Helena and an organizer of the Helena Board of Trade, credited with building the city to permanence after the gold rush days were over. Montana Historical Society Collection

This 1907 view, taken from the music room, looks out to the hall and staircase of this home, built at 520 Harrison Avenue in 1898 by Henry Sieben, pioneer stockman and rancher. The house was faced with fine pressed brick from Nick Kessler's brickyard, west of Helena, and the interior featured finely-crafted cherry, walnut, bird's-eye maple, and oak woods. Today this house is the home of Mrs. William A. Brown. Montana Historical Society Collection

Music Room and Hallway, Henry Sieben Home

Samuel T. Hauser, Montana financier and entrepreneur, was appointed territorial governor in 1885, about the time this twenty-nine-room mansion at 720 Madison Avenue was completed. This is a view of the grand reception room, where Governor Hauser and his wife greeted guests, both personal and official. Today this mansion, which was the home of Catholic sisters for many years after 1914, is the residence of former Montana Governor Tim Babcock and his wife, Betty. Montana Historical Society Collection

Reception Room, Hauser-Babcock Home

William A. Chessman, a Helena businessman who was deeply involved in water development, built this mansion at 304 North Ewing in 1885, and in 1913 it was purchased by the state of Montana as the first official Governor's Mansion. It was the home of nine Montana governors, beginning with Samuel V. Stewart in 1913 and ending with J. Hugo Aronson in 1959, when the modern Governor's Mansion was completed at 2 Carson Avenue. The house was owned for a time by Mrs. Peter Larson and later by George H. Conrad, an official of the Conrad Trust and Savings Bank. Today it is open as a public museum, with much of the interior renovated and furnished with period furniture. Montana Historical Society Collection

Original Governor's Mansion

Dining Room, Original Governor's Mansion

This is the dining room of the William A. Chessman home, which was the official residence of Montana governors from 1913 to 1959. Although this is a gracious residence and was a favored place for entertainment, the nine chief executives who lived here often found the quarters inadequate for official entertaining. This home was replaced by the modern Governor's Mansion at 2 Carson Street. However, when Montana's present governor, Ted Schwinden, was elected in 1980, he and his wife would have preferred living here rather than in the colder, more modern Governor's Mansion. Montana Historical Society Collection

Helena Public Library and Auditorium

An adequate public library had long been a concern of Helena citizens, especially men like Cornelius Hedges, who lived in Helena and was Montana's first superintendent of public instruction. The cornerstone for the building was laid in March 1892, after the city council awarded the $23,000 contract to E. W. Fiske. Located at the corner of Seventh Avenue and Warren Street, this combination library and auditorium served many purposes, including appearances by such notables as Theodore Roosevelt in 1900, when he was campaigning for the vice-presidency, and Franklin D. Roosevelt in 1920, when he was campaigning as the running mate of James Cox. The structure suffered irreversible damage in the earthquakes of 1935 and was demolished. Courtesy of Helena Water Department

Public Library Interior

Patrons of the Helena Public Library are seen here reading periodicals and other materials on file. Among the magazines in the rack on the back wall are Scribner's *and* Engineering Magazine. *Courtesy of Helena Water Department*

Ming Opera House

John H. Ming, a man of myriad interests, built this three-story building in 1880 to house what was described at the time as "a real, simon-pure Opera House—minus the opera, like the play of Hamlet with the character of the Melancholy Dane omitted." This became, however, Helena's earliest and only viable place to hold live entertainment—musicals, stage performances, and lectures. Ming imported the best traveling troupes he could afford, and they were enthusiastically received by a town thirsting for culture. Today this is the site of the Consistory Shrine Temple. Courtesy of the Montana Historical Society Collection

EARLY-DAY SOUVENIR

SOUVENIR

GRAND OPENING

MING'S

OPERA HOUSE

HASENWINKLE DRAMATIC CO'Y

MISS KATIE PUTNAM

Old Curiosity Shop

LITTLE NELL, THE MARCHIONESS, Miss KATIE PUTNAM
DICK SWIVELLER, ... H. A. FERRIS
QUILP, ... FLINT KENNICOTT
SAMPSON BRASS . . . . C. A. HASENWINKLE
GRANDFATHER TRENT, ... CHAS. COON
KIT, ... WILL O'KEEFE
NED TRENT, ... ED HOWARD
MASTER HUMPHREY, ... A. HASEN
STRANGER, ... BARRY ADAMS
BURTON, ... OSCAR WILLIAMS
HIGGINS, ... J. ROLLINS
SALLY BRASS, ... Miss ADA LAWRENCE
MRS. QUILP, ... Miss AGNES KENNICOTT
MRS. WOBBLES, ...

M. O'REARDON!

PAUL C. BLUM,

The above program is reproduced from a valued relic preserved by Mrs. E. K. Preuitt after the opening of the Ming Opera house Sept. 2, 1880. The theater was renowned in the west for many years. On its site today stands the Consistory temple.

John H. Ming

An early resident of Virginia City, John H. Ming was one of Helena's first businessmen, engaging in such diverse pursuits as the book and stationery business and ranching, besides his deep interest in bringing the best of entertainment to his Ming Opera House on Jackson Street. He died late in 1887, according to the Helena Weekly Herald, *of a chill he suffered while overseeing winter operations on his ranch north of Helena. Montana Historical Society Collection*

John H. Ming, Jr., Violinist

Music was the art most stressed in the education of the young people. Almost every home had a piano, which was the focal point of the living room, and most children had to learn to play the piano or violin. Montana Historical Society Collection

Chinese in Helena

Hard-working Chinese people were a factor in the development of the early West, where they often followed white miners, going through the mine dumps and tailings left by prospectors who had moved on to more promising diggings. In Helena most of the Chinese lived in enclaves on Helena's South Main, like the two pictured here in front of their log dwelling at the foot of Reeder's Alley. These people, whose costumes and traditions were starkly alien to strict Victorian codes, suffered open prejudice and hostility, even in the press, which was quick to point out that two of Helena's great fires in the 1870s had started in a Chinese dwelling on South Main. At a meeting held in Helena in April 1892, prejudice against their employment was evident when employers were urged to dismiss their Chinese help. Eighteen were employed in seven of the city's hotels and restaurants, it was reported; nine were servants in private homes; and ninety-six worked in the city's fourteen laundries. Courtesy of Helena Water Department

A Well-Dressed Oriental

This unidentified Helena Chinese man, dressed in native costume, posed for photographer E. H. Train with his native pipe and tea dishes at his side. Although they lived under notable prejudice at the time, the Chinese people persisted in their industrious ways and eventually became highly respected in Helena as elsewhere. Montana Historical Society Collection

Chinese at the Mullan Tunnel

Hundreds of Chinese worked on the westward pushing railroads in the 1880s. This group lined up in their Sunday best in 1883, when the Mullan Tunnel near Helena was dedicated. The Chinese willingly undertook the dangerous and arduous work of building this 3,800-foot tunnel. Montana Historical Society Collection

Chinese Working with Other Miners at Spokane Bar

Chinese were to be found in almost every placer mining region. After the rich surface placers had been hastily worked, the Chinese would come in and rework the tailings or hire out for work on placer mining crews. In this photograph, taken by E. H. Train, Chinese miners are working the overburden gravel deposits with hydraulics at Spokane Bar of the Missouri River, which is now covered by the impounded waters of Hauser Lake. E. H. Train photo; courtesy of Esther Olson Robinson

Helena's Black Citizens

Although relatively small, the black population of Helena has been surprisingly lively, educationally oriented, and almost universally beloved by the city. St. James Church was established in 1879 at Fifth and Hoback, and it formed the nucleus for the establishment of many groups, such as a literary society, a women's benevolent association, a theatrical group, a nine-piece band, and a baseball team.

In this remarkable photograph, taken by Edward M. Reinig in the Galen Building, now the site of the Yat Sun Restaurant, a ladies' cultural group staged a pageant of many nations. The young lady on the throne, representing America, is Julia Palmer, whose family homesteaded near Lincoln, Montana. Ladies in the back row have been identified as, left to right: Alice Fisher, Emma Dorsey, Marie Baker, Corrine Souls, Almira Kelly, Charlene Kelly, and Inez Williams. Front row: Etta Bowles, Rebecca Anderson Palmer, Sadie Ford, Ruth Hooper, Sarah Ingram, Olga York, and an unidentified lady. On the right front: Geraldine Lee, Hazel Cottles, Carrie Dorsey, Mattie McGinnis, Ella Anderson, Mrs. Mathews, and Polly Lee. Mattie McGinnis became the wife of Julian Anderson, veteran and beloved bartender at the Montana Club. Ella Anderson later married Ed Banks, and Sadie Ford was the wife of Nathaniel Ford, the skilled groom and horseman Senator T. C. Power brought back to Helena with him from Washington, D.C. Emma Dorsey operated a store at Eighth and Hoback, and the Kelly sisters, Charlene and Almira, lived with her. Reinig photo; from the Jean Baucus Collection

Clarissa Jane Crump

Born into a slave family in Booneville, Virginia, in 1854, Clarissa traveled with her family to Helena by horse and mule team in 1865. Clarissa married James W. Crump in 1869, and at the time of her death in 1941 at the age of eighty-seven, she had been a Helena resident for seventy-six years. A woman of charm and character, Mrs. Crump was a member of St. Peter's Episcopal Church, the Pleasant Hour Club, and other cultural and social organizations. Courtesy of the Norman Howard Collection

James Wesley Crump

In the 1870s James W. Crump freighted from the end of track at Corinne, Utah, to Helena. After his marriage, he established headquarters in Helena, where he became a successful miner and built a house at 1003 Ninth Avenue, which today is the home of his grandson, Norman Howard, and his wife, Maxine. Crump and his grandchildren, Lawrence and Norman, were photographed about 1903. Courtesy of the Norman Howard Collection

Pleasant Hour Club

Ladies of the Pleasant Hour Club were photographed at the front of the James W. Crump home at 1003 Ninth Avenue at the close of an afternoon's meeting. Mrs. Crump is believed to be the lady second from the right. Courtesy of the Norman Howard Collection

Nathaniel Ford Family

Nathaniel Ford, skilled horseman and teamster, accompanied Senator T. C. Power back to Helena from Washington, D.C. with a handsome black coach and a team of matched black horses. Born a slave, Nathaniel continued on Senator Powers's staff and became a solid Helena citizen. The aging Mr. Ford is seen here in about 1950 with his wife, Sadie, and daughter, Carlotta, with members of the Power family. At left is Charles B. Power, only son of the senator, and standing in front of Carlotta is young Judy Tobin, granddaughter of Charles. The Fords lived in rooms over the rose granite carriage house on the grounds of the T. C. Power mansion, and raised their two children, Carlotta, and a son, Arthur, who later served for many years as commissioner of the New York City Water Works. This picture was taken in the back yard of the Charles B. Power home on Dearborn, now the residence of Mr. and Mrs. Tom Tobin. Courtesy of the Jane Power Tobin Collection

Livestock Men of Helena

A number of Helena's pioneer businessmen combined activities such as mining, banking, and merchandising with ranching. Notable were A. M. Holter, Samuel T. Hauser, T. C. Power, Henry Cannon, Louis Stadler, and L. E. Kaufman, all of whom were identified with many business interests. Stadler and Kaufman, who were Helena merchants, ran their cattle under the O-H brand near Utica, in central Montana. It was during the disastrous winter of 1886-87 that a young night herder named Charles M. Russell sketched a postcard-sized picture which informed them of conditions on the range. The picture, which he titled *Waiting for a Chinook,* depicts a starving cow about to fall prey to waiting wolves; its wide circulation brought recognition to Russell, who quit the range in 1893 to become Montana's famed Cowboy Artist.

Typical of those who devoted themselves almost entirely to ranching were such men as Dan Floweree, Conrad Kohrs, Norman Chevallier, and Henry Sieben, all of whom established substantial homes in Helena. Kohrs, whose Grant-Kohrs ranch at Deer Lodge is now a National Historic Site, administered as a working ranch by the National Park Service, made his home after 1900 at 804 Dearborn. Henry Cannon, whose interests included mining, railroads, gas works, and electric power, had extensive livestock holdings near Cascade, which he sold in 1907 to Henry Sieben. This is the Adel ranch operated today by Sieben's great-grandson, Chase Hibbard.

Sieben, who came to Montana in 1864 and once rode the range for Granville Stuart in central Montana, gradually built up his livestock interests until they included, besides the Cannon ranch in Cascade County, the Mitchell ranch twenty-five miles north of Helena near the entrance of Little Prickly Pear Canyon. This ranch is operated today by the founder's great-grandson, John Frederick Baucus.

Descendants of Phillip Chevallier have, like those of Henry Sieben, continued to operate the family ranch fifteen miles northwest of Helena. These family ranches have been diversified hay and livestock operations, specializing in both cattle and sheep. Thus although the colorful days of the open range period are long gone, descendants of the founders keep up the tradition while keeping abreast of modern technology and complicated corporate procedures. ■

A Jolly Lot of Cowboys

This fine 1904 stereopticon view shows working cowboys as they were, minus the Texas-style hats and new cowboy boots stylized by Hollywood. Library of Congress photo

A Herder and His Sheep

Armed with a walking stick and depending on his faithful dog, a herder watches his sheep in this graphic 1904 stereopticon view. Library of Congress photo

Settlers Shack

With plenty of kindling wood, some faithful canine friends, a barrel of water, and a small but snug log shack, this couple seems content enough trying to put down roots in a snow-covered landscape. Like many others, they may well have given up the struggle later, but may have been among those who stayed and prospered as a part of Montana's leading industry, agriculture. Courtesy of the Mark McBride Collection

Trappers and Hunters

Although Helena and all Montana are still considered prime hunting ground, the bonanza of these early-day hunters and trappers would stagger modern nimrods and officials of the Montana Fish and Game Department. Note the long skiis propped up against the roof of the log shelter and the array of firearms and trophy heads. In early Helena, local butcher shops handled wild game across the counter before livestock raising became a major industry. Courtesy of the Mark McBride Collection

Mark of Permanence

Pride in a substantial home and good breeding stock are evident in this picture of a ranch near Canyon Ferry. Montana Historical Society Collection

Haying at the Gates of the Mountains

Pleasure boats are moored now at this spot near the Gates of the Mountains north of Helena, in waters of the Missouri River backed up by Holter Dam, located some thirty-five miles downstream. This picture, taken by Ralph DeCamp, well-known Helena artist and photographer, shows haying operations at what was then known as Holter Meadows. Nicholas Hilger, whose pioneer ranch was established here in 1867, is the man in the white shirt. On all early maps, this location was referred to as American Bar, and the Hilger family, which still ranches here, have found many Indian artifacts, indicating that this was a favored tribal campground. This picture was taken in about 1912, before Holter Dam had time to back up the Missouri to form Holter Lake at this spot. Montana Historical Society Collection

Henry Sieben Herding Cattle

Dressed as he always was in white shirt, vest, and business hat, Henry Sieben is seen here herding cattle at the Adel ranch of the Sieben Livestock Company near Cascade. Note Square Butte, made famous by many C. M. Russell paintings in the right background. This quiet, skilled stockman never wore cowboy boots or a Texas-style hat, and even in his early bull team freighting experiences, never used a bullwhip. He kept ranch records in a notebook in his vest pocket for many years as he built up his ranching operations, bowing to modern bookkeeping systems only towards the end of his life in 1937. He was survived by two daughers, Berneice, who married Fred Sheriff and is the mother of Jean Sheriff Baucus, and Margaret, still a revered resident of Montana and the widow of banker A. T. Hibbard. It is the grandchildren of the two Sieben sisters who operate the two major Sieben ranches today. From the Jean Baucus Collection

Sieben and Granddaughter Jean

A new spring lamb holds the interest of Henry Sieben and his granddaughter, Jean Sheriff, in this picture taken at the Sieben ranch north of Helena in 1917. From the Jean Baucus Collection

Hilger Band of Sheep

David Hilger looks over a band of sheep from a horse-drawn wagon in this photograph, taken at the Hilger ranch in central Montana. Montana Historical Society Collection

After a summer visit to the Sieben ranch north of Helena, this group of people, including members of the family, prepares to return to Helena in their dark blue Stevens Durea automobile. The lady without the hat is Mrs. Henry Sieben, and seated in front of her is her daughter, Berneice, who married Fred Sheriff in 1915. The white barn on the left was the

stage station in the 1880s at this historic ranch, while the large barn partially seen on the right, built in about 1910, is now due for demolition. The Sieben family lived in Helena most of the year but every summer came to the ranch to spend several weeks, living in tents. From the Jean Baucus Collection

After a Hiatus at the Sieben Ranch, 1914

Montana's statehouse looked much as it does today in this picture, taken in 1930, except for the many trees which have grown to large proportions. The east and west wings, faced with granite, were completed between 1909 and 1912. John L. Maloney photo; Montana Historical Society Collection

Chapter Seven

Dawn of a New Century and a Capitol for Montana

As the twentieth century began in Helena, work was progressing rapidly on the state's new capitol building, but reports it would be ready in time for the 1901 session of the legislature proved overoptimistic. Shock radiated throughout the city on September 6, 1901, when it was learned that President William McKinley had been shot in Buffalo, New York, by a demented anarchist.

Helena newspapers kept the citizenry informed about his condition until eight days later, when the *Helena Independent* sadly used McKinley's last words, "Goodbye, all, it is God's Way, His Will Be Done," in its headline announcing his death, less than a year into his second term. In Helena, and throughout Montana, there was grief but general approval of the robust political posture of his successor, Theodore Roosevelt, the great outdoorsman, rancher, and Rough Rider who took it as a compliment when Old Guard party boss Mark Hanna referred to him as "that damn cowboy."

In its issue of Friday, July 4, 1902, the *Helena Independent* devoted columns of space to the rain-soaked dedication of the new capitol building. "A handsome building it is," the article said, "a credit to the state. Three years ago, its cornerstone was laid with impressive ceremony. Today it is dedicated to good state government, a reminder of the inherent right of the people to self government."

Aside from the rain, which forced postponement of the mammoth parade until the next day, the *Independent* found only one flaw: "There is but one thing about the whole building that puts a bad taste in the mouth," the editor said in the middle of his front page news story, "and that is the motto on the cornerstone, 'Ora y Plata'—gold and silver. That is not a good motto for any state. It is a good motto for a miser."

The ceremonies, at which Governor J. K. Toole presided, turned out to be lengthy, in spite of the rain. The Reverend W. W. Van Orsdel, beloved pioneer Methodist minister, gave a long invocation, followed by orations by Wilbur F. Sanders and U.S. Senator Paris Gibson, who in 1883 had founded the city of Great Falls. Secretary of State George M. Hayes described the odyssey of the building and the generosity of Thomas Cruse in taking the full issue of $350,000 in bonds in April 1898, after other investors had spurned them. He described the search for Montana building materials and the decision finally to use sandstone from a quarry near Columbus, Montana, for the exterior walls.

The parade was held the next day, with dozens of floats and flower-laden vehicles assembled in Haymarket Square to begin the march. One artistically decorated buggy, the newspaper said, was occupied by Mrs. T. J. Walsh, Miss Kleinschmidt, Miss Young, and "little Miss Genevieve Walsh." Thomas J. Walsh, who in 1912 was to become Montana's most respected U.S. senator, had arrived in Helena in 1890 and was rapidly building a reputation for legal genius, especially in the area of mining law.

William A. Clark, who had finally won his seat in the U.S. Senate, was somewhat reluctantly taking care of the home folks in the office he had wanted so badly but which failed to greatly interest him once he had it. Indeed, Clark seldom visited Montana after 1900 in spite of his continued adulation in Helena, which he had supported in the capital city fights. He bought one of New York's finest Fifth Avenue mansions and endowed institutions as far flung as the University of Virginia and the University of California, but not Montana. He left his mark on the state's journalism one more time when, in August 1902, he purchased the *Helena Independent*, which had invariably supported him.

The national public debt stood at $968,091,321 late in 1902, a fact deplored in the press, as Theodore Roosevelt was entering the second year of his presidency. Helena's population dropped from the high of 13,834 in 1890 to 10,770 in 1900, and the Victorian age came to a close with the death of Queen Victoria. Newspapers were full of references to the delay in the coronation of her aging and ailing son, Edward VII, who finally became king on August 8, 1902.

The Montana Club's building, "the most magnificent building this side of Chicago devoted to club purposes," was completely destroyed by a mysterious fire on the night of Monday, April 27, 1903. All firemen could do was contain the blaze to the imposing building, valued at $150,000, on the corner of Sixth and Fuller. Aside from the building, its furnishings and the belongings of a number of prominent Helena men who kept rooms and offices there raised the figure to great proportions.

Inspired by the vigorous new leadership in Washington, waves of progressivism swept the Montana political scene early in the century, and in 1910 a young woman from Missoula, Jeannette Rankin, gained national prominence when she worked for women's suffrage in the state of Washington. The next year, she was granted an appearance before the Montana House of Representatives to plead for a suffrage amendment to the Montana Constitution. The amendment narrowly passed in the election of 1914, the new homestead counties in eastern Montana making a decisive difference. Two years later, Jeannette Rankin became the nation's first congresswoman and cast her first vote against American participation in global war in 1917.

By 1910, as America emerged as a major world power under the two-fisted "big stick" policies of Theodore Roosevelt, Helena had gained a 16.2 percent rise in population, from 10,770 in 1900 to 12,515 in 1910. War clouds were gathering in Europe, but few in Montana realized that in the next decade, her sons, in record numbers, would serve and many lose their lives in the war that would "make the world safe for democracy."

Capitol under Construction, 1900

Building materials and temporary construction shacks littered the grounds of the capitol building in this picture, taken when the framework of the dome was in place but still lacking the copper sheathing which was to become its exterior surface in honor of Montana's copper mining prominence. The figure of Miss Freedom, *the origin of which still puzzles historians, is already in place. Architects Charles Emlen Bell and John Hackett Kent of Council Bluffs, Iowa, had become Helena residents after they won the contract to design the building in 1898, a move intended to placate resident architects who had been passed over for the assignment. Bell and Kent managed, however, to keep within the cost of a little less than a half million dollars appropriated by the 1897 legislature. More ambitious plans in 1895 had called for a building which would cost well over a million dollars. Montana Historical Society Collection*

At the Capitol Dedication, 1902

Crowds ascending the front steps of the capitol on July 4, 1902, were dressed for the drenching rains which failed to diminish dedication day attendance or oratory but which forced postponement of the colorful parade until the next day. Montanans had to wait more than a decade for completion of their domed seat of government. Intervening was a plan of 1895 for a more elaborate building than the new state could afford, as well as a shameful scandal two years later, when it was discovered that members of the first capitol commission were planning to use inferior materials to defraud the state of large portions of the building's cost. It was during the administration of Democrat/Populist Robert B. Smith that a new commission was appointed and an economy-minded 1897 legislature appropriated funds for a more modest building, but one which, with the addition of east and west wings between 1909 and 1912, has served the state well and because of its classic design, is now on the National Register of Historic Places. Montana Historical Society Collection

Horse-drawn Capitol Landscaping

Black dirt, hauled from Big Indian Placer No. 66, is seen here being spread on the front yard of the capitol building, preparatory to landscaping, soon after completion of the building, without east and west wings, in 1902. Landscaping, which includes trees and shrubs of many varieties, and a distinctive flower display which spells out MONTANA *early each summer, has continued to the present day. Blue spruce, planted on the grounds of the building and throughout the city, have proved to be one of the most attractive features of Helena. Montana Historical Society Collection*

Rotunda and Main Staircase

Architects Bell and Kent and interior decorator F. Pedretti envisioned a nineteenth-century opera house setting when they planned the impressive rotunda and broad staircase at the main floor entrance of Montana's capitol. The theatrical history pageant which artist Charles Pedretti and his assistants painted around the rotunda dome reflect scenes of early Montana history, including a placer miner, a trapper, a cowboy, and an Indian. There are also paintings of the driving of the golden spike at Gold Creek, Montana, west of Helena, in 1883, and portrait busts of such notables as Senators Thomas J. Walsh and Burton K. Wheeler, Governor Joseph M. Dixon, a larger-than-life statue of Wilbur F. Sanders, and most recently, a heroic sculptured likeness of Jeannette Rankin. Throughout the building, historic paintings and murals by Pedretti and Montana artists Edgar S. Paxson and Ralph De Camp follow through the history pageant theme. Montana Historical Society Collection

Montana's capitol grounds have provided the arena for a number of July Fourth celebrations, including laying of the cornerstone in 1899 and dedication of the completed building in 1902. On July 4, 1905, crowds gathered to view the unveiling of the equestrian statue of Thomas Francis Meagher, the colorful Irish revolutionary and Civil War hero who came to Montana in 1865 as territorial secretary and twice served as acting governor. Often mistakenly listed among Montana governors, Meagher nonetheless played a controversial and crucial role in his acting capacity, even attempting to guide the new territory to statehood long before either sufficent population or orderly government warranted the status. Concerned with defending the territory against what he believed were growing Indian troubles, Meagher was at Fort Benton awaiting shipment of arms when he apparently fell from a steamboat and drowned. His body was never found.

On the day his statue was dedicated, over 2,500 out-of-town visitors arrived in Helena to observe the procession, which gathered at the courthouse and proceeded up Sixth Avenue to the capitol. Four companies of soldiers fired salutes as the flag drapery was removed before this gala crowd, obviously more comfortable in the sunshine of 1905 than they had been at the capitol dedication three years before. The statue was donated by the people of Montana, particularly those of Irish descent. A continuing problem for state officials, aside from explaining why an acting governor of brief residence was so honored, has been to prevent destruction by vandals of Meagher's upraised sword. Montana Historical Society Collection

House of Representatives

This picture of a recent session of the Montana House of Representatives shows the durability of Charles M. Russell's great mural Lewis and Clark Meeting the Indians at Ross' Hole, *which he completed on commission in 1911. Attached directly to the wall, this great painting, the most valuable Russell original known to exist and the only one of mural proportions, has been recently restored by experts who detected deterioration during its lifetime of over seventy years. Len Eckel photo*

Fourth of July Parade, circa 1904

The initials of Lewis and Clark County are intertwined atop the patriotic arch which framed a colorful Fourth of July parade moving north along Last Chance Gulch. Uniformed police, followed by a marching band and flower-bedecked floats, are at the corner of Sixth and Main. Courtesy of Helena Catholic Diocese

This colorful patriotic parade, moving south on Last Chance Gulch, was one of the many opportunities for Helena ladies to vie with each other to display their finery and their hothouse flowers, and at the same time evoke patriotic sentiment. The two young ladies who have just passed through the arch are Berneice and Margaret Sieben, daughters of Henry Sieben, riding their horses, Doctor and Cricket. The large sign on the building at the left proclaimed a liquidation of merchandise at the Weinstein Brothers' store. This was the Ashby Block on the corner of Sixth and Main, which was completed in 1883 at a cost of $50,000, representing one of the largest building expenditures in Helena history to that time. The building was torn down in 1929 to make room for the present First National Bank Building. Culbertson photo; from the Jean Baucus Collection

Flower Parade, 1908

Teddy Roosevelt in Helena, 1903

Popular President Theodore Roosevelt, whose early hunting enthusiams and open-range cattle interests gave him a special affinity for Montana, was a Helena visitor on a number of occasions, including this outdoor appearance in front of the Helena High School late in 1903. The three-story high school building was decorated with flags and bunting for the occasion, with Roosevelt's portrait set in the large star outline above the speaker's stand. Culbertson photo; courtesy of Helena High School

President Taft in Helena, 1909

During a presidential visit to Helena on September 9, 1909, the ample proportions of President William Howard Taft towered as he stood in the back of an elegant open car owned by Helena physician B. C. Brooke. Sitting in the back seat of the car is Montana Governor Edwin L. Norris, and next to the president is state fair chairman T. O. Hammond. On that day, President Taft laid the cornerstone of Mount St. Charles College, which was to become Carroll College, and was apparently a visitor as well at the Montana State Fair, at which Great Northern Railway president James J. Hill was also an honored guest. Library of Congress photo

Nils P. Walters, who arrived in Helena from his native Sweden in 1880 at the age of sixteen, is seen in his private office in the old Union Bank Building in August 1908, surrounded by memorabilia of his career, including a picture of Abraham Lincoln visiting the headquarters of General George McClelland of the Army of the Potomac, accompanied by Allen Pinkerton, who founded the famous detective agency. Walters, who was the maternal grandfather of Dr. Clem L. Shafer of Helena, was a notably skilled lawman, credited, among many things, with solving a perplexing Union Bank robbery in 1920. Walters served as a Helena Police Department plainclothes detective and city police chief before becoming a Pinkerton detective. Courtesy of Clem L. Shafer

Pinkerton Detective N. P. Walters

Ladies Luncheon at the Broadwater, circa 1909

A social season highlight was luncheon at the Broadwater Hotel, with many of Helena's prominent ladies present. Almost complete identification, with the help of a number of pioneer residents still living, has been made. The three ladies on the porch at the left are, left to right: Miss Fortune (in black), Mrs. Norman B. Holter, Mrs. Will Wallace, and Miss Hebe Ashby. Standing on the steps: Mrs. S. C. Ashby (in dotted dress), Miss Mary Cruse (almost obscured), and an unidentified lady. Standing in the full row: Mrs. William Word, Mrs. Henry Sieben (in dark dress with white bodice), Mrs. John Longmaid, Mrs. Clara Kennett, Mrs. John T. Murphy, Mrs Theodore Brantley, Miss Bella Sharpe, Miss May Flanigan, Mrs. Sibley, Mrs. C. J. McNamara, Mrs. Alonzo K. Prescott, unidentified, Mrs. T. C. Power (in black), and unidentified. In the front row, seated: Mrs. Harry Pigott, Mrs. J. M. Neill, Mrs. Edward C. Babcock, Mrs. Frank K. Turner, Miss Helen Word, Mrs. H. B. Ives, Mrs. C. A. Broadwater, unidentified, Mrs. William Biggs, Mrs. William Chumasero (seated on the ground, in black), Mrs. J. E. Bower (seated on the ground, in white), Mrs. David Wallace, Mrs. W. A. Chessman (seated on ground, in black), Mrs. Tom Marlow, and Miss Sarah Power. From the Jean Baucus Collection

Balloon Ascension at the Fair

Professor Oscar Hunt thrilled visitors to an early Montana Agricultural, Mineral, and Mechanical Fair, which had been held continuously since the late 1860s at the fairgrounds on the northwest edge of Helena. In 1891 the facilities were sold to the Montana State Fair Association, which staged official state fairs here for many years. Following a period of decay and non-use when the official events were moved to Great Falls, these historic grounds were renovated and the facilities improved annually for the Last Chance Stampede under the leadership, in the 1960s, of the late William A. Carson. Montana Historical Society Collection

Notables at the 1909 State Fair

Mrs. Charles M. Russell, wife of Montana's famed Cowboy Artist, was chairman of the art department at the 1909 fair and posed in front of the fair secretary's office with other notables, including Governor Edwin L. Norris, seen at her left. Others in the picture are, front row, left to right: Thomas A. Marlow, John Borkin, James Wood, Martin Martin, Governor Norris, Mrs. Russell, Police Captain L. Bailey, and fair marshal Cal Hubbard. In the back, left to right: James Shoemaker, Chief of Police N. P. Walters, N. Nathanson, Bud Storey, Judge William E. Biggs, George Huffaker, and fair president T. O. Hammond. C. E. Hedges photo; Montana Historical Society Collection

Pioneer Rest Tent at the Fair, circa 1913

Area pioneers were always honored at annual Montana state fairs in Helena, a log "rest tent" providing for their comfort and as a gathering place to share reminiscences. The man wearing a black bowler hat, fifth from the right, is Anton M. Holter. Courtesy of the N. J. Holter Collection

Seamstresses and Babies Compete at the Fair

*W*inners of county sewing competitions and some happy and some reluctant babies all vied for honors at the 1913 state fair in Helena. The young seamstresses, most of them busy with handwork, pose in front of some garments which received high marks from the judges. Contenders for the Beautiful Baby title are posed with their mothers, some of whom seem more anxious for the recognition than do their well-dressed tots. R. H. McKay photo; Montana Historical Society Collection

Crowds at the State Fair, 1915

R. H. *McKay took these photographs of crowds in front of the grandstand and on the grounds of the Montana State Fair in Helena in 1913. The city took great pride in the mile-long racetrack, which boasts dirt from the storied racetracks of Kentucky. When state fairs were moved to Great Falls, these historic grounds and grandstand fell into decay but were renovated in the 1960s for the annual Last Chance Stampedes, which have become so successful that facilities have been enlarged and the grandstand made structurally sound once again. R. H. McKay photo; Montana Historical Society Collection*

Car Racing, circa 1918

Race cars are lining up at the starting line under the watchful eyes of occupants of the judges' stand in this picture, taken at the fairgrounds in about 1918. Notice the press corps had its headquarters at the finish line. From the Jean Baucus Collection

Last Chance Stampede

The renovated grandstand at Helena's fairgrounds is filled with modern-day enthusiasts for the annual Last Chance Stampede and Fair which gets bigger and better every year since its inauguration in the 1960s. Courtesy of Gene Fisher

Bagging Big Game, circa 1903

Helena's great woman rodeo champion, Fanny Sperry, is seen with two antlered deer she bagged at the foot of Bear Tooth Mountain north of Helena, site of the Sperry ranch, in about 1903. The young woman's weapon was an 1894 Winchester saddle gun. She was a world champion saddle bronc rider, taking top prize in this category in 1912 at the Calgary Stampede. In 1913 Fanny married Bill Steele, and together they operated a dude ranch in the Lincoln area. After Steele's death, Fanny continued operating the ranch and big game outfitting operation until 1965, when she retired at the age of seventy-eight. Since 1974 she had been a resident of a Helena rest home, still alert until her death in February, 1983 at the age of ninety-five. Courtesy of the Mark McBride Collection

Helena High School Orchestra, 1906

Fred Kuphal, the German-born musician who became a leading violinist with the Los Angeles Philharmonic later in life, posed here with members of the Helena High School Orchestra when he was their conductor in 1906. Many of these young musicians continued in the city's musical and cultural circles throughout their lives. In the back row, left to right: Dorothy Green, H. Crampton Jones, Fay Kent, Verna Green, Donald Berry, and Genevieve Walsh (Gudger). Middle row: Miss Jackson, Virginia Kennett (Fletcher), Conductor Kuphal, Ruth Carpenter, and Palmer Jahr. Seated in front are Margaret Carpenter and Octavia Ryder (Haraldson). From the Jean Baucus Collection

Young Ladies on Mount Helena

The late Elizabeth Nelson Greenfield is the young lady taking aim from a path on the way to the summit of Mount Helena in about 1908 as newly-planted Douglas fir trees begin to grow on the slopes. Courtesy of the Clarence DeWalt Collection

May Pole Dance, circa 1910

Spectators had even climbed to the upper levels of the capitol building in about 1910 to witness this colorful and popular May Day festival. Umbrellas suggest that a May shower was in progress, which failed to dampen the fun or diminish the crowds. Florence Holter photo

Ladies Participate

Three well-dressed and equipped lady fishermen ply the waters of the Missouri in this early photograph, which includes one male fisherman and two armed hunters with their hunting dogs between them. Courtesy of the Mark McBride Collection

City Park atop Mount Helena

In 1903 the Helena Improvement Society conceived the idea of creating a city park on top of Mount Helena, which has formed the city's distinctive mountain backdrop since the gold discoveries of 1864. By 1906 the city had title to 360 acres of the mountain, and plans were under way to increase that to about 1,000 acres. Members of the society obtained the services of two foresters from Washington, D.C., to report on the feasibility of reforesting the mountain.

A plan was eventually approved to supply 50,000 two-year-old Douglas firs which today cover the slopes of the mountain where there were once barren expanses, believed to have been caused by prospectors harvesting original trees to build cabins and flumes. With help from the noted landscape artist Warren Manning and General Chittenden, facilities for the park eventually included benches placed every 1,000 feet along the trail to the top and a shelter, seen here, erected at the summit. Two hundred citizens climbed to the top on July 4, 1904 to dedicate the shelter house, which is no longer standing. Montana Historical Society Collection

Helena High Football Team, 1910

With their coach and leather-helmeted mascot, the Helena High School football squad of 1910 posed on the steps of the Seventh Avenue gymnasium. The first player in the back row, left, is Lester Loble, noted legislator and jurist who gained national attention for his work in controlling juvenile delinquency. After forty-two years as a Helena lawyer, Loble was elected judge of the First Judicial District in 1956. He died in December 1974 at the age of eighty-one. Courtesy of Bruce Loble

Wading in Prickly Pear

Four young ladies, dressed in the popular middy blouses of the day, were having a great time frolicking in the waters of Prickly Pear Creek in about 1905. Margaret Sieben (Hibbard) is the girl on the far right. From the Jean Baucus Collection

Montana Club

One of the Northwest's most enduring membership social clubs is the Montana Club, organized and incorporated early in 1885 "for literary, mutual improvement and social purposes." Membership was restricted to "gentlemen," with ladies invited only for very special occasions. With a membership of 130, the club held its grand opening on April 13, 1895, at quarters on the third floor of the Parchen Block. The Fourteenth Territorial Assembly had just vacated the rooms, which were hastily redecorated and furnished for the occasion. In May 1888, when membership had reached 160, the club moved to the fourth floor of T. C. Power's new Gold Block, which was completely redecorated and furnished. The Gold Block, which boasted Helena's first passenger elevator, was destroyed in the great fire of 1928.

Meanwhile, in 1891, the club at last decided to build its own quarters, and with the help of banker S. T. Hauser, purchased the lot at the corner of Sixth and Fuller for $45,000. In spite of the financial panic of the time, the first Montana Club building was completed and officially opened on July 15, 1893. Among the new employees was a former slave named Julian Anderson, who had arrived in Helena in 1881 and worked at a number of jobs, including shoeshine boy, porter, and night manager of the Broadwater Hotel. In the summer of 1893 he was hired as a bartender at the Montana Club, a job he held for sixty years.

The club entertained such notables as General Nelson Miles, Theodore Roosevelt, and Mark Twain in its beautiful quarters, even as the members struggled with continuing financial worries in keeping the club going. Then about midnight on April 27, 1903, fire was discovered on the top floor, and the flames quickly spread to the lower floors as bachelor residents and guests fled for their lives.

The next morning, as an April snowstorm hid some of the black ruins, the Montana Club was destroyed, with only the first floor exterior walls standing. The loss was a staggering $150,000, with only $63,000 covered by insurance. To add to the agony, the fourteen-year-old son of bartender Anderson confessed he had set the fire as well as an earlier abortive one in order to "see the fire horses run and help the firemen work."

Club directors immediately met and planned a new building at the same site, meanwhile renting the unused and palatial Samuel Word mansion at 626 Madison for $200 a month. The services of the eminent architect Cass Gilbert were engaged and after an expensive plan was replaced with a more modest one, debris from the old building was removed and construction began. Members moved in on June 24, 1905, and the building was formally dedicated on December 30 of that year.

Fortunes of this historic club have fluctuated with the times, but the "rising like a phoenix" philosophy has seen it through modern-day renovation to bring the building, now almost eighty years old, to conformity with building and fire codes. Women have long since become voting members, and the founders are gone from the stag dinner tables of long ago. But much of the flavor remains, articulated in the club's own song, "We thrill with pride in our Rocky Mountain home, Land fairest of all the Lord has blessed; Tho' in foreign climes we may chance at times to roam, We are oft returning here for rest."■

First Montana Club Building

Occupying the corner of Fuller and Sixth Avenue, the first Montana Club building looked like this when it was open to the membership and guests on July 15, 1893. Montana Historical Society Collection

Montana Club Dinner, circa 1900

B. H. *Tatem, who paid for the oak flooring of the Montana Club's first building, was honored at a stag dinner party with a distinguished group of Helena leaders hosting the affair. The man holding the side of his chair in the left foreground is Governor Sam Hauser. Next to him, from left to right around the table: T. A. Marlow, M. S. Gunn, Al Smith, B. H. Tatem, D. P. Patenaude, Norman B. Holter, R. A. Lulse, W. A. Chessman, Montana Club president E. C. Day, A. J. Davidson, and J. B. Miller, with back to camera. Montana Historical Society Collection*

Reading Room of the First Montana Club, circa 1900

The second floor of the original Montana Club contained this reading room and library, furnished with all the latest periodicals and national newspapers. No food or drink was allowed in these quiet quarters, but food was available on the sixth floor where a formal restaurant was opened in charge of a Chinese cook in 1902. The first club also contained a bowling alley, which helped keep the club afloat during the panic years of the 1890s. For financial reasons, the first crack in the armour of an all-male club also came, when ladies developed an enthusiasm for bowling and were admitted at certain hours, escorted or unescorted. Taylor photo; courtesy of the Montana Club

Montana Club Ablaze, 1903

Fire, which started on the top floor of the Montana Club during the night of April 27, 1903, is completely gutting the ten-year-old building in this picture. By morning the walls had collapsed except for the blackened arches of the first floor. Montana Historical Society Collection

Montana Club Smokers

Annual stag smokers were a historic tradition at the Montana Club. Helena artist/cartoonist Fanny Cory created both of these examples for special occasions involving loss of the former club building in 1903 and inauguration of the new in 1905. Courtesy of the Montana Club

Present Montana Club

The Montana Club building, which rose over the ashes of the old on the corner of Sixth and Fuller, looked like this when it was completed in June 1905. When the costs of building and the services of famed architect Cass Gilbert were toted up, it was found the building cost over $117,000. But members were pleased with the design, which followed that of the former building in many respects. A Dutch-style rathskeller was a popular feature of the basement. The other six floors contained a library, billiard and meeting rooms, a card room, private apartments for bachelor members, staff quarters, and dining facilities on the top floor.

Membership soared early in the new century, and the club remained a haven for men. But in 1913 the new Placer Hotel opened, and ladies began persuading their men to accompany them there. Thus in December of that year, the club held its last stag night. With the coming of Prohibition, even more strictures were imposed, and as the year 1916 dawned, women were permitted to full participation. Throughout the Prohibition era, the club kept its faithful bartender, Julian Anderson, but membership fell and debts mounted.

The club suffered along with other segments of the economy during the Great Depression, but with the repeal of Prohibition, things began looking up again. Slot machine gambling in the 1940s brought an unprecedented prosperity to the club, and by 1938 membership rose to 1,150 from the all-time low of 139 in 1934. In 1948 the crackdown on gambling brought a new decline, but the famed Montana Club hospitality, presided over by Julian Anderson, continued. In June 1953 Anderson was honored on his 90th birthday and the 60th anniversary of his service to the club. Anderson, known as "the master of mixers" and author of a book of his famed recipes for libations, was honored as the club celebrated his 100th birthday in 1960. He died in 1962. Courtesy of the Montana Club

Russell Painting *When the Land Belonged to God*

Charles M. Russell is seen here completing the great oil painting commissioned by the Montana Club in 1915. The artist executed the picture in his studio in Great Falls and entrusted its delivery to his friend, author Frank Linderman. As the members gathered to inspect the painting, for which they paid Russell $3,000, there was general approval except from B. H. Tatem, who complained that the lead animal was a "miserable bull." When Linderman returned to Great Falls and recounted what long-time member Tatem had said, Russell replied, "Well, mebby he is a bum bull, but he's the best buffalo bull I ever painted." This great canvas, which hung in the Montana Club for many years, eventually was damaged in the smoky atmosphere and upon restoration was placed in the Montana Historical Society's Russell Gallery. When the Montana Club faced financial pressures in recent years, the Montana legislature, in an unprecedented artistic move, appropriated funds to buy the painting for the state. Today it is appraised at $750,000. Montana Historical Society Collection

Last Chance Gulch, Looking North, circa 1910

A newsboy hawks his papers in the lower left corner of this picture, very near the narrow street, known as Wall Street, coming in from the left, with the Music Hall on one side and the Colwell Building, still standing, on the north side. At this time, the Colwell Building was known as Uncle Sam's Building, with U.S. Lodging rooms upstairs and the Kessler Brewery warehouse and office on the street floor. This unusual old building is best known today as the Weggenman Building, since it housed that family's grocery business until recent years. The three-story building down the street on the left was originally the new York Store and later the Quincy Hotel, which still later housed the Independent Record newspaper office. This building was razed in 1982.

The streetcar lines point directly to the Atlas Block on the right side of the street. Latest information is that this historically important structure will be saved and renovated. The four-story building with horizontal white stripes was the Gans and Klein store on the corner of Broadway and Main. The twin towers of the now-demolished Novelty Block are prominent on the skyline on the right side. The vertical Theatre sign is on the building which now

houses the Ghost Art Gallery, and next to it is the Boston Block with its bay windows, fortunately still standing. All structures beyond that, including the Cosmopolitan Hotel which is the site today of the new Aspen Building, were demolished during the urban renewal period. Courtesy of the Mark McBride Collection

Chapter Eight

The Decade of World War I

Early in 1912 Helena residents were stirred with the news that the giant liner *Titanic*, thought to be unsinkable, had struck an iceberg off the Newfoundland Banks and gone down with over 1,200 passengers, many of them affluent Americans. Scholarly Woodrow Wilson became the twenty-eighth president that year, promising to administer the country in "a progressive era of New Freedom in domestic affairs," and to keep America out of the war which now threatened to engulf Europe.

Edward VII, Queen Victoria's oldest son who ascended the throne in 1901, died in 1910, and the new monarch was his sincere but somewhat colorless son, George V, who sat for his portrait with his redoubtable Queen Mary. Standing alongside was his oldest son, who was to become Edward VIII in 1936 and abdicate for love of a commoner the same year.

In its issue of Sunday, August 2, 1914, headlines in the *Helena Independent* announced that the German kaiser had declared war against Russia, and a dispatch from London said that "now the die is cast, and Europe is to be plunged into a general war which has been the apprehension of European statesmen for a year."

As the kaiser lost 25,000 men in a bloody battle at Liege, Belgium, troubles in the copper mines of Butte climaxed in August 1914. Governor Sam Stewart called out the Montana National Guard and companies from throughout the state began gathering at Fort Harrison for deployment to Butte.

In Helena, construction of St. Helena Cathedral was nearing completion, and an aging Thomas Cruse, one of its prime benefactors, was able to attend the first mass, celebrated in the basement, on November 8, 1914. He died on December 20, five days before the great Gothic building was dedicated on Christmas Day. Helena lost another of its pioneer builders, perhaps the most influential entrepreneur of them all, when Samuel T. Hauser died at his home on November 10, 1914.

A few months after the woman's suffrage amendment had narrowly passed in the Montana legislature, the leading suffragettes met in Helena in January 1915 and organized the Montana Good Government Association, which in later years was to become the Montana League of Women Voters. In the 1916 election, the victorious ladies demonstrated their power by electing three women to Montana legislative seats and their own Jeannette Rankin to a seat in the U.S. Congress.

Montana prohibitionists, many of whom were identified with the suffrage movement, had their way in November 1916, when a referendum prohibiting the sale of alcoholic beverages passed overwhelmingly. Prohibition officially went into effect in Montana in 1918, and as the country struggled out of the dislocations of war in 1920, the "noble experiment" which proved to be anything but noble, became the law of the land with the passage of the Eighteenth Amendment. It would be thirteen years of rumrunning, illegal stills, and rising gangland crime before Montanans could join with their countrymen in a glass of legal whiskey and beer instead of the dangerous "moon" or the hated "near beer."

In the winter months of 1917, the regime of Tsar Nicholas of Russia collapsed in revolution, and America moved ever closer to war with Germany, stung by submarine sinking of its ships and the plight of its allies. On April 6, 1917, President Wilson asked for and got a declaration of war. Montana's Jeannette Rankin was among a handful of dissenters; she was to be alone in a similar vote a little less than a quarter-century later.

Mobilization of troops began at once, and in August, Fort Harrison became the receiving and training point for members of Montana's Second Regiment. In its issue of August 2, the *Helena Independent* said that more than 7,000 soldiers chosen by selective draft in Montana would be mobilized at the post.

In August 1917, as Montana was mustering for war, self-styled vigilantes in Butte dragged labor leader Frank Little from his rooming house and hanged him from a railroad trestle on the edge of town. This killing of Little, a leader in the radical Industrial Workers of the World, brought appeals to the Washington offices of Senator Walsh and Congresswoman Rankin for federal troops and intervention in troubled Butte, where early in June 1917 the Speculator Mine had exploded and killed 164 persons.

All these events whipped emotions to a frenzy in Montana as the search began for subversives and "traitors." With the new U.S. district attorney for Montana, Burton K. Wheeler, in charge of enforcing federal law, a witch hunt was advanced which, in spite of Wheeler's cool handling of affairs, led to a dark chapter in Montana history and, indeed, the nation's. The Montana Council of Defense, demanding more prosecutions of those they considered subversive, finally induced Governor Stewart to call a special legislative session, during which Montana's incredible sedition law was passed. It was later used as the model for the federal sedition law of May 1918. The German language was prohibited in Montana, and there were many cases of trampled civil liberties as the war continued.

Finally, in its issue of November 11, 1918, the *Helena Independent* used type three inches high to proclaim PEACE. "Cowardly Kaiser and Son Flee to Holland!" exclaimed the paper as it reported that the terms of surrender would be severe, that "Germany will be absolutely deprived from further military power of action on land and sea and in the air."

Even as the idealistic President Woodrow Wilson was in Europe promoting his League of Nations, which his own country was to repudiate, an obscure soldier named Adolf Hitler was already hatching plans to restore

Flag-Bedecked Last Chance Gulch, circa 1910

American flags flying from many store windows and overhead suggest this might have been a July Fourth observance in 1910. Vintage automobiles lining the streets seem to have largely replaced the few horse-drawn conveyances visible in this picture, which looks north from near the corner of Main and Broadway. From the Jean Baucus Collection

Germany to power and saw his efforts crowned only fifteen years later when he wrested leadership from the aging von Hindenberg and became German chancellor.

Feted in Europe but disappointed at home, Woodrow Wilson was touring the country trying to sell his League of Nations dream to the American people when he suffered a physical breakdown from which he never recovered and during which his vigorous wife, Edith Bolling Galt, was the leader of the country.

Montana, along with the rest of the nation, suffered in the aftermath of the great war. Farmers had ridden a wave of good crops, ample rainfall, and prime markets for eight years before the war. Spurred on by the Lever Act which froze wheat prices at two dollars a bushel to aid the war effort, patriotic Montana farmers plowed and planted every acre they could, a practice which eventually led to the dust bowl days in many parts of the west.

The war had also come at a time when Montana's great eastern prairies were filling with homesteaders, altering forever the Montana legislature as it met in Helena and sat representatives from twenty-eight new counties which had been created since 1910.

Postwar depression began with the collapse of wartime markets and a continuing draught, which culminated in 1919 with one of the most devastating farm calamities ever seen in Montana. As global and deadly influenza hit here as elsewhere, the price of wheat went from $2.40 a bushel in August to $1.25 in October. Winds whipped over-plowed fields and triggered disastrous forest fires in the western mountains.

Governor Stewart called the legislature into special session in midsummer 1920 but little was done except to authorize county commissioners to issue road construction bonds in the hope that some destitute farmers could find paying jobs. Much the same was true on the national scene, as the Wilson administration extended seed loans which, though the totals sounded grand, had little impact.

The ominous news of mortgage foreclosures, abandonment of farms, failure of banks, and an exodus of Montana's population all presaged more of the same, and in grimmer proportion, in the decades to come. As it turned out, Montana was the only state in the Union which lost population during the 1920s; perhaps because it was the seat of government, Helena lost only a meager 3.8 percent of its people. But in many ways, the end of World War I saw Montana leave the frontier of free plowing of marginal farmlands and as the legislators from newly formed and now nearly destitute counties gathered in Helena, there was an air of caution and a loss of optimistic self-confidence. ■

Fifth Avenue, 1911

Fifth Avenue was once the principal street going east out of Helena. This is a view of it looking west from the state capitol building. Courtesy of the N. J. Holter Collection

St. Charles Aero Club, 1911

Young men of Helena were fired up, as were young men everywhere, about the excitement of aviation when the St. Charles Aero Club was formed in 1911 as the result of talks given at Helena High School, St. Vincent's Academy, and Mount St. Charles College, the forerunner of Carroll College, by pilot Bud Mars. The enthusiasm of Mars had not dimmed in 1910, when he failed but survived an attempt to cross the Rocky Mountains in this Curtis pusher airplane, a feat which was to be accomplished the next year by Cromwell Dixon. Courtesy of Carroll College

Cromwell Dixon and His Historic Biplane

Nineteen-year-old Cromwell Dixon of Columbus, Ohio, sat in his fragile biplane at the Montana State Fairgrounds in Helena in 1911 before taking off westward to become the first man to fly over the Continental Divide. A party of observers at Blossberg, at the top of the divide, kept a fire going to guide him as his craft finally attained an altitude of 7,000 feet. Some tricky wind currents almost flipped him over, but thirty-four minutes after take-off, he landed at Blossberg. Dixon walked over the hill to the Northern Pacific telegraph and wired the sponsoring Curtis Exhibition Company of his success, and then wired anxious State Fair officials that he had landed safely and would "return before four o'clock." The daring young flier arrived at the race track landing spot at 3:30 p.m. to the cheers of a standing crowd and a check for $10,000. Two days later Dixon appeared at the Inland Empire Fair in Spokane and was killed when his biplane crashed. Artist Bob Morgan of Helena caught the excitement of this September day in 1911 in a mural for the new Helena Airport terminal building. Courtesy of Morrison Flying Service

Katherine Stinson at the Fair

Petite Katherine Stinson, one of the country's most highly-skilled and daring pioneer pilots, posed in 1913 at the state fair in Helena. Miss Stinson, a sister of aviator Eddie Stinson, carried the first air mail in Montana as a feature of the 1913 fair, when she flew from the grounds to the Helena Post Office. R. H. McKay photo, Montana Historical Society Collection

Flag-Bedecked Main Street, 1914

Patriotic sentiment was especially evident as Helena celebrated Independence Day in 1914. With war raging in Europe and America moving ever closer to involvement, Helena merchants went all out in decorating their buildings with bunting and American flags. Note the many automobiles lining the streets and the electrified streetcar proceeding south on brick-paved Last Chance Gulch. Montana Historical Society Collection

Militiamen Heading for Butte, 1914

Labor troubles in copper mines of Butte got out of hand late in June 1914, when rival unions clashed and the old Miners' Union Hall was dynamited. Governor Stewart, in response to pleas for help in restoring order, declared martial law and called up the National Guard, who were mobilized in Helena. In this picture, a contingent of guardsmen board Northern Pacific boxcars in Helena for the trip to the troubled city. Many of the same men would be called up again to serve on the Mexican border in 1916 and, a year later, to participate in World War II. Florence Holter photo

Montana National Guard, 1917

Company M of the Montana National Guard assembled at Fort Harrison for training as America entered the European conflict early in April 1917. National Guardsmen were the only troops with any prior military training the country had available, and they were the first to go to Europe. By the end of the year, 175,000 men were overseas. The draft, which started in July, called up millions of others who needed training at posts throughout the country, including Fort Harrison. By July 1918 over a million Americans were fighting in Europe and the country's industrial might in high gear turned the tide of war and led to the armistice on November 11, 1918. Courtesy of Montana National Guard

Montanans Off to War

Helena residents turned out en masse to watch members of Montana's 163rd Infantry, 41st Division, march north along Last Chance Gulch on October 24, 1917, to join the fighting in Europe. Leslie Lyle photo; Montana Historical Society Collection

St. Helena Cathedral

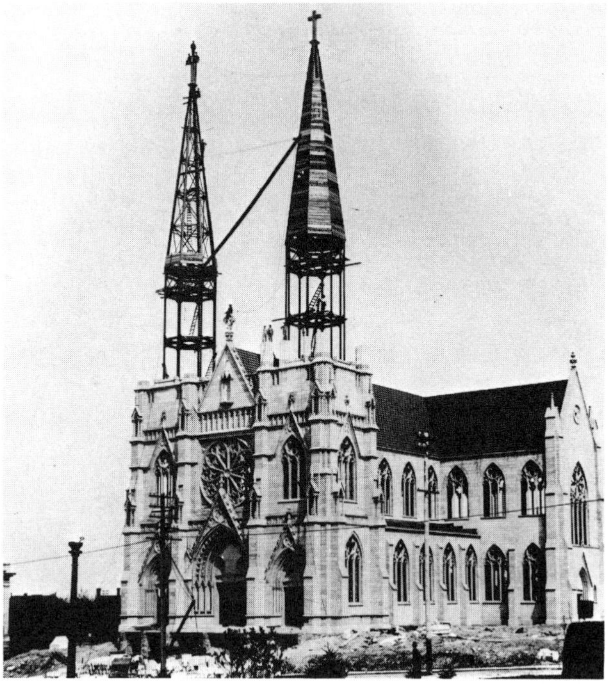

One of the most beautiful examples of Gothic architecture in the country is the twin-spired St. Helena Cathedral, seen here in exterior and interior stages of construction. Patterned after the Votive Cathedral of the Sacred Heart in Vienna, the church was designed by Albert O. Von Herbulis, an Austrian-born architect who also designed the main building on the campus of Mount St. Charles College (now Carroll College). The cathedral's Indiana Bedford limestone cornerstone was laid at the site at the head of Lawrence Street on October 4, 1908, and work began at once. In the exterior view (above), daring workmen are constructing the twin spires, which rise 230 feet above the Warren Street sidewalk. Three workmen are poised on one of the massive gold crosses which surmount the spires.

The magnificent stained-glass windows, crafted by F. X. Zettler and Company of Munich, Germany, had yet to be placed in the pointed arch openings. Also missing are statues of many scientific and religious figures, which were later placed in exterior wall niches. Workmen on the inside of the cathedral (left), are in the midst of constructing the great vaulted sanctuary, which for many years contained altars, statuary, communion railing, stations of the cross, and a baptismal font made entirely of Carrara marble. Now a priceless landmark and repository of sacred art, the cathedral cost a total of $645,590. Courtesy of Helena Catholic Diocese

Thomas Cruse at Unfinished Cathedral

Mining magnate Thomas Cruse is assisted down the front steps of the unfinished St. Helena Cathedral on November 8, 1914, after taking part in the first mass which had been celebrated in the basement. He died at his Helena home on December 21, and his funeral mass was the first celebration of its kind in the church to which he had contributed so much. Formal dedication came on Christmas Day of 1914, with formal consecration held a decade later. Courtesy of Helena Catholic Diocese

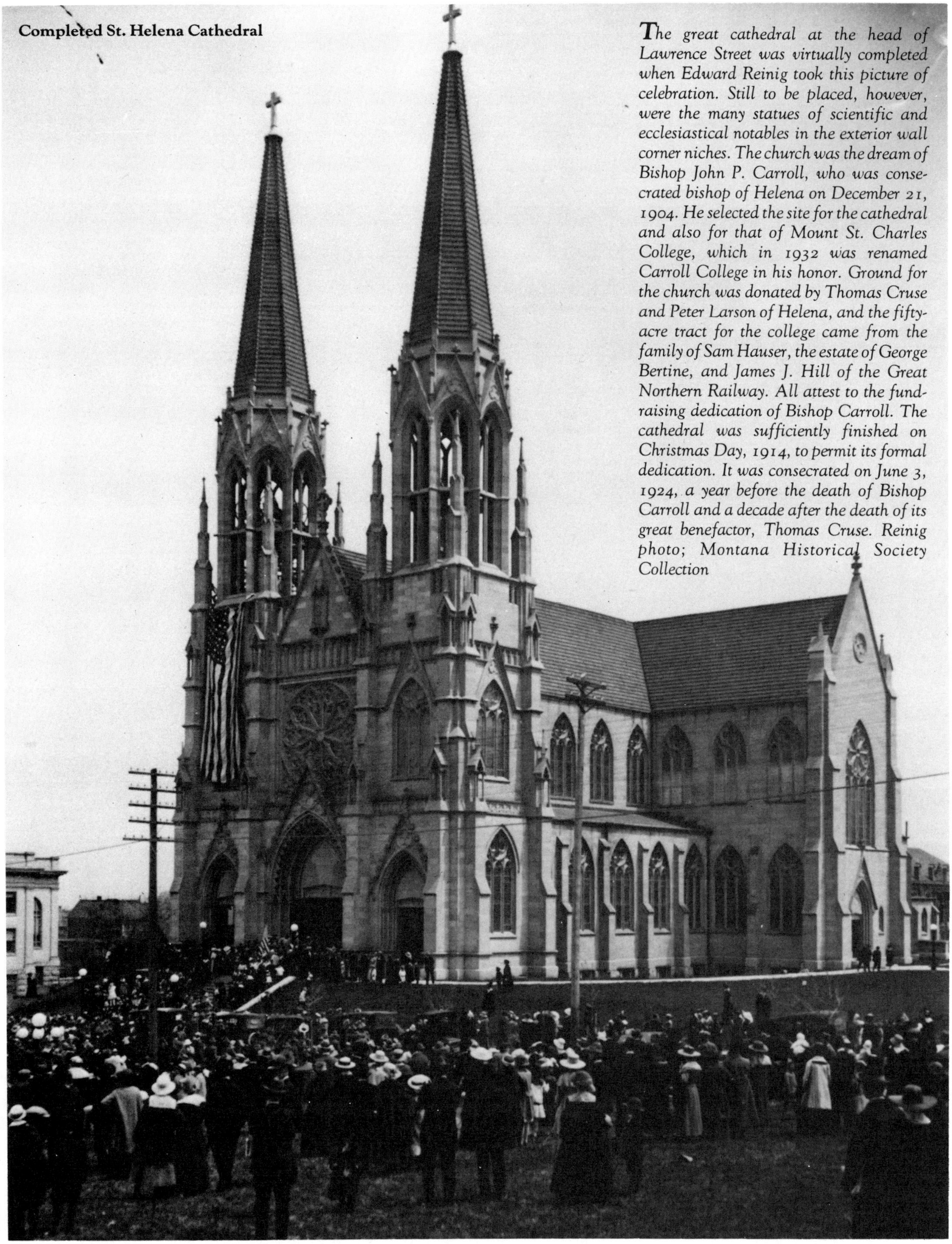

Completed St. Helena Cathedral

The great cathedral at the head of Lawrence Street was virtually completed when Edward Reinig took this picture of celebration. Still to be placed, however, were the many statues of scientific and ecclesiastical notables in the exterior wall corner niches. The church was the dream of Bishop John P. Carroll, who was consecrated bishop of Helena on December 21, 1904. He selected the site for the cathedral and also for that of Mount St. Charles College, which in 1932 was renamed Carroll College in his honor. Ground for the church was donated by Thomas Cruse and Peter Larson of Helena, and the fifty-acre tract for the college came from the family of Sam Hauser, the estate of George Bertine, and James J. Hill of the Great Northern Railway. All attest to the fund-raising dedication of Bishop Carroll. The cathedral was sufficiently finished on Christmas Day, 1914, to permit its formal dedication. It was consecrated on June 3, 1924, a year before the death of Bishop Carroll and a decade after the death of its great benefactor, Thomas Cruse. Reinig photo; Montana Historical Society Collection

Groundbreaking at Carroll College

Bishop John P. Carroll is breaking ground for the gymnasium on the campus of Mount St. Charles College in this picture, taken on commencement day June 13, 1917, with visiting dignitaries in attendance. Bishop Carroll had performed a similar chore eight years before, when he broke ground for the main building, still the imposing centerpiece of the campus. At the cornerstone-laying of the main building on September 27, 1909, a special guest was President William Howard Taft, who remarked that while he was not of the Catholic faith, he applauded the educational efforts of Bishop Carroll and his staff. The school was first devoted to teaching at the high school level, but in September 1911 the first college-level students were admitted.

Clergy in this picture have been identified, left to right: Monsignor Joyce, Father John O'Kennedy, Father Denis Meady, Father Lambertus, Father Norbert Hoff (the priest in the background, wearing glasses, Carroll College president from 1920 to 1934), Father McDonald (in black robes), Father Patrick Casey, Bishop Mathias C. Lenihan (in light-colored robes), Father Gilmore, Father Casey, Bishop Carroll, Father Tracy (the tall man, college president at the time), Father Stephen Sullivan (the stout priest in the front row, the college's first president in 1911), and Monsignor Victor Day, standing bareheaded. Courtesy of Carroll College

Army Training on Campus in 1918

The fifty-acre campus of Carroll College looks bleak and unlandscaped in this picture, taken in 1918 as World War I troops were in training down the hill. Directly behind them is the gymnasium, built a year earlier, with the impressive main building, completed in 1910, rising in the background. This building, designed by Albert O. Von Herbulis, the Austrian-born architect who at about the same time was perfecting plans for the St. Helena Cathedral, still dominates the campus today. The small utility building at the left proclaimed that this was still known as Mount St. Charles College.

Renamed Carroll College in 1932, the campus added buildings through the years, including a library and residence facility in 1923, a convent for Sisters of St. Dominic in 1924, an astronomical observatory in 1937, and others in more recent years, including O'Connell Hall, a new gymnasium in 1967, and a new library. In 1939 a civilian pilot training program under the auspices of the Civil Aeronautics Administration was instituted, and during World War II these facilities were used to train hundreds of army and navy pilots. Thus in yet another world conflict, the college served as a training center. During the years after World War II, as the campus continued to expand and a department of nursing was established, Carroll College became a fully accredited coeducational institution. Courtesy of Carroll College

Farewell to the Founder of Carroll College

Bishop John Patrick Carroll, who succeeded the pioneer prelate J. B. Brondel as the second bishop of Helena in 1904, died on November 2, 1925, in Switzerland at the age of sixty-one. His body was brought back to the city to which he had contributed so much, and his funeral mass was celebrated at St. Helena Cathedral on December 2, 1925. Standing at the foot of the stairs as the great educator's casket is borne out of the cathedral is Father Taugus, pastor of St. Helena. Bishop Carroll, trained as an educator, organized St. Aloysius Institute in 1906, and two years later, through the generosity of prominent landowners, acquired the fifty-acre site on which Mount St. Charles College was built. Bishop Carroll celebrated the twenty-fifth anniversary of his priesthood on September 21, 1914, and promptly donated gifts he had received to pay off the $23,000 debt the college owed at the time. In 1932 Bishop Carroll's successor, Bishop George J. Finnegan, changed the name of the college to honor its founder. Courtesy of Helena Catholic Diocese

Carroll College, 1982

Seventy-three years after its inception, Carroll College has become Montana's largest privately endowed college and has earned an enviable reputation for excellence, ranking in the top ten among independent colleges of the Northwest for the quality of its entering students. Although it remains rooted in Catholic tradition, over forty percent of today's students are of other faiths. St. Charles Hall still dominates the hill, although it is flanked today with a wing containing a chapel and a little theater.

In the background on the right is Science Hall. Borromeo Hall is only partially visible, as is Carroll Commons in the lower right of the picture. The administration building, O'Connell Hall, is in the left foreground, and to the left is Guadalupe Hall. The football field, the new physical education center, and the new library are all out of view, to the left. Courtesy of Carroll College

An Evening with Dickens

The 100th anniversary of the birth of Charles Dickens was celebrated on February 7, 1912, by a gathering of the Current Topic Club, held at the Spruce Street home of Mrs. Theodore Brantley, wife of the chief justice of Montana's Supreme Court. Characters and the ladies who played them have been identified, although not in sequence. Mrs. H. B. Ives, standing on the right side, portrayed jovial "Mr. Pickwick." Others are "Dolly Varden," Mrs. M. S. Gunn; "Mrs. Varden," Mrs. Katherine Warren; "Mrs. Jarley," Mrs. Frank Powell; "Mrs. Podsnap," Mrs. James Deering; "Mrs. Belinda Pocket," Mrs. F. K. Turner; "Mrs. Crummies," Mrs. Brantley; "Mrs. Colonel Wugsby," Mrs. Lockwood; "Little Dorrit," Mrs. Morton; "Mrs. Cratchitt," Mrs. Kyle; "Dora," Mrs. Rudolph Horkey; "Little Nell," Mrs. W. N. Sloan; and "Betsy Trotwood," Mrs. Clara Kennett. Other male Dickens characters were "Sam Weller," portrayed by Mrs. J. K. Scott, and "Wilkins Micawber," by Mrs. James Shoemaker. Courtesy of the Joan Holter Collection

Helena Ladies in New Packard, circa 1912

Seven Helena ladies, dressed to the "nines," are obviously enjoying a ride in a shiny new Packard touring car stopped in front of Hill Park. Among those recognized are the three in the back seat, from left to right: Margaret Sieben (Hibbard), Dorothy Smith, and Lenore Loble. Courtesy of Bruce Loble

Celebrating the Fourth, 1917

Henry J. Edgar, one of the discoverers of gold at Alder Gulch (Virginia City) in 1863, was escorted to the July Fourth parade of 1917 by a group of prominent Helena men, driving the old Canyon Ferry Stage with four dappled and decorated horses furnishing the power. Edgar is the man seated in the center on the front seat, with J. U. Sanders and B. H. Tatem on either side. Behind them are M. Reinig and M. L. Milligan. The towered building, seen in the background, was the headquarters for the Helena Water Department in the early years. Located on the southeast corner of the Carroll College campus, it is still standing, minus the towers. The building served as a barn for horses used by the department to draw the old round water tanks through town. Reinig photo; Montana Historical Society Collection

Main Street before the 1928 Fire

This view, looking south from the corner of Sixth and Main, was taken shortly before fire destroyed a number of buildings on the right side of the picture. The building with the flagpole, just south of the barely-visible Power Block, which went unscathed, is T. C. Power's Gold Block, completed late in 1888 and equipped with Helena's first hydraulic passenger elevator. It was completely gutted in the fire. The low white building is the New York Store, and further down, fire victims included the LaLonde Building, the Granite Block, and the Bailey Block. Reinig photo; Montana Historical Society Collection

Chapter Nine

The Decade of Boom and Bust

In 1920 the Nineteenth Amendment gave women the right to vote, just in time to help elect a handsome man named Warren G. Harding to the presidency. It was the administration of this misguided and gullible man which led to national prominence for Thomas J. Walsh, Montana's coolly intelligent U.S. senator who had been adding to his reputation steadily since he took his seat in 1913.

By now one of the most respected men in Congress, Walsh led the investigation of the Teapot Dome oil leasing scandal, which led to the jailing of Albert B. Fall, Harding's interior secretary. Walsh's younger colleague, Burton K. Wheeler, joined him in 1923, the year of Harding's sudden death and the beginning of the administration of quiet Calvin Coolidge. Less than a year later, Wheeler also gained national attention when he investigated Attorney General Harry M. Daugherty for malfeasance in office and generated enough pressure so that President Coolidge dismissed him from office.

Thus as Montana entered the Flapper Age of the 1920s, two of its senators were propelled to national reputations which would lead to their prominence in the Roosevelt period of the next decade. In Montana, Governor Joseph M. Dixon, who had defeated Wheeler in the acrimonious election of 1920, followed his progressive leanings as he governed from Helena. In 1924, in a speech near Butte, he lambasted the Ku Klux Klan and other radical groups which were springing up in postwar America, and tried valiantly to pass tax reform measures in Montana.

Dixon, one of Montana's more able governors, was still faced with postwar depression in Montana that was to persist well into the decade when he pointed out that the metal mines had paid only $13,559 in state taxes in 1922, when the value of production had reached over $20 million. He thus became the target of mining interests and was soundly defeated in 1924 by tall, handsome John E. Erickson, who on the death of Senator Walsh in 1933 went to Washington as a U.S. senator.

The country and the world were thrilled in May 1927, when a shy young man from Minnesota flew the Atlantic alone in his silvery *Spirit of St. Louis*. Charles A. Lindbergh arrived at LaBourget, France, a record-breaking thirty-three-and-one-half hours after his gasoline-laden monoplane barely cleared the trees on foggy Long Island. On September 6, 1927, Helena was included in his triumphant tour of the country.

In November of that year, the *Helena Independent* ran an interesting news story about an order for Montana bison which came from the brash premier of Italy, Benito Mussolini, who had held Fascist sway in his country since 1922. "Three bison were dispatched from the National Bison Reserve headquarters at Moise yesterday," the paper said in its issue of November 4, 1927. "The buffalo, each secured in an individual crate, are being shipped by express and were handled through the American Express Company," the article continued. "The bison are of the surplus stock on the national range northwest of Missoula, and some of the best specimens were chosen for the Mussolini order."

Later in the month, it was announced that the railroad commisson granted a permit to R. P. Crago and L. F. Schroeder to operate passenger busses in Helena and environs to replace the old Helena street railway system. And on November 29, 1927, a full-page ad sponsored by the Ford Motor Company announced the new Model A Ford automobiles to replace Henry Ford's cherished Model T. "Nineteen years ago we made the first Model T Ford car," the ad said. "We have now built a new car to meet modern conditions." On December 2, 1927, the first pictures of the radically different new Fords appeared, with four-door sedans priced at $570, roadsters at $385, coupes at $495, sport coupes at $550, and phaetons at $395, all prices f.o.b. (free on board) Detroit.

In Helena the new cars were displayed at Capital Ford, the agency which young Carl Anderson had opened in 1925, barely in time to survive the radical change from the dependable Model T to the sleek new Model A's which came in a variety of colors and were of an entirely new design. Anderson, whose agency is still operated by his son, Ralph, recalled that there was a period of some eighteen months when no new cars were available at all, but when the new models arrived in early December 1927, some 4,000 people jammed his showroom.

On December 4, 1927, Helena newspapers announced the world's first slag-treating plant to recover zinc would open in East Helena, and on December 8, the paper's columns were filled with accounts of a record cold snap. Scores were marooned in the blizzard, including a motorbus, filled with children, missing in the Brady area. Temperatures dropped fifty-eight degrees between 1:30 p.m. and 9:15 that night. As temperatures fell to more than thirty-five degrees below zero, the deaths of a boy and a herder were reported and the storm spread eastward, causing numerous deaths and the statement that "a great part of America is chilled."

After that terrible winter ended, Helena experienced one of the worst fires in its history, a history noted for devastating blazes. In its issue of July 16, 1928, the *Independent* headlined the horror: "HEART OF CAPITAL IS ABLAZE!" and went on to say that the fire started in the early morning hours at the Curtis Cafe, and by 4:30 a.m. was still unchecked as it spread rapidly to the Granite Block and the Bailey Block. On the east side of Main Street, the Pittsburgh Block was fired as strong winds carried "a hail of sparks and embers." Meanwhile a deluge of rain began falling, and roomers in the Granite Block and in the building to the south of the Curtis Cafe began moving out into the storm "bearing trunks, grips and what not which were soon drenched." The flames hit the Woolworth store next to the Curtis Cafe, and stores in the lower level of the Bailey Block, including Nifty Bill the Tailor's store, Reeves' Music House, and a shoeshine parlor went up in flames, along with the Gold Block and the New York Dry Goods Store.

In its issue of the next day, the paper said that even as the "embers were still alive," most of the owners of lost buildings were making plans to rebuild. This time the structures would be "more modern and well equipped." Stating that loss estimates were in the millions, the paper went on to say, "Following conferences held during the day, announcements were made by C. B. Power of the T. C. Power Company, owner of the Gold Block; Aubrey M. Holter of the Holter interests and owner of the New York Store building; Herman Fligelman, president of the New York Dry Goods Company; and Charles Hartwig of the W. J. Hartwig Company that they will rebuild." It added that similar announcements were expected from the Kleinschmidt interests which owned the Granite Block, and by Napoleon LaLonde, who controlled the Bailey Block.

Gangland crime hit a climax in February 1929, when rival gangsters, dressed as police, mowed down seven members of the "Bugs" Moran mob in Chicago on St. Valentine's Day. Herbert Hoover was beginning his second term as bootleggers and speakeasies flourished and the country rode a wave of paper prosperity. The dizzy spiral on Wall Street went unchecked as marginal investors, many of them millionaires only on paper, celebrated with illegal booze and laughed when showgirl Texas Guinan greeted them with "Hello, Sucker."

The crazy honeymoon came to an end along with the decade when, on Tuesday, October 29, 1929, the New York stock market plunged and with it the nation's financial apparatus. In panic selling, over 16 million shares changed hands on Wall Street that day, the Dow Jones average dropped to 198.69, and paper declines for all securities throughout the country totaled well over $100 billion.

Impact of the crash itself did not hit Montana and especially Helena for a time, but the familiar dry cycle began afflicting farmers, and before the new decade was underway, there was genuine suffering, and a concerned Governor Erickson in Helena was powerless to help. The Great Depression had begun, and from Helena were administered new federal programs which would affect the lives of Montanans for all time.■

The unusual mosque-like Algeria Shrine Temple, now Helena's civic center, looked like this in the early 1920s, when it functioned as headquarters for the Masonic order. Link and Haire, who operated architectural firms in both Billings and Helena, designed this unique building with the ancient rituals of the Shrine in mind. Note the mystic moon and star representations at the top of the tower. The building was severely damaged in the 1935 earthquakes, and the Shriners could no longer afford its renovation and upkeep. It was purchased by the city for use as a civic center and a place for city offices. Still city-owned, it is being upgraded and refined as a cultural center. Except for the police department, city offices have recently been moved to the former Federal Building at the head of Sixth Avenue, and federal offices have been moved to a new building in the urban renewal area. Reinig photo; Montana Historical Society Collection

Weiss Cafe, circa 1923

Weiss Cafe, at 20 North Main, was one of Montana's famous eating places after it was established by Maurice Weiss, who once operated the Old Stand Bar farther up Last Chance Gulch. Open twenty-four hours a day, the cafe had private oak booths in the back part of the building, where waiters such as these provided excellent service. They have been identified, left to right: Lewis J Teddy, Nick Kabalin, Nell Finnigan, Tommy Burke, and John Kabalin. Weiss's partner in the business for many years was Zeb Melhorn, who carried on the cafe after Weiss sold out in 1913 to become manager of the new Placer Hotel across the street. Another colorful waiter at the Weiss Cafe for many years was Tom Neagle, who lived to be ninety-three years old and often recalled how, as an inveterate runner, he would don heavy shoes after work and run as much as fifteen miles, often to the top of Mount Helena. In the days when ham and eggs were twenty-five cents and a cup of coffee and a doughnut could be had for a nickel, waiters were respected friends, and hundreds attended Neagle's funeral.

Across the street was another famed Helena restaurant, Eddy's Cafe, which used a steaming cup of coffee as its logo. Formerly known as the Capital Cafe, it was purchased in 1910 by Ed Gallivan and James E. "Eddy" O'Connell, who had been a waiter at the Broadwater Hotel. For a time O'Connell was manager of the Montana Club as well, and in 1908 he and a brother, Frank, established a small bakery in Missoula. Three years after buying the restaurant in Helena, the partners moved Eddy's Cafe to the Grand Central Hotel, which they had purchased, and in 1916 they moved to 16 Edwards Street. Beginning in about 1919, O'Connell began buying up small bakeries and eventually developed a chain of twenty-one Eddy bakeries throughout the Northwest. A heavy backer of Carroll College, O'Connell lived to see a campus building named in his honor. He died in 1972 at the age of eighty-six. Jorud photo; courtesy of the N. J. Holter Collection

Graduation Day at Intermountain Union College

Charles M. Russell and Friends, circa 1925

Camp Vigilante Swimming Hole, 1927

Capped and gowned graduates of Intermountain Union College lined up to greet family and friends in this picture, taken in the mid-1920s. The college was established in 1923 with the union of Methodist-sponsored Montana Wesleyan and the Presbyterian College of Montana, which had operated in Deer Lodge since 1883. Intermountain Union provided a full, four-year course of study to a student body which included both men and women. Helena Hall, the classroom building on Eleventh Avenue which is still standing, later served as a dormitory for Intermountain Deaconess Home for Children and today is used as a state office building. Other parts of the campus have given way to development of shopping areas across the street. Interestingly, if the 1935 earthquakes had not seriously damaged the college, it is possible that it would have had many more years in Helena. As it was, classes moved to Great Falls temporarily after the October 31 earthquake, and eventually it merged with Polytechnic in Billings to form present-day Rocky Mountain College in that city. Montana Historical Society Collection

Helena's long-time Pinkerton detective Nils P. Walters and artist Charles M. Russell had much in common and were close friends, as evidenced by this picture, taken about 1925. Both were born in 1864 and came to Helena in 1880 as sixteen-year-old adventure-seekers. Death came to both men in 1926, when they were sixty-two years old. In this picture, Walters is the man with the cane at the left, and Russell is at the right. The man in the center has been identified as Robert Johnson of Great Falls. Percy Raban photo; courtesy of Clem L. Shafer

The creek water was cold and the swimming hole often riled up with the black dirt surrounding it, but young campers always enjoyed the "dip." Florence Holter photo; courtesy of Barbara Kirkland

Popular Motorcycle Cop

Chub Munger was Helena's first speed cop, and the children of Helena were filled with both admiration and affection for him. These youngsters, who called themselves Coxey's Army, were great fans of the friendly law enforcement officer who was later Lewis and Clark County sheriff and is still a Helena resident. From left to right, beginning with the fourth child: Jack Power, Joan Treacy (Holter), Doris Holter (Burmingham), Chub Munger, Pauline Holter (Shumate), "Tiss" Holter (Clary), Tom Power, and Elizabeth Treacy (Bauer). Florence Holter photo; courtesy of Barbara Kirkland

Lindbergh Arriving over Helena, 1927

Flying into the wind, indicated by the windsock on the corner of Helena's original one-plane hangar airport on September 6, 1927, Charles A. Lindbergh guides his biplane to a landing as eager residents, like their counterparts throughout the country, waited to greet the shy hero. Florence Holter photo; courtesy of Barbara Kirkland

This famous plane, now hanging in the Smithsonian Institution, was tied down with a rope at the first Helena airport, today the site of Bill Roberts Golf Course. Florence Holter photo; courtesy of Barbara Kirkland

***Spirit of St. Louis* on the Ground in Helena, 1927**

Lindbergh in the Parade Car

Flanked by Governor John E. Erickson on the left and Mayor Percy A. Witmer on the right, leather-coated Charles Lindbergh rides in the open car which took him to a parade and planned festivities during his Helena visit. Florence Holter photo; courtesy of Barbara Kirkland

Refueling the *Spirit of St. Louis*

Lindbergh's plane is being refueled with cans of Conoco gasoline, manually lifted to the wing tank. Ed Follensby, standing on the ladder, watches the crowd's reaction on the field. Jorud photo; courtesy of Morrison Flying Service

Biplanes of the 1920s

This biplane, partially built by Ed Follensby, was photographed at the original Helena airport. Ed Follensby was a well-known Helena pilot. Courtesy of Morrison Flying Service

Pioneer Rancher Flies to Ranch

Henry Sieben, who had traveled much of Montana by horseback and stage, later took to travel by car, train, and then air. About 1924 he was flown to his ranch at Adel, in Cascade County, in this biplane with two open cockpits. His daughter, Margaret Sieben Hibbard, records the event. From left to right: Fred B. Sheriff, Bill Ferguson, A. T. Hibbard, and Henry Sieben with his two grandchildren, Jean Sheriff (Baucus) and Henry Hibbard. The landing field was a pasture by a sheep shed. Bill Ferguson was a barnstorming pilot as well as the secretary of the Helena Chamber of Commerce. He made many parachute jumps at fairs throughout the state. From the Jean Baucus Collection

Views of the Fire

Citizens tried to help man hoses, and officials were busy trying to protect a curious public in these views, taken at the height of and in the aftermath of the fire of July 16, 1928, which destroyed four major buildings and a number of smaller ones south of the Power Block on Main Street. In a city noted for devastating fires throughout its history, this was a major and costly conflagration.

Leslie Lyle photo; courtesy of The Parrott

Florence Holter photo

Florence Holter photo

Montana Historical Society Collection

After the Fire

This panoramic view was taken when the great 1928 fire was still smoldering. Barricades are in place in front of the remains of the Granite Block, the New York Store, and the gutted Gold Block. Jorud photo; courtesy of the John Wheeler Collection

Square-bodied automobiles lined West Sixth Avenue on June 19, 1930, when L. H. Jorud took this picture, looking west towards the Federal Building, now the City-County office headquarters. The prominent building on the right, built in 1883, housed a farm implement firm owned by S. C. Ashby and C. A. Broadwater until it was sold in 1894 to Weinstein Brothers. Today this is the site of the First National Bank Building. Across the street, west of the Power Block, can be seen the Western Union office, Claflin Furniture, Starz Pharmacy, and the Electric Block minus its historic smokestack and now site of the municipal parking ramp. Jorud photo; Montana Historical Society Collection

Chapter Ten

The Depression Years

As the country's economy reeled after the stock market crash of October 1929, the nation as a whole lost its confidence in big business. Such industrial leaders as Samuel Insull were in disgrace, banks failed, farm mortgages were foreclosed, and business proved incapable of providing jobs.

Oddly enough, as the new decade dawned, Helena newspapers were filled, instead of news of economic distress, with stories about a rash of student walkouts on college campuses, including Mount St. Charles College, now Carroll College. Students went on strike, according to the *Independent*, on November 15, 1930, demanding seven changes in governing rules, including one requiring that students be in early on weekends. The strike was especially widespread at Montana State College in Bozeman, where the president threatened to resign and only intervention by the governor brought the students back on campus.

In 1932 the clear voice of Franklin Delano Roosevelt ("the only thing we have to fear is fear itself") was heard on the radio airwaves as the New York governor campaigned for the presidency. Swept into office by a landslide vote in November, Roosevelt quickly declared a bank holiday and began pushing the first of his New Deal programs through Congress.

The country was stunned in March 1932, when news was flashed of the kidnapping of Charles Lindbergh's young son. Every Helena newspaper for many weeks carried front-page stories about progress in the case and the eventual execution of Bruno Hauptmann for the "crime of the century." Helena residents recalled that it had been only five years since they had welcomed the aviation hero after his daring flight.

In January 1933, when John E. Erickson began his third term as Montana governor, a group of hunger marchers descended on the capitol in Helena as the legislature met. Their spokesman was allowed to speak before the senate, but when it was all over, the *Helena Independent* summed up the effort in these sardonic words: "They have accomplished exactly as much as did the King of France in the nursery rhyme who 'marched up the hill with 20,000 men and then marched down again.'"

As the new president in Washington asked for an immediate half-billion dollars in aid for the needy, Montana's newly appointed chairman of the Emergency Relief Board, Tom Spaulding, announced in Helena that in some counties of the state, one out of every two families was in need of relief.

Prohibition neared the end of its nearly fourteen years of unpopular existence, and the *Helena Independent* editorialized against the hated 3.2 percent beer. "The trouble with the stuff," the editor said, "is that it's too weak for the wets and too strong for the drys. Thus it pleases no one. This newspaper is for beer—legal beer—not because it will 'help the farmer' or raise billions, but simply because the American people have the right to drink what they please, when they please."

In February 1933 a joint congressional resolution repealed the Eighteenth Amendment and passed the Twenty-First, once more legalizing liquor. Within ten months, state conventions had ratified the repeal of the old and the institution of the new, and on December 5 of that year, President Roosevelt officially announced the death of Prohibition.

Meanwhile, gangster Al Capone, who had risen to gangland power largely because of the Eighteenth Amendment, was sent to federal prison in Atlanta for income tax evasion, where he was to die from the effects of syphilis. In Northampton, Massachusetts, former President Calvin Coolidge died of a heart attack at the age of sixty, and in Madrid, Spanish loyalists and rebels clashed as a prelude to the three-year civil war which was to become a dress rehearsal for the dictatorships of Adolf Hitler and Benito Mussolini. With their help, the rebel general, Francisco Franco, became the Spanish dictator in 1939.

On January 29, 1933, Amelia Earhart and Colonel L. H. Brittin visited Helena and were guests at the home of Mr. and Mrs. Fred Sheriff. Brittin at the time was general manager and vice-president of the new Northwest Airways and with Miss Earhart was flying westward from St. Paul across the northern tier of states to determine feasible routes for passenger and airmail service. Miss Earhart, who had been the first woman to fly the Atlantic alone, piloted a Flying Ford tri-motor plane with Wasp engines during the 1933 Western trip. Four years later, she and her navigator were lost on a reconnaissance Pacific flight, their plane never found.

In January 1933, Adolf Hitler was named chancellor of Germany, and, according to a German quote in the *Independent*, "Nationalist Germany was thrown into a paroxysm of joy at the union of President von Hindenburg and the Nazi leader in a common effort to pull the Fatherland from the mire."

In February, as Norma Shearer and Clark Gable were appearing at the Marlow Theatre in *Strange Interlude*, newly-elected President Roosevelt was in Miami when an assassin fired at him and Chicago Mayor Anton Cermak, who was in the presidential party. The president was unhurt, but Mayor Cermak, grievously wounded, died a month later in Chicago.

Later in the month, Montana Senator T. J. Walsh, designated to become attorney general in the new cabinet, was in Havana to marry Senora Mina Perez Chaumont Truffin, wealthy widow of a prominent Havana businessman. The usually taciturn Senator Walsh told reporters, "I expect to take two months or ten weeks vacation in order to show my wife the beauties of my state, Montana."

On March 2, 1933, Senator and Mrs. Walsh were bound for Washington when he died of a heart attack as their train was passing through North Carolina. He was seventy-three years old, one of the country's most respected statesmen. Accorded appropriate honors in Washington, Senator Walsh was returned to Helena, where his body lay in state in the capitol rotunda before funeral mass was said at St. Helena Cathedral on March 9. He was buried in Resurrection Cemetery beside his first wife, who had died in 1917. The stricken new Mrs. Walsh told reporters she was unable to attend.

Amid considerable controversy, Montana Governor Erickson became the new U.S. senator from Montana on the death of Walsh, and was succeeded by Frank H. Cooney of Missoula. On March 24, as Hitler set himself up as dictator of Germany and called for the first boycotts against Jews, H. F. Sheehan Company of Helena was issued the first wholesale license to distribute beer after Prohibition. The firm arranged to have a truck at Ogden, Utah, site of the nearest operating brewery, to speed legalized beer to thirsty Helena residents.

In 1935 Helena residents were coping with the Depression, taking heart when they listened to President Roosevelt's weekly "fireside chats" on the radio, when they began to feel a series of earth tremors. On October 3, a noticeable tremor awakened a few residents, but most were unaware of it until they were informed the next day. A week later, at one o'clock in the morning, no one in the city failed to wake up to tumbling dishes, moving furniture, and a deep rumble.

Hasty inspections showed little damage, and newspaper and radio announcements sought to calm fears. Fifty-seven vibrations occurred, none of them serious, during the next week. Then on October 18, on a particularly beautiful and warm Indian summer evening, a violent tremor struck a few minutes after eight o'clock, but when it passed without damage, residents breathed easier, put their children to bed, and relaxed to read or listen to the radio. By now they were accustomed to the earth movements and told themselves they were experiencing familiar aftershocks.

But at ten o'clock came the violence which was to plunge Helena into darkness and panic and see many of her public buildings and homes destroyed. Two men were killed by falling debris and many panic-stricken residents piled possessions in their cars and headed out of town. Business houses and schools closed, troops patrolled the streets, and Montana's congressional delegation wired promises of relief. In its issue of Sunday, October 20, the *Helena Independent* took up its entire front page describing the damage, beginning one story of estimated damage in these words: "Helena, the capital city of Montana, whose streets and hills have yielded upwards of $100,000,000 in gold, has suffered a loss of fully $2,500,000 in property damage. It is certain that each day will reveal new damage not at the present time perceptible."

In an accompanying box, Will A. Campbell, the paper's chief executive, said that while the *Independent* building had not apparently been damaged, he felt that the staff, which worked around the clock to produce papers on Saturday and Sunday, should not be expected to work another night. "Human life is more important than publishing a paper during the night when earthquake shocks of terrorizing proportions might again be felt in Helena," Campbell wrote.

Damage appraisals which quickly followed showed that the west side slopes of the city had escaped virtually unscathed, but on Helena Avenue and Rodney, the city's new high school building, opened for the first time early in September, was virtually a total wreck. The damage in the central and east sides and out into the Helena Valley was staggering.

Reconstruction began almost immediately. High school students attended class in railroad passenger cars, and state and local police and National Guardsmen still patrolled the streets even as they tried to find temporary quarters for their operations. Engineers and workmen were climbing buildings, assessing damage, sometimes shooting weakened chimneys and stacks with rifles to demolish them. Two men were inspecting the top of the Kessler Brewery stack when, at noon on October 31, the last great tremors struck. The two men at the brewery were killed, bringing the earthquake death toll to four.

Many buildings, weakened in the quake of the eighteenth, toppled or were rendered unusable. Patients were evacuated from St. John's Hospital and from Fort Harrison Veterans Hospital. Intermountain Union College moved to Great Falls, never to return to Helena. While many public buildings, including schools, were damaged severely or beyond repair as the terrible month ended, it was found that St. Helena Cathedral had suffered so little damage that city engineer Oscar Bearson declared it safe for the funeral of Governor Frank Cooney, who had died of a sudden heart attack.

Tremors were felt throughout the rest of the year and into the first months of 1936, but Helena was done with earthquake violence, even though geologists point to the fault which crosses Helena Valley and hold out the real possibility of future tremors. All told, during the 1935 and 1936 nightmare, well over 1,000 tremors were recorded.

As Helena residents began reconstructing their fallen or damaged homes and places of business, administration of the New Deal programs of Franklin Roosevelt centered in Helena, and state government itself underwent the greatest change in its history. Because of its vast expanses of federal lands and the political clout of its Democratic party representatives in Congress, Montana received an inordinate share of federal moneys until well towards the end of the decade.

The Works Progress Administration, which sponsored all manner of make-work projects, employed over 14,000 Montanans until mid-1939, while in northeastern Montana, the mighty Fort Peck Dam was rising on the Missouri to become, at the time, the largest earthfill dam in the world and a virtual "crown jewel" in President Roosevelt's public works program.

With the repeal of Prohibition in 1933, lawmakers in Helena hastened to create the Montana Liquor Control Board, which to this day operates a liquor monopoly in the state. Other new agencies, all the result of federal programs and money, included a water conservation board, a grazing commission, a state planning board, and a state highway patrol board. The Social Security Act of 1935 triggered creation of Montana's Department of Public Welfare and the Unemployment Compensation Commission.

Meanwhile, officials in Washington witnessed with growing apprehension appeasement in Europe and the growing arrogance of Adolf Hitler and his lackey, Mussolini. In its issue of May 7, 1937, the *Helena Independent* ran a front page picture of the great silver *Hindenberg*, the world's largest dirigible, with the Nazi swastika decorating its tail rudder, along with the story of its destruction as it sought mooring at Lakehurst, New Jersey.

Mrs. Franklin D. Roosevelt, a world traveler on behalf of her husband's programs, stopped briefly in Helena on May 7 aboard a Northwest Airlines plane, en route to Chicago from Seattle, where she had been visiting her daughter, Anna Boettiger. "She was dozing as the plane landed," the paper said, "but awoke and glanced from the window as the ship taxied up to the administration building. She yawned, leaned back in her seat again and apparently slept through the stop here."

No one in Helena took offense because the First Lady rested instead of granting yet another interview. There was plenty to do, helping her handicapped husband administer a country now on the brink of another war, a war which would provide a tragic but built-in finale to the years of Depression and isolationism.■

Aviation in the 1930s

In spite of Depression, aviation enthusiasts in Helena began growing in number and accomplishment since World War I had trained some and fired the imagination of others. Since 1928 National Parks Airways had been running from Salt Lake City to Great Falls, via Helena, using a fleet of classic planes, such as a two-cockpit open biplane and a six-passenger high wing monoplane. In 1932 the Montana Aero Club had an active membership and was training pilots in this high wing monoplane, designed and built by Henry and Jack Lay of Helena. Powered with a five-cylinder Siemens-Halske motor which developed seventy-five horsepower, this plane featured ball bearing engine construction, an innovation at the time. Courtesy of Morrison Flying Service

Amelia Earhart Visits Helena, 1933

Amelia Earhart Putnam, the country's leading woman flyer, landed in Helena on January 29, 1933, in a tri-motor Ford biplane, accompanied by Colonel Brittin of Northwest Airways, who was seeking out feasible routes for a mail and passenger line across the northern tier of states. In the picture above, Fred Sheriff, one of the leaders in the development of aviation in Helena, gives the pilot landing signals and, at the right, officially welcomes the great aviator to Helena. Sheriff, a civil engineer, married Berneice Sieben, daughter of pioneer stockman Henry Sieben, in 1915 and assumed management chores in the ranching operations of his father-in-law. Many people remember him best, however, for his role in establishing Helena's airport and his service as Montana's first commissioner of aeronautics. From the Jean Baucus Collection

Dedication of the Helena Airport, 1938

With the completion of the small administration building, seen at the far left, it was time to dedicate the Helena Airport on May 2, 1938, although the landing strips had been used for a decade. National Park Airways flew in a shiny new twin-engine plane for the occasion. Contrasting transportation from another era was provided by the Canyon Ferry Stage, pulled by a four-horse team driven by Court Sheriff of Canyon Ferry. The stage had been accompanied by four riders, including Josephine Sheriff and Whitney Smith, seen fourth and third from the right, and Fred Sheriff, at the extreme right. Others in the picture who have been identified include Mayor Jack Haytin, wearing a Shriner's fez, and high school principal A. J. Roberts, wearing a light overcoat and a very large western hat. From the Jean Baucus Collection

The Morrisons, 1933

The late R. E. "Red" Morrison and his wife, Elizabeth "Biddy," were photographed in the summer of 1933 alongside a six-passenger Lockheed Vega plane at the Helena airport. Morrison, a crack pilot and flying enthusiast who had been a pilot for William Randolph Hearst in California, came to Helena in 1931 and established the Morrison Flying Service, which is still in operation. Morrison and Bill Fahrner are credited with establishing the high school aeronautics school at the airport, the first fully accredited school of its kind in the country. Still in operation, the school is noted for excellence and rate of pilot placement. Red Morrison lost his life in a plane crash at Tampa, Florida, while he was serving in the U.S. Air Force in 1943. His widow, who still resides in Helena, was active in management of the Morrison Flying Service for many years until her recent retirement. Their son, Jeff Morrison, now manages this pioneer aviation service. Courtesy of Morrison Flying Service

Mount St. Charles Champion Football Team, 1931 and 1981

Not a single opponent was able to score against this championship football team of 1931, which carried the letters of Mount St. Charles College. Opponents included Montana State University, Montana Wesleyan, Montana Normal, Montana School of Mines, and Montana State College. In 1981, a half-century later, ten members of the team held a reunion at Carroll College, successor of Mount St. Charles. Players in the championship lineup, photographed in the college dining hall on December 17, 1931, are identified as follows, with men who were present for the reunion in capital letters. Top row, left to right: Coach William B. Jones, Helena; "Cal" Snyder, North Platte; LARRY SCHEEWE, Helena; Gene Connors, Townsend; Floyd Meyer, Polson; Lou Dvorsky, Iowa City; Tom O'Connor, Miles City; Fred Fox, Hollywood; Al Donich, Deer Lodge; Brad Seeley, Helena; John Johnson, Idaho Falls; James Conway, Livingston; Assistant Coach SIDNEY T. SMITH, Philipsburg; and Assistant Coach JOHN GOOD, Butte.

Middle row: Al Pascol, Helena; Ed Foley, Butte; DONALD A. NASH, Bozeman; GEORGE DOYLE, Miles City; ART DOYLE, Miles City; Gene Dunnigan, Miles City; Charles Garner, Pocatello; Coleman Mulligan, Anaconda; WARREN NELSON, Great Falls; BEN EVANS, Helena; Leary Mills, Garden Valley; Frank Harrington, Butte; George Moses, Butte; and Manager Bill Dunn, Miles City.

Front row: Rex Budel, Philipsburg; John "Harp" O'Neil, Butte; Philip "Red" Davidson, Anaconda; Clarence Mayer, Havre; WALTER MACK, Havre; Bill Nugent, Miles City; Raymond Botch, Wibaux; James Freebourn, Butte; John McDonald, Helena; James Cronin, Sioux City; and Philip Botch, Wibaux. Not pictured were Matt McMahan, JOHN McGILLIS, Frank May, Joseph Laux, William Sullivan, Tony Niklas, and Adolph Zuelke.

In the 1981 reunion picture, the former champs were: back row, Ben Evans, Walter Mack, John McGillis, and Art Doyle. In front: Warren Nelson, Larry Scheewe, John Good, Sid Smith, George Doyle, and Don Nash. Gene Fischer photo; courtesy of Carroll College

St. Vincent's Academy, 1932

Established in 1870 as a Catholic boarding school, St. Vincent's Academy moved into its new brick building on Ewing Street in the 1880s. This picture, taken in May 1932, shows the building a short time before it was seriously damaged in the 1935 earthquakes, which led to its demolition. The academy offered high school classes only from 1909 until its destruction in 1935. Courtesy of Helena Catholic Diocese

Vigilante Parade

Since 1924, Helena High School students have staged annual Vigilante parades in May, with local merchants donating a variety of prizes. Industrious students have vied with each other in recreating historic scenes and events, with the result that both ingenuity and an interest in the city's colorful history have been evoked as a substitute for such clandestine activities as "sneak day" when the school year draws to a close. The annual events have taken place for nearly sixty years, except for the years of World War II.

These pictures, all taken in the 1930s, reveal the kind of imaginative planning that still characterizes the parades. At the top, two period-dressed teamsters drive the black coach which Senator T. C. Power brought back to Helena in the 1890s. The boys were able to borrow the coach, but could hardly be expected to emulate the four, perfectly-matched black horses which once drew this historic coach. In the center, comic relief, a traditional aspect of the parades, was provided by a sway-backed horse drawing a sulky. At the lower left, some busy high schoolers created the starving cow and waiting wolf made famous in C. M. Russell's postcard depiction of the terrible winter of 1886-87. In this picture, two participants are busy putting the finishing touches on the simulated snow.

Top
From the Jean Baucus Collection

Middle
Courtesy of the Helena Chamber of Commerce

Bottom
From the Jean Baucus Collection

Costume Party, circa 1937

If prizes were given for the most beautiful and elaborate attire at this costume party at the Montana Club in about 1937, one no doubt went to Mrs. Belle Winestine, seen in the right foreground wearing her grandmother's wedding dress. Others who have been identified are Edmund Patenaude, seated at left in cowboy hat, with his wife, Mary Agnes, standing at his left. Wearing period costume with top hat is Ted Collins with his wife, Fritz, in white standing at his left. Next to her is Lucille Thompson, wife of Dr. John Thompson. Far back behind Mrs. Winestine is Marion Holter Barbour, standing at the left front of C. M. Russell's great oil painting, When The Land Belonged to God. *Next to her, further to the front, is Virginia Kennett Fletcher, wife of Robert Fletcher; Mrs. Brent Rickard, wife of the East Helena Smelter manager; and Margaret Sieben Hibbard. Montana Historical Society Collection*

Senator Thomas J. Walsh

Time magazine ran a picture of Montana's Senator Thomas J. Walsh on the cover of its issue of May 4, 1925, when the reserved, brilliant lawyer was at the height of his twenty-year career in Washington. A year before, investigative work by Senator Walsh had resulted in the downfall of President Harding's secretary of the interior, Albert B. Fall, along with a number of his associates in the Teapot Dome oil leasing scandal. A native of Wisconsin, Thomas J. Walsh came to Helena in 1890 after teaching school for a time and taking his law degree from the University of Wisconsin. He built a remarkable record as a lawyer, especially in cases of injured workmen, and in 1912, after two previous failures as an office seeker, defeated Joseph M. Dixon in a race for the U.S. Senate. Walsh was widely respected throughout the country before he had been in Washington for very long. His career apexed in 1933 when President Franklin D. Roosevelt appointed him attorney general in the new administration. Walsh died en route to Washington to accept the appointment. History's verdict on this austere, brilliant man has been one of profound respect without the usual easy-going, first-name familiarity by which Montanans are often characterized. A familiar saying, attributed to a newsman, was that asking T. J. Walsh for a political favor would be "like asking the statue of Civic Virtue for a chew of tobacco." Courtesy of the Steve Browning Collection

Senator Walsh with his Granddaughters

The senator with the children of the late Admiral and Mrs. Gudger. Genevieve Gudger was the senator's only daughter, and up to the time of her marriage she served as her father's assistant. Courtesy of Helena Catholic Diocese

Funeral of Senator T. J. Walsh

The body of Senator Thomas J. Walsh was brought back to his Helena home after eulogies in Washington, D.C., for services at St. Helena Cathedral and burial in Resurrection Cemetery. Pallbearers were close personal and political friends, among them Lester Loble, leading the line at the right. Later a district judge, Loble was prominent in the Democratic party, as was the late Senator Walsh. Behind Loble is Wellington D. Rankin, a close personal friend of the senator but a nationally prominent Republican. To break the tension of this sad day, Loble was quoted as saying to Rankin, "Hang on tight, Wellington, this is as close as you will get to the U.S. Senate." The fourth man in that line was Fred B. Sheriff, an old family friend, while the third man from the front on the left side is Raymond Nagle, who had practiced with Walsh's law firm in Helena for many years.

In this picture, left above, the beautiful interior of St. Helena Cathedral was filled beyond capacity for the funeral mass of Senator Walsh, held March 9, 1933. One of the mourners was an Indian in full dress, his bonnet trimmed with eagle feathers. The only other occasion known in which an Indian attended a prominent funeral in Helena in full dress was at last rites for Frontier Town builder John Quigley in 1979. Courtesy of Helena Catholic Diocese

National Biscuit Factory in Ruins

Helena had prided itself on a modern biscuit factory on Boulder Avenue, although at the time of the 1935 earthquakes, it was used mainly as a distributing center by the National Biscuit Company. Apparently in the direct path of the violent quakes of both the eighteenth and thirty-first of October, the brick structure was totally ruined. The Northern Pacific depot district, where this was located, was among the hardest hit in the city, virtually every home and building, including the Bryant School, sustaining extensive damage. Indeed, Helena's schools were especially hard hit by the quakes, but none of them was occupied at the time of either major quake. Jorud photo; courtesy of the N. J. Holter Collection

Mortally Stricken Home

Countless homes in Helena were severely damaged or totally ruined during October 1935. Brick sheathing from this and other buildings fell away, and in many cases those weakened earlier in the month were destroyed or made inhabitable by tremors on the last day of that terrible month. Jorud photo; courtesy of the N. J. Holter Collection

Shattered High School

Helena had pridefully dedicated its new high school at Rodney Street and Helena Avenue on September 21, 1935, only to see it severely damaged in the earthquake of October 18. Inspection of the school showed that the brick structure had been subjected to terrific wrenches and strains in every direction. The town was stunned at the devastation but grateful that no classes were in session and that a dramatics teacher, who had been in charge of an evening session of students, had dismissed them early as if by premonition. The building, now site of Helena's Junior High School, suffered further damage in the last great tremor on October 31. Jorud photo; courtesy of the N. J. Holter Collection

Four Years after the Quakes

This picture, taken by Les Jorud on March 20, 1939, is looking north toward the Helena Valley and the snow-covered chest of the Sleeping Giant Mountain. The flat-topped building in the left foreground is the A. A. Garage, formerly site of the streetcar barns and now location of the new Federal Building. Main Street begins just beyond the oval, snow-covered park and runs diagonally across the right hand side of the picture. The large windowless building in the right center is the back of the Marlow Theater. Jorud photo; Montana Historical Society Collection

Commando Trainees at Rest

After a thirty-mile hike to Marysville, members of the First Special Service Force in training at Fort Harrison cooled their feet in a small stream above the town. Although none of the volunteers knew of their ultimate assignments, their rigorous training in parachute jumping, mountain climbing, cliff-scaling under full pack, grueling mountain marches, after-dark maneuvers, and ski instruction by a team of Norwegian experts all suggested preparation for guerilla warfare. John Marshall photo

Chapter Eleven

The 1940s and World War I

Joseph B. Poindexter, once associated with the pioneer Poindexter and Orr cattle ranch in Beaverhead County and a Helena resident during a 1915 to 1917 term as Montana's attorney general, was the man directly responsible for civilian defense and welfare in Hawaii on Sunday, December 7, 1941, when the Japanese attacked Pearl Harbor and plunged the country into World War II. Appointed a federal judge in Hawaii in 1917 by President Woodrow Wilson, Poindexter had been governor of the Territory of Hawaii since 1934. Now, as his tenure in the islands spanned the time period beginning with World War I, he saw his country, and his territorial charge, embarked on a new and even more devastating global holocaust.

In its issue on Monday, December 8, the *Helena Independent* devoted its entire front page to the sneak attack on Pearl Harbor and its worldwide ramifications. Included was a news story about a number of Helena vicinity residents who were in the combat zone. Among them were Lee Dickey and Richard O'Hearn, both of whom were captured during the initial occupation of Wake Island and interned by the Japanese throughout the war. Dickey, who is still a Helena resident, had written a letter to his parents a short time before the attack, describing how 1,200 civilian Americans, himself included, were just completing work on an airbase on Wake.

Senator Burton K. Wheeler, who had been an antagonist of administration policies for a number of years and an outspoken isolationist, was quoted as saying that "the Japanese have chosen war and thus we must exert our every energy, not only to win but to give the Japanese such a whipping that they will not want war again." In Washington, President Roosevelt addressed a joint session of Congress on Monday morning, asking for a declaration of war against Japan, characterizing Sunday, November 7, as a "day that will live in infamy."

As the full impact of the war hit Montana residents, mobilization was taking place at war plants on the West Coast and elsewhere, and there was a considerable exodus of population from the state. A major airbase at Great Falls, Malmstrom Air Force Base, was activated, but the work of arming the country was elsewhere, and many Montanans left to take jobs in the war industry. Helena, however, which had been losing population since 1890, reached its highest peak in 1940, when it counted 15,056 residents, a rise of over 3,000 since the beginning of the Depression years.

In July 1942 the First Special Service Force, the brainchild of General George Marshall and British Prime Minister Winston Churchill, began training at Fort Harrison. It was to become, in a real and dramatic sense, Helena's close encounter with war training, and indeed because a number of force members elected to return and make their homes here, it was to have a lasting effect.

The rationale for training these tough, resourceful Canadian/American troops in the techniques of guerrilla warfare, winter survival, and commando tactics was the Nazi takeover of Norway. As it turned out, the troops were not needed there, but they served with incredible valor in the Aleutians and especially against the Germans in the Italian campaign.

Commander of the force was Robert T. Frederick, who became one of the country's youngest general officers, one who inspired Winston Churchill to say, "If we had a dozen like him, we would have smashed Hitler in 1942." General Frederick had conferred with Allied leaders early in the war to plan the organization, and not only named it but was in Helena to train the men and command them throughout the war.

Helena was also wartime host of another unique military entity, Camp Rimini, where dogs and men trained for arctic war conditions. Located in the mountain canyon nineteen miles southwest of Helena, this was the only army dog training center activated during the war. Staffed by seven officers and 120 enlisted men, the camp was housed in former CCC camp buildings and eventually trained thousands of dogs and handlers for duty in arctic regions. An outstanding and little-known mission of these men was accomplished in December 1944, when they helped evacuate wounded from the snowbound battle sector in Belgium which was the scene of the bloody Battle of the Bulge.

Eddie Barbeau, who still lives in the Helena Valley and for many years has operated a kennel and training center for dogs, was purchasing agent for the sledge and pack dogs used at Camp Rimini. In this capacity, he scoured Canada, Alaska, and the northern tier of states in search of Siberian huskies, Alaskan malamutes, and other Eskimo breeds trained at Camp Rimini.

As Helena emerged from the war with the highest population in its history, it found itself appallingly short on housing for returning veterans. Such builders and developers as W. A. Carson, L. P. Barney, and others hastened to build modest-size bungalows to fill the need and in the process closed the considerable gaps between older residential sections and the Lenox Addition on the east and the Kenwood Addition on the west. These areas had been developed in the 1890s and contained a number of large gingerbread mansions favored by men of means who sought to outdo each other.

Today, growing trees and landscaping obscure the presence of many postwar houses which are interspersed with historic homes. Nevertheless it is a phenomenon which once more makes Helena a unique and colorful city, blending the old with the new. Only in very recent years have areas been developed which contain homes of similar size and type of construction.

The most notable event in Helena as the decade ended was a gigantic community celebration called

Golden Canyon Days in which historical pageantry, gatherings of pioneers, and the presence of celebrities marked the eighty-fifth anniversary of the gold discoveries in Last Chance Gulch. From July 21 through July 24, 1949, actor Gary Cooper was proclaimed governor of the celebration, while Dinah Shore sang at Vigilante Stadium and her husband, George Montgomery, was declared mayor of Helena.

A major happening was a dynamite blast at the Canyon Ferry damsite, marking the beginning of construction of the second dam on the Missouri to replace the historic barrier which had been completed in 1898. Besides motion picture celebrities, dignitaries included Secretary of the Interior Julius Krug and Montana Governor John W. Bonner. A mock battle between Indians and the U.S. Cavalry was followed by an Indian messenger rowing across the Missouri to present a gold key to Secretary Krug.

Helena residents were poised for a new decade which was to see some of them going off to fight yet another war, this time a "police action" in Korea, as others sought to catch up with building and renovating a city which had been slumbering in that department for nearly half a century.■

First Special Force Encampment

The elite, all-volunteer force of Canadian and American troops began training in July 1942 at Fort Harrison, seen in this panoramic view. The force was first conceived by high British and American military officials as a commando force which would parachute into Norway, knock out strategic installations, and fight its way back to neutral territory. However before the men were fully trained, the war situation changed in that sector and in Alaska, so assignments were changed to southern France and Italy. It was here that these superbly trained men contributed so much to breaking the back of German resistance that one general was moved to say, "They won the war in Europe." John Marshall photo

Mountain Maneuvers

The snow-covered slopes of Mount Helena furnished rugged terrain for mountain maneuvers of this segment of elite First Special Service Force troops, who underwent similar training at York, Wolf Creek, and Marysville before they were ready to strike such terror among German troops in Europe that enemy commanders circulated a memorandum which read: "You are fighting an elite Canadian-American force. They are treacherous, unmerciful and clever. You cannot afford to relax. The first soldier or group of soldiers capturing one of these men will be given a ten-day furlough." John Marshall photo

Parachute Training at Fort Harrison

Speeded-up training to get the volunteer force ready for action in Europe included a six-day, parachute-jumping course instead of the normal three-month preparation, according to recollections of General Emil Eschenberg, who is still a Helena resident. Major General Robert T. Frederick, commander of the force, took his first jump after only ten minutes of instruction, landing in his bedroom slippers because jump boots for the men had not yet arrived. Eschenberg also recalled his own experience, when he had his men singing the song "Granada" as each took his turn, himself included. He said he could understand some of the pale faces when his own "moment of truth" arrived. John Marshall photo

Governor Sam C. Ford stands on the reviewing stand with hat to chest in this photograph, taken April 6, 1943, as members of the crack First Special Service Force, trained at Fort Harrison, march in review. At the governor's left, wearing light trousers and a combat helmet, is Brigadier General Robert T. Frederick who led his Canadian/American commando force, affectionately known as Black Devils in Baggy Pants, in heroic fighting in the Aleutians, southern France, and Italy. This photograph, looking east, was taken by Les Jorud at the corner of Sixth and Main. Jorud photo; courtesy of the Margaret Hibbard Collection

General Frederick Reviewing His Troops

Commandos March off to War

General Robert T. Frederick led his crack First Special Service Force north along Last Chance Gulch on April 6, 1943, on their way to combat in southern France and Italy. They were in the thick of things from the beginning of the assault on Italy, which began in July. In November and December, they lost roughly a third of their number in taking Monte de Difensa, an Italian sector in which the Germans were dug in and where assault was possible only by climbing "practically straight up," in the words of a contemporary account. The mountain training they had received in Montana was a factor in their skill and determination in the face of incredible odds, as the force finally secured Monte de Difenso on December 6, 1943. It was only one of many victories for these feared troops who, although they suffered heavy casualties by enemy fire as well as by falls from the treacherous terrain, "captured the imagination of the entire Fifth Army," their action "overnight making them almost legendary figures in a battle area where heroism was commonplace."

The First Special Service Force has had many reunions in Helena, comrades from faraway places joining those who chose to return and live here. Major General Frederick joined them for two notable reunions, one in 1955 and one in 1964, when over 400 gathered to relive their experiences and visit Helena's Memorial Park, where the force's insignia and Canadian and American flags are on display as a remembrance of heroism. Jorud photo; courtesy of the Margaret Hibbard Collection

Officers and Men at Camp Rimini

Housed in CCC buildings constructed during the Depression and augmented by others, Camp Rimini was established in the spring of 1942 in Rimini Canyon, nineteen miles southwest of Helena. In this picture, taken outside the headquarters building, some of the staff of seven officers and 120 enlisted men pose in winter garb. The commander was Major Purfield, seen second from left in the front row. Fourth from the right, second row, with fur-collared coat, is Eddie Barbeau, still a Helena resident and noted dog handler who was charged with recruiting dogs for training. Courtesy of the Eddie Barbeau Collection

Individual kennels were provided for dogs in training on the snow-covered slopes of Rimini Canyon. Many Helena residents still recall the "symphony of sound" issuing from the area as the Siberian huskies, Alaskan malamutes, and other Eskimo dog breeds were fed after intensive dog-team training. Dog teams and their handlers, who trained here, were extensively used in search and rescue work in Arctic regions during the war and played a little-known role in evacuating wounded from the frozen sector of the Battle of the Bulge in Belgium, December 1944. Todd photo; courtesy of the Eddie Barbeau Collection

Dog Shelters at Camp Rimini

Testing for Endurance at Camp Rimini

Sled dogs underwent strenuous endurance training at Camp Rimini, while sleds, equipment, and clothing were carefully checked for weight-carrying and survival qualities. Eddie Barbeau of Helena is seen at the left manning his dog team led by the husky Kenya, who was the sire of Barbeau's team. At the right is Herbert Wilkenson putting his teams through training as carriers of heavy loads and at the same time furnishing wood for fuel at the camp. Courtesy of the Eddie Barbeau Collection

Naval Training at Carroll College

The facilities of Carroll College were given over to military training throughout the war, and it was not until November 1, 1945, that the college returned to its primary purpose of education and reopened its doors to an all-civilian, full-time student body. Besides the Civilian Pilot Training program, under which 127 civilian pilots, 38 army pilots, and 550 navy V-5 pilots were trained, the college was designated as a V-12 training school in 1943, and during the next two years 704 trainees underwent instruction. In this picture, taken August 7, 1943, some of the naval trainees are seen in marching maneuvers on the campus. Jorud photo; courtesy of Carroll College

Girl Scouts Learning about Flying

This group of advanced Girl Scouts in Helena were given a course in aircraft familiarization in 1948, under leadership of Helen Willard, who was a licensed pilot. Although they did not take flight instruction, the girls learned the mechanical aspects of this Stinson plane, including instrumentation, and were briefed about flight training procedures. In the front row, left to right: Marcia Chezick, Dorothy Carlson, Donna Skor, Helen Willard, Beverly Easbey, Gay Fredregill, Shirley Bausch, Sue Wiley, and Pat Kindrick. In the back row, left to right: Donna Pugh, Polly MacDonald, Beverly Sherlock, Nancy Mason, Dawn Wood, Nancy Wood, Lila Hartzog, and Louise Peterson. Courtesy of the Helen Willard Collection

National Guard Commander S. H. Mitchell

Soon after the outbreak of World War II, Governor Sam Ford appointed Colonel Spencer H. Mitchell as commander of the Montana National Guard and administrator of Selective Service throughout the war years. Later this tough but capable officer became adjutant general and before his death in January 1964 had served the National Guard for over two decades. Jorud photo; courtesy of the John Willard Collection

Flight Training Class, Carroll College, 1940

Instructors Red Morrison and Dr. Newman pose in front of this class of aeronautics students, sponsored by the Civil Aeronautics Administration at Carroll College, in this picture taken on April 12, 1940. Standing in the front row, left to right: Monsignor Emmett J. Riley, Raynor Roberts, Francis Murphy, Jean Caillet, Helen Willard, Andrea Magnus, Lawrence McCarty, A. D. Hahn, Paul Chaquette, and an unidentified priest. In the back row, left to right: Charles Harrell, Cal Sampson, Milton Johnson, Dan McCarthy, Frank Keim, and Earl Mueller. Charles "Chuck" Harrell tried to enlist in the air force when the war began but was rejected, apparently because of his color. He stayed on in Helena as a flight instructor throughout the war years and later was killed in a plane crash. Jorud photo; courtesy of the John Willard Collection

Jack Dempsey Hosted by Governor

Roy E. Ayers had just lost the governorship to Sam C. Ford when he hosted boxer Jack Dempsey at dinner in the Governor's Mansion at 304 North Ewing on December 4, 1940. It had been seventeen years since Dempsey defeated Tommy Gibbons in the ill-conceived title fight in Shelby, and the fighter's popularity had since soared. On this occasion, with a number of Governor Ayers's Lewistown friends in attendance, the country was almost exactly a year away from Pearl Harbor and total involvement in World War II. At left in the picture is Mike Thomas, holding a young man wearing Dempsey's boxing gloves. Next in line are two Lewistown men, Mr. Wassell and Mr. Beardsley (whose grandson was wearing the gloves), Dr. Sid Cooney, Joe Markham, Dempsey, Governor Ayers, Tom Ulleg, J. Burke Clements, Fred Heinecke, Don McKinnon, A. T. Hibbard, and Charles B. Power. Jorud photo; Montana Historical Society Collection

Charity Ball Committee, 1943

Pictured in front of the old St. Peter's Hospital on a winter day during World War II are members of the Charity Ball Committee, charged with planning an annual event long held in Helena to benefit the community hospital. From left to right, the members have been identified as: Dorothy Talbot, Helen Willard, Beryl Kaiserman, unidentified, Dorothy Anderson, Mrs. Bennion, and Louise Cashmore. Jorud photo; courtesy of the Helen Willard Collection

Hospital Guild Tea, circa 1940s

An annual event for many years has been the St. Peter's Hospital Guild membership tea. The one pictured here was at the home of Mrs. Beryl Kaiserman at 628 Dearborn. Mrs. Helen Willard is pouring, and talking to her is Mrs. Tanna Keller. Standing, in long white dress, is Mrs. Jane Reynolds, talking with Mrs. Duncan Galusha, seated at the far right. Courtesy of the Helen Willard Collection

Military Tom Thumb Wedding

Army and navy uniforms were worn by the young male participants in a Tom Thumb wedding, held May 12, 1942, to benefit St. Peter's Hospital. Staged at the Methodist church, the wedding was conducted by a young Mr. Campbell, who became a minister as an adult. The bride and groom cannot be identified, but the "older" couple in formal dress, obviously "parents" of the bride, are Elizabeth Fahrner and Dick Morris. Sarah Cashmore is the bridal attendant third from the right in the front row, and directly behind her are Jan and Gretchen Buterbaugh. John Etchepare is the naval officer on the far left, front row; Eric Lindstrom is the army officer, third from left in the back row; and Jean Painter is the "older" woman, perhaps "mother" of the groom, eighth from the left in the back row. Jorud photo; courtesy of the John Willard Collection

Current Topics Club's Golden Anniversary

In 1892 women of Helena launched a social and educational organization called the Current Topics Club. On September 17, 1942, they gathered at the home of Mrs. T. B. Weir at 510 Dearborn to observe the organization's fiftieth anniversary. According to an item in the Helena Independent, *a luncheon was served at 1:30, the table laid with a handmade Italian cutwork and lace tablecloth and matching napkins, with each guest's name initialed in gold. Popular songs of five decades were sung during the luncheon by Mrs. Hazel Hitchcock. After lunch the members gathered in the yard, and Les Jorud took their picture.*

Standing in the back row, left to right: Mrs. Howard Johnson, Mrs. Frederick S. Sell, Mrs. S. McKenna, Mrs. J. S. Boardman, Mrs. Frank K. Turner, Mrs. Charles Reifenrath, Mrs. Cora Lee Burke, Mrs. William A. Brown, Mrs. J. C. Archibald, Mrs. John Carlson, Mrs. William Campbell, Mrs. J. G. Reitche, and Mrs. William A. Copenhaver. Seated in chairs, left to right: Mrs. T. O. Hammond, Mrs. Clara H. Kennett, Mrs. J. E. Bower, Mrs. Frank Bogart, Mrs. Fred Heinecke, Mrs. T. B. Weir, Mrs. Hal Ives, and Mrs. D. P. Patenaude. Seated on the ground, left to right: Mrs. R. E. Towle, Mrs. Myron Wilson, and Mrs. Sam V. Stewart. Jorud photo; courtesy of the Joan Holter Collection

Wartime Smoke-filled Room

Bartenders were busy, and smoke filled the historic air of the Montana Club during World War II, when its facilities were thrown open to First Special Service Force members and other servicemen and their ladies. Membership in the club skyrocketed along with revenue as slot machines and wartime gatherings filled the once-sedate "club for gentlemen only." Courtesy of the Montana Club

Stag Party at the Montana Club, 1948

With the end of World War II and the crackdown on gambling yet to come, the fourth floor of the Montana Club was the frequent scene of stag parties, reminiscent of the early days of the private club when activities were for men only. Dr. Ray Lewis and Dr. Walter Doering are seen in the foreground, while Scott Harrison is the tall man, standing at the far left. In the center of the room in white is George Williams, bartender, and just behind him is Jack McCluskey. Tom Tobin and Hal Cain are at the far right, and walking towards the camera is Ernest Palmquist. Dave Wallace is the man at the right center, facing the camera. The picture was taken on April 10, 1948. Courtesy of the Montana Club

Shooting Craps at the Montana Club

Wide-open gambling, before the crackdown came just before the decade of the 1940s ended, kept things humming at the Montana Club and other "private" clubs. This group of observers and participants are intent at the crap table at the club in the late 1940s. To the left of the table are Dr. D. J. McKillican of Townsend and Jack Tucker (partial profile). Judge John Harrison is the man with pipe in the background, and in front of him are Dick Ronan, Bill Clarke, and Dr. Bill Finley, far right in partial profile. Leaning over the table are "Dibbs" Mitchell, Mr. Nash of Townsend, and Earl Tucker. Courtesy of the Montana Club

Birthday Party for a Pioneer Lawyer

Milton S. Gunn, pioneer Helena lawyer, was honored on his eightieth birthday on February 19, 1948, at the Montana Club with many of his contemporaries and the younger generation participating. The men have been identified as follows. Seated, left to right: Charles Kessler, Norman B. Holter, Mr. Gunn, Harry Piggott, Frank Bogart, and T. B. Weir. Standing, left to right: Fred Sell, Dave Wallace, N. J. "Jeff" Holter, Milton C. Gunn, Tom Patterson, and Edmund Toomey. C. M. Russell's oil painting When the Land Belonged to God, *hangs above the fireplace in the background. Jorud photo; courtesy of the Thursday Club*

New Water Line from Ten Mile

The original water line, made of wooden staves held together by metal bands, is seen exposed in the picture above, ready for replacement with a modern conduit. The last of the historic wooden pipe was not removed from the side of Mount Helena until 1981. In the picture at the right, Helena Mayor Jack Haytin stands by as two young helpers turn the valve of the new line, releasing water from Ten Mile Creek to the city in 1943. Courtesy of Helena Water Department

A confident Thomas E. Dewey of New York got off his special campaign train at the Northern Pacific depot in Helena in 1948 on a Western trip during which he hoped he was garnering more than enough support to defeat Harry S. Truman. Posing with the candidate and his wife were Governor and Mrs. Sam C. Ford, both wearing Dewey Victory Special buttons. In the background at the left is Lieutenant Governor George H. Gosman; at the extreme right are Michael S. Koich and Frank S. McIntyre. Not long after this picture was taken, a triumphant Harry Truman displayed headlines prematurely announcing that the former New York governor had won the election. Courtesy of the John Willard Collection

Thomas E. Dewey Campaign in Helena

Colonel Broadwater's Bank a Fire Victim

A winter fire on January 11, 1944, destroyed Colonel C. A. Broadwater's Montana National Bank, later known as the National Bank of Montana, at the corner of Main and Edwards. Later this was the location of the Livestock Building, also now gone with the urban renewal elimination of Edwards Street. Broadwater organized this bank in 1883, and in 1890 added a stone buffalo head over the entrance in apparent answer to a comment of the time that he was foolish to spend so much money on the massive building when "buffalo will be grazing in the streets of Helena before long." Broadwater died only two years after installing the buffalo head, but his faith in the future of Helena was justified. Jorud photo; Montana Historical Society Collection

Helena's Motion Picture Celebrities

Myrna Loy and Gary Cooper, both natives of the Helena area, were frequent visitors to the city during their stellar motion picture careers. Above, Cooper visited with his brother, Arthur, at the Cooper ranch, north of Helena. Below, Myrna Loy, wearing a miner's hat, visited the Spring Hill mine, leading a working mule which had spent all its life underground. Both pictures were taken in the 1940s. Cooper, who was born in Helena in 1901, spent some of his early youth in Helena and worked as a cartoonist for the Helena Independent. *He died in 1961. Miss Loy, born Myrna Williams at Radersburg in 1905, has made several visits to Helena in recent years, including an internment service for her mother, who died in the 1960s. Montana Historical Society Collection*

Helena Little Theatre, 1940s

Judge Peter Meloy directed a notably active Little Theater group in Helena from 1939 through the early 1940s, with rehearsals held in rooms in the Pittsburgh Block and performances at the Junior High School Auditorium. In this picture, the cast of the play "Kind Lady," is taking a curtain bow. From left to right: Helen Willard, George Nink, Justine Pfeiffer, Art Trent, Florence Waterman, Noral Whittinghill, Florence Molrine, Wilma Muth, Paul Miller, Elizabeth Gilbert, Marvin Flatow, Harriett Meloy, George Niewoehner, and Minne Mae Shaeffer Michelson. Courtesy of the Helen Willard Collection

Blast to Start the New Canyon Ferry Dam

Smoke curled into the sky on July 23, 1949, as a dynamite blast signaled start of construction of the new Canyon Ferry Dam, which would replace the original, completed in 1898. The blast and a ceremony to follow were part of a four-day celebration of Golden Canyon Days, which marked the eighty-fifth anniversary of gold discoveries in Last Chance Gulch. At the damsite, as the new decade began, crews worked around the clock to complete the new multi-purpose dam, not financed by Helena entrepreneurs as was the first dam, but by federal funds under the aegis of the Bureau of Reclamation. Photo by John Willard

Eisenhower Campaigning in Montana

Dwight D. Eisenhower was riding the crest of unprecedented public popularity when his special campaign train toured Montana in 1951 and made a stop in Helena. Prominent Republican Wellington D. Rankin of Helena is seen sharing the rear platform with Ike, who went on to win the presidency with the largest majority ever won by a candidate, including the Depression years' triumphs of Franklin D. Roosevelt. Photo by John Willard

Chapter Twelve

The 1950s: Returning Veterans and a Decaying Inner City

On June 25, 1950, forces of North Korea crossed into South Korea, and thus began the first of postwar "police actions" which have led to America's unpopular foreign involvements. President Harry S. Truman, a World War I captain, fired General Douglas MacArthur, who had sought to break the stalemated no-win deadlock in Korea, leading to an emotional split in the country as MacArthur returned home to retirement.

Truman himself chose not to run again, and in the elections of 1952, General Dwight D. Eisenhower defeated Adlai Stevenson with the largest vote ever accorded a presidential candidate, surpassing even Franklin D. Roosevelt's landslide victories of the 1930s. One of Eisenhower's campaign pledges was to extricate American fighting men from Korea, a pledge he kept.

The national shift to Republicanism was reflected in Montana when J. Hugo Aronson, a native of Sweden and a former oil field heavy equipment operator at Cut Bank, defeated John W. Bonner. The only major Democrat in Montana who tasted victory was Mike Mansfield, who emerged from five consecutive terms as a congressman to defeat Republican Zales Ecton for a seat in the U.S. Senate. Thus began another distinguished Montanan's Senate career.

In the election, voters gave overwhelming approval for a new high school to be built at a cost of $1,720,000. Location of the school, in the former Chinese Gardens site on Montana Avenue, barely passed. At Canyon Ferry, crews worked around the clock in the early 1950s to speed construction on the dam which would eventually generate 315 million kilowatt hours of power and furnish source water for the 19,631-acre Helena Valley irrigation project.

Life in Helena resumed its normal tempo, even as decay stalked the inner city and shoppers were drawn in increasing numbers to stores located away from downtown. Population rose to 17,581, a 16.7 percent increase since 1940, due in part to large numbers of returning soldiers who were seeking housing. There were parties as always at the Montana Club, and growing in popularity was John Quigley's unique boulder and log village on the eastern slopes of the Continental Divide which he had started building, almost singlehandedly, on his return from the service in 1946.

There were community concerts to attend, all manner of home-talent pageants and plays staged by the notably lively JayCees, and the Montana Historical Society moved into a handsome new limestone building across the street from the capitol. Its dynamic director, Dr. K. Ross Toole, built a new museum and filled a C. M. Russell gallery with the Mackay Collection, deemed to be the finest private collection of Russell art in the country.

J. Hugo Aronson moved into the coldly modern new Governor's Mansion with his wife, Rose, and his young daughter, Rika, and the former official home of governors on Ewing Street was left to fall into decay until concerned residents acted to restore and refurnish it. The same kind of decay, but on a much more pervasive and pernicious scale, had brought virtual abandonment to the south end of Last Chance Gulch. The next two decades were to see drastic changes as demolition crews leveled historic but decaying buildings, many of them owned by absentee landlords. All this engendered nostalgia, if not outright defiance, as former residents returned to see the historic gulch changed, almost beyond recognition. ■

Missouri River Dams near Helena

The Missouri River in the Helena area was changed for all time from the way Lewis and Clark first saw it in 1805 when the first Canyon Ferry Dam was completed in 1898 east of the city. Today the waters of the second Canyon Ferry Dam, built during the 1950s, are impounded almost to the town of Townsend, to the southeast.

In 1908 the Upper Missouri Power Company, in which Sam Hauser, A. M. Holter, and others were deeply involved, began working on Holter Dam, located some thirty-five miles to the north. Only a small amount of work was completed, however, and the project was taken over by Montana Power Company in 1912 and completed in 1918.

Meanwhile, in 1901, Sam Hauser began dreaming of a dam a few miles north of the city which would be completed in January 1907 and bear his name. Faulty engineering, notably the use of steel plates as barrier material, doomed Hauser Dam a little over a year after its completion in 1907. On April 14, 1908, water began seeping between the plates and the bedrock, and in less than ten minutes, water had destroyed five company houses, an office building, and a stable.

Thirty men employed at the dam escaped with their lives, but frantic calls were made to residents of Craig to evacuate, and even Cascade and Great Falls officials were warned that the dam had failed and flood waters released. Montana Power officials at Rainbow Dam in Great Falls worked a crew throughout the night to build a wing dam as a precautionary measure.

Stoutly, the once-powerful Hauser vowed he would rebuild the dam, but the expense and agony of failure only added to the decline in fortunes and influence which was to plague this pragmatic man until his death in 1914. Hauser Dam was rebuilt and functions today as a facility of the Montana Power Company. Part of the water held back by the dam flows into Lake Helena, an artificial lake where two pumping plants used to draw water for irrigation prior to the construction of Canyon Ferry Dam. ■

These pictures show the failed Hauser Dam in 1908, when water seepage between its steel plates and bedrock brought ruin and a release of flood waters, and a rebuilt Hauser Dam, north of Helena, which is operated today by the Montana Power Company. Courtesy of Montana Power Company

Building the Second Canyon Ferry Dam

These views of construction at the modern Canyon Ferry Dam include a night view, taken on September 26, 1952, when crews were working around the clock. The daytime view, photographed on March 24, 1953, shows the powerhouse in the right foreground which rises 115 feet above the river level. Canyon Ferry is a key unit of the Bureau of Reclamation's Missouri River Basin project for the control, conservation, and hydroelectric power use of the Missouri, authorized by Congress in 1944. Courtesy of Helena Chamber of Commerce

Dedication of the Helena Valley Project

Mrs. Wanna Thompson, newly-elected mayor of Helena, accompanied Governor J. Hugo Aronson and Bureau of Reclamation officials in inspecting and dedicating the 17,361-acre Helena Valley irrigation project on April 1, 1959. They are witnessing the first delivery of water through the Helena Valley Tunnel, a concrete-lined seven-foot horseshoe 2.7 miles long. Frank Clinton, regional director of the Bureau of Reclamation, is seen at the right side, explaining some of the features of the project. Others in the picture, left to right: T. E. Mann, construction engineer; H. E. Aldrich, project manager of the Upper Missouri District; N. A. Rossiter, president of the irrigation district; Mayor Thompson and Governor Aronson. Courtesy of Bureau of Reclamation

Commissioners of the Helena Valley Irrigation District, 1955

The Helena Valley Irrigation District was formed in 1955 to manage the distribution of the water taken from the Missouri River by the Canyon Ferry Dam to be used in the Helena Valley. Under its supervision is the Helena Valley Canal, which is thirty-five miles long and has a system of laterals sixty-five miles in length. This terminates with a wasteway into Lake Helena. The commissioners were, front row: Henry Hibbard, William A. Rossiter, president, and Robert Ellis. Back row: Albert Hrella, Allen Shumate, and John J. Baucus. Courtesy of Bureau of Reclamation

Irrigation Pumping Plant at Canyon Ferry

This dramatic picture, taken in 1959, shows the Helena Valley Pumping Plant, located 500 feet downstream from Canyon Ferry Dam on the left bank of the Missouri, as it pumps irrigation water for the Helena Valley unit and the supplemental supply of municipal water for the city through a gigantic, steel, six-foot, three-inch pipeline anchored in the steep canyon walls. A concept of the gigantic size of this installation can be had by noting the man standing at the foot of the pipeline. Courtesy of Bureau of Reclamation

Farming the Helena Valley

Dick Peck was discing the soil in the Helena Valley preparatory to planting a crop of alfalfa. Water makes the desert bloom. The water used for irrigation in the Helena Valley has turned a semi-arid valley with an average rainfall of ten to twelve inches into 15,734 acres of alfalfa and other crops. There are 106 full-time farms today plus 152 part-time farms and hundreds of new homes since the water was brought into the valley. Gene Fisher photo

Graduating Nurses, Carroll College

After World War II, when Carroll College introduced an academic program for nurses, the institution became coeducational. This group of graduating nurses are seen entering St. Helena Cathedral for baccalaureate services on May 31, 1953. Jorud photo; courtesy of Carroll College

Students at Carroll College, 1952

Father Raymond Hunthausen, now bishop of Seattle, is standing at the left on the steps of St. Charles Hall on the campus of Carroll College in 1952. Later he was the president of the Helena institution. Students who have been identified include Tom Noel, seated at the left next to Father Hunthausen, Bill Lannan and Liz Bottomly coming down the steps, Pat Thompson, Tom Wilkins, and Tim Calnan standing at the right. Courtesy of Carroll College

Helena High School, 1876

Graduating classes were small and made up mostly of women in the 1870s, when the old Central School at Eighth Avenue and Warren was Helena's major graded school. This is the site of the present-day Central School. High school students attended classes here until the impressive, three-story high school was completed at the head of Lawrence Street in 1893. Courtesy of Helena High School

Helena High School, 1890s

The Romanesque Helena High School building stood out in treeless isolation when this picture was taken by F. Jay Haynes in 1894. This building, at the top of Lawrence Street at Warren, served the city for nearly forty-five years, although at the time of its construction, the Helena Herald *worried that things were going so slowly that perhaps it would be finished "in time for the grandchildren of present scholars to attend school in it." The cornerstone was laid in 1890, and "workmen were not out" until January 1893. Now this building, so typical of the 1890s, has been replaced by a parking lot. F. Jay Haynes photo; courtesy of the Haynes Foundation Collection, Montana Historical Society*

High School on Wheels, 1935-1938

All high school classes ceased for a brief time on October 18, 1935, when earthquakes struck the new high school with unusual fury. Officials of the Great Northern and Northern Pacific railroads offered the use of passenger coaches, moved onto specially built tracks, which served as the world's first "school on wheels" until the high school was restored in late 1937 and early 1938. Courtesy of Helena High School

Restored High School Building

When its new $500,000 high school on Rodney was virtually destroyed in the earthquakes of 1935, students attended classes in railroad coaches and waited nearly two years before their building was reconstructed, as seen here, with federal funds secured for rebuilding this and other schools which were shattered or damaged in the quakes. By the fall of 1937, the first units of the rebuilt school were ready, and by the spring of 1938 the restoration was complete and Helena's 1,000 high school students moved back in. In 1955 this became the junior high school after the sprawling new high school was built on Montana Avenue. Courtesy of Helena High School

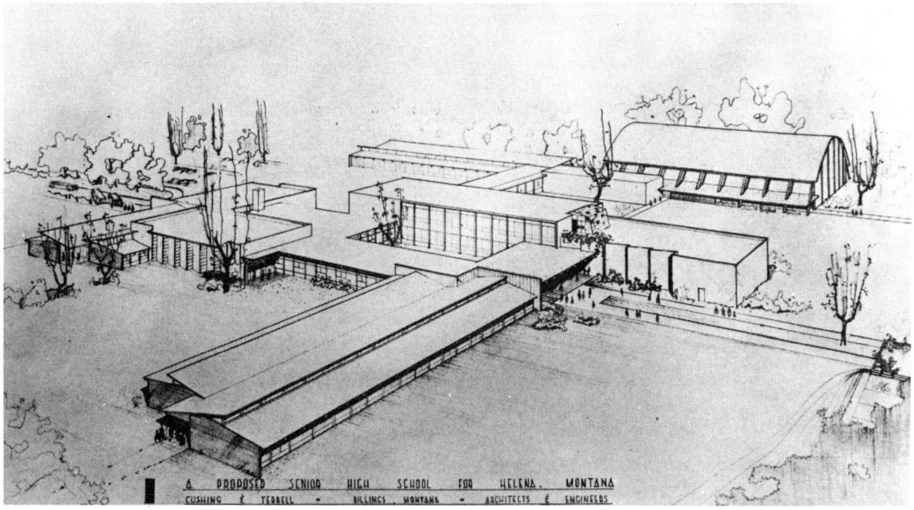

Architect's Concept, Helena High School

An architectural drawing of the Helena High School building, located in a low area between Montana Avenue and Roberts Street, once the site of the Chinese Gardens, is a feasible way to picture this sprawling complex which since 1955 has served as Helena High School. In the 1970s the former Cathedral High School in the Helena Valley became Capital High School, which engages in cross-town scholastic and athletic rivalry with Helena High. Courtesy of Helena High School

Montana Historical Society

Portraits of such territorial governors as Sam Hauser, Robert B. Smith, and Benjamin F. Potts decorated the walls of Montana Historical Society headquarters on the lower level of the capitol building, which at the time was displaying the Audubon Birds of America *series. This picture was taken about 1904, soon after the capitol was completed, and represented the first time the library, museum, and archival holdings of the society, Montana's oldest continuing organization, were all in one place. Established in 1865 by a far-sighted first territorial legislature, the society was directed to collect, preserve, and disseminate materials relating to Montana history. Montana Historical Society Collection*

Montana Historical Society Museum

This sculpture by Henry Lion of Lewis and Clark and the Indian woman Sacajawea has long greeted visitors to the society's Formal Museum, which tells the history of the territory and state in visual sequence. The legend, taken from the 1865 writings of editor Thomas J. Dimsdale of the Montana Post, *is appropriate: "It is for our people now to say whether they will preserve the early history of Montana in an enduring form, so that after times may know the thrilling drama here enacted." Montana Historical Society Collection*

Russell Gallery

In 1952, when the historical society moved into its new limestone building across Roberts Street from the capitol, director K. Ross Toole was making arrangements to acquire the great Mackay Collection of C. M. Russell art which today still forms the nucleus of the society's holdings of original Russell art, displayed in this gallery on the main floor. Montana Historical Society Collection

Archie Bray Foundation, 1952

One of the region's outstanding pottery centers is located on the western edge of Helena, once the site of Nick Kessler's historic brickyard. The pottery was long the dream of Archie Bray, Sr., who owned the brick-making facility. With the help of such artists as Peter Meloy, a Helena lawyer, and Branson Stevenson of Great Falls, an executive with Socony-Mobil Oil Company, Bray established a pottery under the name Archie Bray Foundation, and in 1951 staffed it with two men, Peter Voulkos and Rudy Autio, who were looking for jobs and studio space to create works fired in clay. Both Voulkos and Autio are now nationally recognized potters. Enthusiasm ran high, and many amateur bricklayers constructed the walls of the new pottery.

In this picture, taken in 1952, Archie Bray, second from the left, posed with well-known potters and guests. At the extreme left is Bernard Leach, and next to Bray, left to right, are Soetsu Yanagi, Branson Stevenson, Shoji Hamada, and Peter Meloy. Courtesy of the Archie Bray Foundation

Ballerina at the Pottery, 1952

Ballerina Marina Svetlova was in Helena for a performance in the Community Concert series in 1952 when she was conducted on a tour of the Archie Bray Foundation and stayed long enough to take a lesson in pottery-throwing from Peter Voulkos, seen to her left. Foundation founder Archie Bray, Sr., is the man at the extreme right in the picture. Voulkos, one of many potters whose gifts were developed at the foundation, became internationally known, winning the Rodin Museum Prize in sculpture at the First Bienale in Paris in 1959. Among other distinguished artists who have worked here are James and Nan McKinnell, Rudy Autio, Ken Ferguson, and today's resident potters, Kurt and Christy Weiser. Courtesy of the Archie Bray Foundation

Pottery Kiln at Bray Foundation

Pieces of pottery fashioned at the Archie Bray Foundation are seen in a brick kiln, where they are fired for from thirty to forty hours at very high temperatures. The "moment of truth" for potters comes when the kiln cools enough for the door to be unblocked and the condition of the pots revealed. Len Eckel photo

Symphony Orchestra and Chorus, 1955

Backed by public support and a dedicated board of directors, the Helena Symphony Orchestra and Chorus has flourished for many years. In this picture, taken on December 17, 1955, the orchestra and chorus presented its annual Christmas concert, with the colorful curtain of the Algeria Shrine Temple furnishing a backdrop at the civic center. Conducting was Eugene Andre of Missoula. Montana Historical Society Collection

Helena Symphony Board, circa 1958

Members of the board of directors of the Helena Symphony Society met in the offices of A. T. Hibbard, along with director Eugene Andre, far left. Board members, left to right: Mrs. Otto G. Klein, Dr. Raymond P. Walker, Miss Dorothy Green, Mrs. Ken Todd, Dr. Everett Lynn, Miss Susan Eaker, John Carlson, and Mrs. Vern Cougill. Montana Historical Society Collection

Community Concerts in Helena

Since 1930, the year the Community Concert series was launched nationally, Helena has been a dedicated charter member, bringing fine music and the performing arts to the city. In this picture, members of the board of directors for the 1964-65 season are pictured, left to right, front row: Ruth Kendall, Agnes Screnar, Carrie Drummond Keil, Dr. Clem L. Shafer (president), Fred Ketron (vice-president), and Myrtle Cummins. Back row: Kate Poore, Dick Dightman, Louise Able, Jean Stephenson, Gene Brown, Cecelia Grose, Chase Patrick, Robert Kendall, Sanford Haraldson, Ellen Ryan, and Alice Kraut. Courtesy of Clem L. Shafer

With the Greenwich Quartet

The late Carrie Drummond Keil, Helena's beloved teacher of music and supporter of the arts until her death in 1981, is seen here, second from left, conferring with two members of the Greenwich Quartet after their performance in the Community Concert series in February 1966. With her at the left are Helena pianist Cecelia Grose, violinist Gary VonOsdale and violinist Guy Lumla. Courtesy of the Clem L. Shafer Collection

Helena High School Band, 1953-54

Ninety-nine members of the Helena High School Band, majorettes, baton twirlers, color guards, and flag twirlers posed on the Civic Center auditorium stage with their director (in white uniform), Robert "Scratchy" Clark. The occasion was the performance of a home talent musical drama Calamity Ranch, *written by Dorothy Helton and directed by Robert H. Moss, Jr. Two performances, on November 4 and 5, 1953, were sponsored by the Helena Jaycees. Courtesy of Clem L. Shafer*

The Cast of *Calamity Ranch*

Members of the cast of the original musical play Calamity Ranch, *lined up in costume on November 4, 1953, as they got ready to go on stage for Act II, Scene 1. The three-act musical, written by Dorothy Helton of Helena, was sponsored by the Helena Jaycees, which took the lead in promoting a number of home talent entertainments throughout the 1950s.*

Seated in the front are Joan Shanklin and Bobby Moss, young son of Robert H. Moss, Jr., who directed the play. In the second row is Darryl Lee, who played the romantic lead, Jimmy Shanklin, Clem Chovanak, Avis Ann Tobin, Dr. Clem Shafer, Don Murphy, and Violet Mires. Sue Moss, wife of the director, is standing directly behind Miss Tobin. Courtesy of Clem L. Shafer

Female Members of the Cast

Most of the women members of the Calamity Ranch *cast have been identified. In the back row, left to right: Liz Gilbert, Sue Moss, Avis Ann Tobin, and Marjorie Lindberg. At the left in front is Jean Stock, and in the middle of the front row is Joan Shanklin. Courtesy of Clem L. Shafer*

Stage Crew of *Calamity Ranch*

Many of these hard-working Jaycees who were members of the stage crew of the musical Calamity Ranch, *have been identified. Seated at the extreme left is Kermit Kruse, and next to him, with arms crossed, is Dr. Bob Kuntz. Standing at the right are Milton Dagenais and Robert H. Moss, Jr., who directed the play. In the second row at left is Dale Fuehrer, wearing glasses, and Dr. Jack McLaughlin in the light jacket. At the left in the back row is Fred Featherly, long-time custodian of the civic center, and third from the left in that row is Harry Joslin. Dick Tobin is the man in the right background. Courtesy of Clem L. Shafer*

Helena Jaycees, 1953

A majority of these smiling young men are still residents of Helena, and most have been identified. This picture was taken after a dinner meeting at the old Colonial Club restaurant, a building which was replaced by the modern Colonial Inn in 1971. The old building was moved to Airport Road and became a nightclub known as Mr. Lucky's. A fire late in 1982 destroyed it. At the dinner meeting pictured here, members of the Jaycees were in a happy mood, discussing an original musical play called Calamity Ranch, *in which many of them participated as actors or behind-the-scenes stage crew on November 4 and 5, 1952.*

In the front row, left to right: Kermit Kruse, Dr. Clem "Bud" Shafer, Bob Kuntz, Bert Amsberry, Chase Patrick, and Don Marley. Barely visible at the left, wearing glasses, is Dick Tobin; then Roy Hudson; Harry Joslin; Harold Paulsen; Clayton Herron, looking down; Gene Fehlig; and tenth from the left in the background, Ralph Young. The man in the dark suit is unidentified. Next in order: Dr. Everett Lynn, Milton Dagenais, Bob Johnson, Drew Routzahn, Jim Pool, Jim Higgins, and Dan Dykstra. The two men at the extreme right in the back are Joe Reber and John Mahan. Courtesy of Joseph B. Reber

Variety Show by Helena Talent, 1955

The Consistory Shrine Temple on Jackson Street was set with several layers of tree-festooned backdrops for a home talent performance planned for the entertainment of the Montana Mining Association after a legislative dinner on January 26, 1955. The show was choreographed and directed by Blanche Judge, who gathered together some local talent for the show. In the back row are, left to right: Jim Strom, Dorothy Helton, Tom Judge, Blanche Judge, unidentified, Inez MacMillan, and Harold Paulsen. Some in the second row have been identified. First and second from the left are Helen Wilson and Jean Baucus, and fifth is Marion Moody. At the other end of this row are, reading from the right, Mary Lou Tobin, Liz Gilbert, Marge Thistlewaite, Jack Thompson, Priscilla Thompson, and Sarah Cashmore. Jorud photo; from the Jean Baucus Collection

Dinner Show at Frontier Town, 1954

Blanche Judge blackened a tooth and donned a Girl Scout uniform for a dinner show featuring hometown talent, one of many she directed for Frontier Town's huge, perfectly balanced, revolving stage, which John Quigley had fashioned of logs. This show was another fund raiser for the Girl Scout camp Thunderbird during the 1950s. In this picture, from left to right, the performers who have been identified are: Jean Baucus, Marion Moody, Nancy Scribner, Sarah Cashmore, Blanche Judge, Betty Todd, Helen Wilson, Emily Vucanovich, unidentified, Shirley Gannon, and Gretchen Buterbaugh. Dorothy Helton photo; from the Jean Baucus Collection

Frontier Town and John Quigley

Soon after his return from World War II service in 1946, John Quigley, son and grandson of pioneers, began building his unique log and boulder village on the east side of the Continental Divide fifteen miles west of Helena. Working virtually alone, with a vintage truck and winch his main piece of equipment, Quigley felled trees and moved boulders, creating four blockhouses and a series of buildings down a main street, along with a dining room and a bar made of massive hand-finished Douglas fir. This creative man, often called "that crazy cowboy" by those who did not share or understand his dream, never stopped building until his death in December 1979.

In this scene John Quigley, surveying his Frontier town, stands before the log chapel at the end of the street, which he completed in 1961 as his greatest achievement. Jorud photo; courtesy of Frontier Town

John Quigley Serving Dinner at Frontier Town

Standing on the apron of the huge dining room fireplace, the late John Quigley was ready to serve a unique Frontier Town dinner of baron of beef and trapper chicken. This mammoth fireplace, which draws perfectly, is capped with a 50,000-pound mantle rock. It escaped unharmed in 1975, when fire destroyed the dining room interior. Before Quigley's death in 1979, the room had been completely rebuilt and refurnished with handmade tables and chairs. Courtesy of Frontier Town

Governor Buys Cookies

In this picture, taken in 1955, Governor J. Hugo Aronson buys cookies from a contingent of Girl Scouts, among them his daughter, Rika. Proceeds from this and other fund-raising efforts went towards the purchase of Girl Scout camp Thunderbird, eleven miles west of Helena. Courtesy of the John Willard Collection

Helena's Tour Train

In the 1950s, Helena Unlimited, a civic-minded organization, purchased the colorful, motor-driven Tour Train, which has been a popular tourist attraction ever since. Beginning its tours at the Montana Historical Society building across the street from the capitol, the train takes passengers to historic places in the city, the driver delivering a commentary by loudspeaker throughout the tour. Courtesy of Helena Chamber of Commerce

Montanans Visit the Russell Statue

In 1957 the heroic-sized statue of artist Charles M. Russell was placed in Statuary Hall in the U.S. capitol as Montana's first and only entry. It was executed by John B. Weaver, then curator of the Montana Historical Society in Helena. Two years later, the statue was viewed by Montana's 1959 representatives to Boy's Nation, Max Baucus of Helena and Larry Short of Billings, who posed with members of Montana's congressional delegation.

At the left is U.S. Senator Mike Mansfield, and next to Short on the right are the late Senator James E. Murray and the late Lee Metcalf, then a member of Congress and later a U.S. senator. Twenty-three years after this picture was taken, Max Baucus occupied a seat in the Senate, while Mike Mansfield continued to give distinguished public service as ambassador to Japan. From the Jean Baucus Collection

Founders Night, Montana Club, 1956

The late Robert "Bob" Fletcher, right foreground, was always a popular dinner speaker in Helena. A noted poet, writer, and publicist, Fletcher was responsible for Montana's unique historic marker highway signs and is also credited with the lyrics for the popular song, "Don't Fence Me In." Others in this picture, taken in January 1956 at a Montana Club Founders Day dinner, are from the left, Dr. Sid Cooney, for whom the Cooney Convalescent Home was named, and George Neill, editor of the Helena Independent Record *at the time. To the right of Mr. Fletcher in the background is Bert Felder. The woman in the background is unidentified. Jorud photo; courtesy of the Montana Club*

Dinner Honoring Norman Holter, 1956

With formal dress and Christmas decorations the order of the day, the Montana Club honored Norman B. Holter at dinner in December 1956. At the head table are, left to right: J. E. "Eddy" O'Connell, Robert "Bob" Fletcher, Dr. S. A. "Sid" Cooney, Charles Pew, Charles McCoy, T. B. Weir, George E. Neill, Arthur Ward, Robert Veatch (standing in the back), A. T. Hibbard, Mr. Holter, Charles Greenfield, Ted Collins, and E. A. Phillips. Jorud photo; courtesy of the Montana Club

Veterans Administration Hospital, 1963

This aerial view of Fort Harrison was taken in 1963, at the dedication of the new hospital facility. In the background are barracks and other buildings on the site of the original Fort Harrison, established in 1891 and constructed between 1893 and 1896. Courtesy of Veterans Administration, Fort Harrison

Chapter Thirteen

The Recent Decades: A Time for Celebration and Renewal

Montana took advantage of the World's Fair in New York in 1964 to call national attention to a celebration of its own: its Territorial Centennial. It coincided as well with the 100th anniversary of Helena's gold discoveries, and the city and state went all-out. A centerpiece for celebration was the Centennial Train, the historical parts of which were assembled at the Montana Historical Society. Montanans rode it across the country, eventually to the grounds of the World's Fair.

As the decade came to a close, Helena officials and many leading business people got the good news that applications for Model City and Urban Renewal designation had been approved. In its issue of March 8, 1968, the *Independent-Record* front page headline shouted, "WE HAVE A MODEL CITY!" "It finally came to pass," the lead article read. "After an up-and-down existence rivaling the 'Perils of Pauline' of silent movie days, the application had been accepted and Helena is a Model City. Montana's Congressional delegation notified the *Independent-Record* this noon of the city's selection to receive an $83,000 grant for a year's planning to build a better city."

There was general jubilation, especially on the part of Mayor Darryl Lee and such citizens as Vern Cougill, Alex Cunningham, and Judith Carlson, who had worked so hard to attain the designation, the first step in what was to become Helena's urban renewal period. There was skepticism along Last Chance Gulch, expressed by those who had waited months for official Washington to act on Helena's application. "I don't believe it—when will you be sure?" was the reaction of Jean Weeks, downtown businesswoman and Model City activist.

Early in 1967 Helena residents saw another historic building destroyed when a Sunday morning fire enveloped the Harvey Hotel, once the glorious old Grand Central Hotel at 10 North Last Chance Gulch. It was late that year that a group of concerned businessmen, surveying the new damage and contemplating the decay of so many other buildings, organized Helena First, Inc., initially exploring the possibility of erecting a new high-rise hotel to replace the ones gone and the aging Placer Hotel.

As midnight approached on March 14, 1968, yet another historic hotel went up in flames. The Grandon Hotel, built in 1885 at the corner of Sixth and Warren, caught fire while its residents, many of them elderly, were asleep. Flames consumed the once-stately hotel, and three persons were lost.

Thus, as the federally-funded urban renewal program at last got under way late in 1969, city officials realized that the hour was late to begin a renewal. Demolition began, but there were many dissenting voices. Urban renewal director Larry Gallagher, hard-pressed to find investors and developers to fill the vacancies created when ancient buildings were razed, traveled widely in an effort to drum up interest in Last Chance Gulch. Work continued and eventually Montana's first pedestrian mall was designed, along with a parking plan which included an enclosed parking ramp.

News that a new Federal Building would be built at the south end of the mall stimulated interest which had been flagging at several points in the program. Gradually, new buildings began to rise, including the Neighborhood Center and the City/County Library of innovative design. Some $13 million in grants had been spent to buy land for resale to private investors, to relocate displaced persons, and help renovate historic buildings which were deemed significant and solid enough to warrant restoration.

When the dust began to clear and residents saw an entirely new south end of the gulch, a total of 228 buildings had been demolished. An estimated 142 businesses and 430 families had been displaced. The work of revitalizing and restoring such buildings as the Diamond Block, the Securities Building, the Colwell, the Bluestone House, and the Masonic Temple began, private investors courageously taking the lead.

Helena residents, and those who come back for visits after long absences, still have mixed feelings about what has happened to their gulch. But on reflection, most can see that the inner city had been dying, that most of the buildings that were destroyed were dangerously decayed, one holding the other up, inviting fire and tragedy, and all contributing to a creeping slum.

Indeed, few can argue that a handsome, usable Arcade Building, though struggling with tenancy, is a worthy successor to the sagging Pittsburgh Block, or that the ancient streetcar barns and countless decayed buildings on the south end of the gulch are better replaced by the new Federal Building, the Neighborhood Center, and the beautifully designed City/County Library.

One applauds the tasteful renewal of the Colwell Building, close to the gold discovery site of 1864 and for many years the home of Weggenman's Market, finding that it still "anchors" the south end of the street in history. There were fresh assurances in 1982 that the Atlas Block would be restored. Even more confidence in the area came as another new office building began rising where the fallen Novelty and Parchen blocks at Broadway and Main once stood. An impressive IBM Building near the City/County Building on Park Street was also being constructed.

As savage "100-year" floods struck the Helena Valley in 1981 and a hailstorm, causing $35 million worth of damage, came with sudden violence late in June 1982, Helena residents once more picked up the pieces and restored their homes and places of business. Even though they know that a major earthquake fault slicing through their valley could trigger horrors like those of 1935, most residents still love this colorful city and believe it is worth remembering and preserving. Few would want to live anywhere else.■

Hospital at Fort Harrison, 1952

With the two buildings on the right in this 1952 picture used for hospitals beds, many of them part of an extensive tuberculosis ward, Fort Harrison had achieved designation as a Veterans Administration Center. The facility had gone through extensive damage during the 1935 earthquakes, when patients were transferred to other VA hospitals and renovation of buildings got underway. In 1948 Claude Meredith became director of the center and in 1963 saw the building and dedication of a modern hospital to replace these buildings, one of which is still used for administrative offices. Courtesy of Veterans Administration, Fort Harrison

Sharing Jurisdiction at Fort Harrison

Governor Forrest Anderson met with Fort Harrison Veterans Administration Center officials in March 1971 to sign the instrument which transferred legal jurisdiction from an exclusively federal law enforcement status to one shared by state and local authorities. To the left of the governor is James M. Larson, then chief attorney at Fort Harrison, and at the right is Leon Wallace, then center director. Courtesy of Veterans Administration, Fort Harrison

Montana's Centennial Train, 1964

Ott Tschache, exhibits manager for Montana's unforgettable Centennial Train posed by one of the cars with Kitty Ann Quigley, who held the title Miss Big Sky and accompanied the train throughout the state and to New York City, where it was displayed during the World's Fair of 1964 and 1965. Three units of the twenty-five-car train were filled with historical artifacts, and eight carried colorful outside murals, painted by artist Lyman Rice of Billings. The historical displays, including the display of over $1 million in gold dust and nuggets, were assembled at the Montana Historical Society, with designs and display cases crafted by curator Robert F. Morgan. Courtesy of Kitty Quigley

Centennial Ball, 1964

Governor and Mrs. Tim Babcock were hosts for a colorful Centennial Ball on May 26, 1964, a social highlight of a memorable year in which Montana celebrated the 100th anniversary of its territorial status. In the picture at the top right, the crowded dance floor at the Civic Center ballroom was photographed with some of the 5,000 yards of material in three shades of pink and a large cluster of simulated crystal chandeliers in evidence.

In the center photograph, women guests, dressed in period gowns, posed with First Lady Betty Babcock, second from the left. To the left of Mrs. Babcock is Kitty Ann Quigley, and on her right is Mrs. Don Nutter, widow of Governor Nutter, and Miss Virginia Kirscher. Seen between Mrs. Babcock and Mrs. Nutter in the background is Mary Sarah Stetzner, who was 1964 Miss Anaconda.

In the picture, at the lower right, Governor Babcock, costumed as Abraham Lincoln, stands at the left side of the line, next to the orchestra stand, as members of the Seventh Cavalry, commanded by Robert Kendall, stand at attention. Jorud photos; Montana Historical Society Collection

Two Helena Authors, 1964

John Willard and Betty Babcock compared notes in June 1964 at the Susan Eaker Book Shop, where they appeared to autograph books they had recently completed. Willard, long-time Helena resident, railroad official, and writer-historian, had just finished his Adventure Trails of Montana, *a compilation of historical episodes. First Lady Betty Babcock had virtually sold out the first edition of her* First Lady Cookbook, *which became the most popular single item produced during Montana's centennial year of 1964. Courtesy of the John Willard Collection*

In the Holter Laboratory, 1963

Six rapt Helena students watched a spectacular demonstration in the laboratory of N. J. "Jeff" Holter in 1963 as he used a Teslacoil to generate high voltage electricity. Holter has always been deeply interested in fostering youthful interest in science. Some of the youths in this picture followed scientific careers, including Wayne Lanthorn, seated at the left, who is now a clinical psychologist. Next to him is Rich Buswell, now a Helena physician. The two seated girls are Jean Longmaid and Vicky Thompson; in the back row are Dennis Todd and Tim Meloy. Courtesy of the N. J. Holter Collection

Norman J. "Jeff" Holter, Scientist

An internationally-known scientist and developer of the Holter heart monitor, Jeff Holter had a distinguished career with the navy in World War II, when he was pictured aboard a vessel in the Atlantic engaged in anti-submarine research. The project was to develop a coating for submarines from which sound would not bounce back but would instead be absorbed, thus avoiding detection. Courtesy of the N. J. Holter Collection

Old Friends Gather, 1967

The late Hugh Galusha (second from right), a native of Helena who became president of the Federal Reserve Bank in Minneapolis, returned often to his hometown to visit friends. He is pictured with Joyce Swan (left), well-known publisher and a Federal Reserve member, rancher John J. Baucus, and at the far right, the late A. T. Hibbard, then president of the Union Bank and Trust Company in Helena. From the Jean Baucus Collection

A Dinner to Honor Julian Anderson

One of the events of the Montana Club's seventy-fifth anniversary, 1960, was a dinner to honor Julian Anderson, who with great dignity had presided over the bar since 1893. He knew the preference of almost every member and was highly respected by all. This was the year the Montana Club published a booklet with Julian Anderson's famous cocktail and drink receipes, including the Millionaires Cocktail.

Club manager John Sutphen is the first on the left in the back row; next is the president of the club, Leif Erickson. Continuing down the back row are E. S. "Buck" Haines, Al Brown, John Thomas, Dr. Amos Little, and Bert Felder.

Seated, from left to right, are: Henry Loble, Edmund Toomey, Dr. Cogswell, Julian Anderson, Norman Holter, Charles Kessler, Taylor Weir, and Julian Anderson's daughter, Ella Banks. Courtesy of Leif Erickson

Medicine Tepee and a Princess

This medicine lodge, which Eddie Barbeau erects every year for Helena Indian Days, was originally crafted by him for the Miss Indian America Pageant at Sheridan, Wyoming, in 1974. It won first place in its category at that event, at which all tribes of the area were present and competing. The lodge door is made of elk legs with dew claws, and decoration includes porcupine quill strands. The pattern around the bases of the lodge represents mountains and the Pleiades, the constellation from which the Blackfeet people traditionally derived strength and prosperity. In the picture at the left, Karen Larson, dressed in Wing Crow tribal costume, sits alongside the lodge, set up on the grounds of the Barbeau home in the Helena Valley. Courtesy of the Eddie Barbeau Collection

Eddie Barbeau

Eddie Barbeau, in full Blackfoot regalia, opens a ceremony at Indian Days by smoking the pipe and making an offering to the sun. Included in the prayer are offerings to mother earth and the four winds. Barbeau's handsome war headdress has a double trailer decorated with golden eagle feathers. On October 27, 1982, the Indian Alliance of Helena awarded Barbeau a plaque for his lifetime work in preserving Indian culture. Each fall a celebration of Indian Days is held and Barbeau's many friends, native Americans and "later" Americans, join to relive some Indian customs. Courtesy of the Eddie Barbeau Collection

Historic Setting for Young Performers

Nostalgia was everywhere apparent at the Old Brewery Theatre in 1972 as young performers posed in historic arched windows and contemplated the end of one of the region's unique summer theater settings. After its demolition, this building, once the home of the Helena Brewery, was replaced by modern condominiums. Dave Shors photo

Final Performances

One of the more painful results of urban renewal was the destruction of the brick brewery on the south end of the gulch which, after its original purposes were long since abandoned, became the site of the Old Brewery Theatre. Under the guidance of Walter and Doris Marsolais Marshall, it became one of the finest summer theaters in the region. In this picture, Kay Burkhardt and Glen Sacos, playing Golde and Tevye, sing the haunting duet, "Do You Love Me?" from Fiddler on the Roof, *performed by fifty-three young actors from throughout the country as one of the last four productions staged at the theater in 1972. The singing and dancing cast for* Fiddler *was directed by the talented Ken Marsolais, a nephew of Doris Marshall. Courtesy of Walter and Doris Marshall*

These talented and active Helena residents were honored in 1978 at the annual Electrum show, sponsored by the Helena Arts Council. Walter and Doris Marshall deserved the honor. They came to Helena in 1947, Doris to teach dramatics and English at Helena High School and Walter to begin a long career as a broadcaster, publicist, V.F.W. official, Montana Senate secretary, and Helena's unofficial greeter and promoter. For eighteen years the couple directed, produced, and promoted the Old Brewery Theatre until its urban renewal demise in 1972. Courtesy of Walter and Doris Marshall

Grand Street Theatre

A present-day delight to Helena theater goers is the Grand Street Theatre, worthy successor to the Brewery Theatre, now gone. After a year and a half at the Placer Hotel on Grand Street, the group moved to its present location on Park Avenue in 1976. This historic and handsome building once housed the Helena City Library. Memorable performances have been given by this theater group, managed and directed by Don McLaughlin. Courtesy of Grand Street Theatre

I Do, I Do at Grand Street Theatre

Colleen Mockler and Eric Hansen delighted Helena audiences the winter of 1982 with their portrayals in I Do, I Do. *Colleen, the mother of two children, has a music degree from St. Mary College. Eric Hansen is a professor of history at Carroll College. Colleen was last seen in* Shamrock, *produced for the first time in December 1982. This play, drawn from the story of Thomas Cruse of the famous Drum Lummon mine, was written and directed by Donald C. Ingels, a Helena man, with music score by Dave Maddux with Bud Brown, Gary Wulf, and Pee Wee Weber. Courtesy of Grand Street Theatre*

West Side Story at Grand Street Theatre

Drawing from a large pool of Helena talent, the Grand Street Theatre produced West Side Story *the summer of 1980. From left to right: Jerry Foley, Jim Manning, Ron McDonald, Dave Yalwich, Brett Padbery, Bill Wise, Brian King, Mike Curtis, Chris Weeks, and John Cooper. Helena's community theater presents a varied program, including musicals, as well as modern comedies and dramas, plus classical theater productions. They have produced* One Flew Over the Cuckoo's Nest, Grease, Fiddler on the Roof, *and* Cyrano de Bergerac. West Side Story *was the biggest hit of all. Courtesy of Grand Street Theatre*

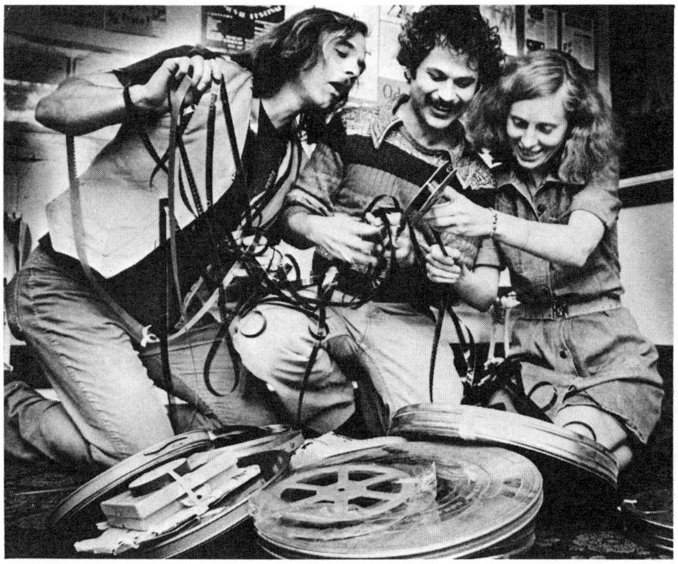

Second Story Cinema/Helena Film Society

A new dimension in entertainment came to the city in 1976 with the founding of the Helena Film Society as an adjunct to the Second Story Cinema, a non-profit, educational organization which has evolved into a community cultural center. Specializing in the presentation of foreign films and American classic films as well as premieres of American independent cinemas, the society also acts as a forum for local artists. It has sponsored numerous plays, such as Equus, The Elephant Man, *and* The Tooth of Crime, *and has brought a series of major performers to the city, including jazz greats Dave Brubeck and Dizzy Gillespie, folk artist Odetta, the Ohio and Hartford ballets, the National Theatre of the Deaf, and the spectacular Chinese Magic Circus of Taiwan. Helena Film Society founder Arnie Malina is seen in the center of this off-stage whimsical photograph, assisting Wally Bivins, left, and Susan Watson untangle film. Courtesy of Second Story Cinema/Helena Film Society*

Mecca for the Arts and Artists

With vigorous public and organizational support, Helena has long been a center for the fine arts, and it has been and is the home for many individual artists who have made their mark far from the city and indeed Montana. Dating back to the days when Charles M. Russell maintained a Helena studio for brief periods in the 1880s, the city has been the home of many artists who have since left, but who deserve more than passing mention.

Among them are Jack Beauchamp, Tom Edwards, and Mabel Bjork, at whose knee many contemporary Helena artists once sat. Dating even further back was the dedicated Mary Wheeler, who taught art to thousands of Helena students. A monumental talent throughout the 1950s and early 1960s in Helena was Butte native John B. "Jack" Weaver, the great sculptor who was curator at the Montana Historical Society and created many of the superb dioramas and fashioned the heroic statue of C. M. Russell which is now in Statuary Hall in Washington, D.C. Weaver, who now lives and works in British Columbia, left a latter-day mark on Helena when he created *The Bullwhacker,* the larger-than-life bronze which stands at the head of the city's Pedestrian Mall.

Many contemporary artists live in Helena today, and while not all can be dealt with in depth, their talents deserve mention. They include Dr. Clem "Bud" Shafer, Kay Lytle, Dyk Grebe, Terry Murphy, Shirley Cleary, Ron Herron, Winfrey Hearst, Bob Zimmerman, Homer Collins, Caroline Laceky, Wayne Whitney, Becky Eiker, and the talented graphics designer who is also a fine artist, Len Eckel.

The fact that Helena today is a growing and exciting center for the arts is due in no small measure to the efforts of the Helena Arts Council, which annually sponsors such events as the Electrum series and the prestigious art show, Western Rendezvous of Art, which ranks among the top three or four exhibitions of art in the region. Proceeds from these events have gone to enhancing the Civic Center as a cultural center, and in 1983, there are even more exciting plans for the future.■

Undoubtedly the dean of Helena artists was the late Irvin "Shorty" Shope, referred to by the Cowboy Artists of America, of which he was a charter member, as "that wonderful little man from Montana." Born in 1900 on a small ranch near Boulder, Montana, Shorty became an expert horseman in spite of polio, which struck him at the age of nine and left his right leg paralyzed. When the family moved to Missoula, after the death of his father. Shorty's youthful artistic gifts were encouraged by pioneer artist Edgar S. Paxson, and even by the renowned Charles M. Russell, whom young Shope visited in 1925. Both artists advised him to stay in Montana. Under a scholarship, however, Shorty studied art at Reed College in Portland, Oregon, and at the Portland Art Academy, and after his marriage to Erva Love of Missoula in 1932, he spent a year in Los Angeles as a cartoonist.

The Shopes returned to Montana in 1935, and established their home only two blocks from the capitol, where until 1961 Shorty was able to keep horses in the yard, on which he taught his four children to ride. Shorty worked as a graphics artist for the Montana Highway Department, illustrated a number of books, created some memorable illustrated maps, and designed some of the first dioramas placed in the Montana Historical Society museum.

Irvin "Shorty" Shope

Shorty Shope is perhaps best known, and certainly remembered, for the many murals he created for Montana public buildings, beginning in 1949, when he created The Four Georgians *for the Helena High School; students had raised the necessary funds. In the next sixteen years, he did twenty murals, including six for the School of Forestry at the University of Montana in Missoula, one for Western Life Insurance Company of Helena, five for the St. Paul Fire and Marine Insurance Company of St. Paul, five for the First National Bank of Helena, two for the State Highway Building in Helena, along with a series of smaller paintings depicting the history of Montana highways.*

Nationally known, Shorty received honors in his home state and elsewhere, his coterie of devoted collectors of smaller paintings growing as he worked at his Helena home/studio, using the easel Edgar Paxson had given him. He and his wife were visiting a daughter in Massachusetts when death came to "the wonderful little man from Montana" on November 22, 1977. He is buried at Boulder.

Since her husband's death, Irva Shope has annually presented the Shorty Shope Award to a participating artist in the Western Rendezvous of Art series in Helena. Beginning in 1982, the award became a popular "People's Choice" and carries a $1,000 honorarium as well as an engraved trophy in Shorty's honor. Courtesy of Great Falls Tribune

Genial, civic-minded, and totally unaffected, Bob Morgan chooses to live and work in his native Helena. A largely self-taught and multifaceted talent, Morgan worked as a store window designer when he was still in high school, freely giving of his talent to creating posters and scenery for school events. Early in 1952, he went to work for the Montana Historical Society as a designer and preparator, and was on the scene when the Society's collections were moved from the lower level of the capitol building to the new Veterans and Pioneers Memorial Building across Roberts Street, which still houses the Society's museum, library, and archival holdings.

Eventually, Morgan became curator and and until his retirement to become a freelance artist in 1973, took the lead in creating displays, dioramas, and the popular Territory Junction street on the lower level. He was of enormous help in redesigning MONTANA the magazine of Western History *to make it one of the most popular and attractive journals of history published anywhere in the country.*

Robert F. Morgan

Bob Morgan, aside from keeping up with a steady demand for his paintings, drawings, etchings, and sculptures, is deeply involved in many civic matters, especially those relating to art. While he was still on the Historical Society staff, he inaugurated the annual Western Rendezvous of Art shows and introduced the popular Quick Draw events which have become part of many other regional art exhibitions.

In December 1982 the talents of this man came full circle, when Dick Duffy's Montana Gallery and Book Shoppe staged the "When I Was a Kid" art show, Morgan's first one-man show in some years. The paintings, which were virtually sold out at the opening, depict scenes from Helena and the Helena Valley which the artist remembered as a boy. They reflect not only his artistic gifts, but his deeply emotional commitment to his town and its colorful past. Courtesy of Montana Gallery and Book Shoppe

Tucker Smith

This talented and rapidly-rising artist lives on a small ranch in the mountains south of Helena with his wife, Jean, and sons, Troy and Dane. A native of Minnesota, Tucker grew up in Pinedale, Wyoming, where his father was the first practicing dentist in that part of Wyoming. Armed with a degree in mathematics and a minor in art from the University of Wyoming in Laramie, Tucker and Jean moved to Helena in 1963, where he worked for eight years as a computer programmer and systems analyst for the state of Montana. In 1971 Tucker, with the encouragement of his wife and a number of Helena friends and artists, became a full-time artist. A founding member of the Northwest Rendezvous Group, which stages its annual events in Helena, Tucker has been seen in a number of other important art exhibitions, including the National Cowboy Hall of Fame in Oklahoma City. He is especially well known for his moving depictions of wildlife and domestic animals, such as horses, cattle, and sheep. Courtesy of Tucker Smith

Quick Draw

A highlight of annual Western Rendezvous of Art shows in Helena every August is the Quick Draw, during which participating artists are given a timed period of thirty minutes to create a work of art in any medium. After the whistle sounds, the works are sold at a public auction. Many artists use models, including modern-day mountain men who attend the events to carry out the fur trade "rendezvous" theme of the shows. In this picture, the noted William Reese of Bellevue, Washington, hastens to finish his Quick Draw entry, while in the background, Kalispell artist Gary Schildt works with a seated model in front of one of the Indian tepees erected on the grounds of Frontier Town, where these events are held after Saturday morning chuck-wagon brunch. Aside from the works created that day, collections of art done by the artists during a week-long campout which precedes the show are auctioned off to eager collectors who have thoroughly enjoyed themselves. Courtesy of Northwest Rendezvous Group

Young Artist Memorializes Jeannette Rankin

Terry Mimnaugh, talented young artist of Great Falls, was chosen in open competition in 1980 to create a larger-than-life statue of Jeannette Rankin, the courageous lady who twice voted against American involvement in global war when she sat as a U.S. congresswoman from Montana in 1917 and again in 1941. At the picture at the left, Governor Ted Schwinden congratulates the artist, who spent many months studying the life and likenesses of her subject before committing her to sculpture and eventual bronze casting.

At the far left, the artist chats with Belle Winestine, who was on Jeannette Rankin's staff when she went to Washington in 1917 as the nation's first congresswoman. Mrs. Winestine, native of Helena and one of its most revered citizens, still voices strong opinions about the rights and civic responsibilities of women, opinions which she enunciated throughout the more than ninety years of her life. Gene Fischer photo

Reeder's Alley

Some of the first permanent buildings still standing today in Helena were individual miner's dwellings built in the 1860s-1880s of brick, much of it purchased in St. Louis from the father of Charlie Russell and shipped up the Missouri by riverboat. In 1962 three Helena women, Jane Tobin, Eileen Harper, and Pat Boedecker, saved the street and converted the area into an arts and crafts center. This was a privately financed Helena urban renewal project. Courtesy of Jorud Photo Shop

Before Urban Renewal

The Fire Tower loomed above a scene of decay in this picture, taken shortly before demolition during the urban renewal period began. In the background are the ruins of the Bluestone House, damaged in the earthquakes and uninhabitable for many years. It is among the restored structures today, its renovation posing one of the most costly and complicated projects undertaken. Courtesy of Donald W. Becklin

Demolition Begins

This scene, looking north, shows much of the area where demolition and some restoration has occurred on the east (right) side of the street. The twin towers in the foreground cap the bay windows on the facade of the Boston Block, which has been restored for office space. At this time, efforts were still being made to save the Novelty Block, whose smaller twin towers are visible down the street. Structural weaknesses in the building showed restoration to be impossible, and it was destroyed along with other buildings to the north of it. Visible next to the Placer Hotel further down the street is the colorful Atlas Block, which has been saved. Len Eckel photo

Ancient Mural Revealed

This faded mural was exposed on the side of a wall of Big Dorothy's Rooms when the demolition crew razed the adjoining building. Courtesy of Helena Water Department

Buildings Now Gone

Every building seen on the right side of this picture was demolished down to the tallest on the skyline. This is the Goodkind Building, which today houses the Cassidy-Grand Interior Design store. This entire area, between Cassidy-Grand and the new Arcade Building, is now a parking lot. DeWalt photo; courtesy of Helena Chamber of Commerce

REDEMPT
CENTER
JACOBY'S

Marlow Theatre Demolished

The Marlow Theatre on Edwards Street stood empty in one of the last pictures taken of it, in May 1972, before demolition began. In the picture at the right, taken a month later, the once beautiful stage arches stand in the midst of falling brick and mortar. Edwards Street, a very narrow street the width of a mining claim, was one of the first to be closed during the urban renewal period.

Chuck Johnson photo; Montana Historical Society Collection

Peter Meloy photo; Montana Historical Society Collection

Restoration of the Diamond Block

One of the finest old structures in Helena is the Diamond Block on the northeast corner of Sixth and Park. This 1889 building was the first in the downtown area to be restored. The two-story, oriel windows are copper-based and the wrought-iron balconies and tiny, faceted mirrors on the facade are handsome embellishments. St. Helena Cathedral and the old Helena High School, completed in 1893 and minus its original towers, can be seen in the left background. The high school has since been razed, primarily because of the poor condition of its masonry. Len Eckel photo

Vacancies after Demolition

The distinctive, long, thin Colwell Building at the south end of the gulch where gold was discovered by the Four Georgians in 1864 still had the marquee of Weggenman's Market when this picture was taken shortly before the urban renewal program began. The street cutting across the hill below the Fire Tower was Jackson Street, and today it is replanned for parking and part of the new Cruse Drive. The gold discovery was made at what is now the west end of the Colwell Building. The small Last Chance Stream was above ground then, and the four down-and-out prospectors found gold along a bend in the stream.

The street in the foreground was originally known as Wall Street in honor of Helena's first bank, the First National, located at the corner of Wall and Main. When Sam Hauser built his new bank, now the restored Securities Building, the old building was used by Nick Kessler for storing beer on the street level. At one time, the top two stories of the Colwell Building were used as public rooms by Celia Karatofsky, who is said to have mortgaged the building several times in order to pay for the added floors of French Empire design. Today this unique structure is restored as an office building and contains the Helena headquarters of Senator Max Baucus. Len Eckel photo

Novelty Block Ready for Demolition

This landmark building on the east side of the gulch was one which residents were especially interested in restoring, because of its elaborate Victorian facade and its twin towers soaring above a mansard roof. Investigation soon revealed that saving it would mean taking it down stone by stone and rebuilding it with better mortar. The towers were saved, however, and today they are roofs of kiosks set at either end of the North Mall. The popular Yat Son Noodle Parlor and the building next to it were demolished, but Yat Son built a new restaurant across the street at the site which is bare in the foreground of this picture. The building to the south of the Novelty Block, known as Big Dorothy's, has been restored and now houses the Windbag Saloon and the Ghost Art Gallery. Len Eckel photo

South Mall Area under Construction

Scaffolding covers the front of the new Aspen Building on the left in this photograph, looking south. New trees were getting a start, the new street lamps are in place, and the open-air streetcar, donated by Mr. and Mrs. Charles Bovey, is the focal point of the South Mall. The Independent Record building, the tall structure third from the right, was razed in 1981 after efforts to save it proved fruitless. Len Eckel photo

Mount Helena Fountain

Residents have had mixed feelings about the Montana Park fountain which stands in the middle of the mall and is intended to depict Mountain Park, once a popular attraction on the top of Mount Helena. Here an early morning hiker soaks up some sun before starting out. This is the point where the recently popular Mount Helena races begin. Jean Baucus photo

Bullwhacker

The larger-than-life statue of a bullwhacker, created by sculptor John B. Weaver, stands between the Securities Building on the left and the Placer Hotel on the right, as a symbol of the overland commerce which helped make Helena a solid city long after its placer gold had played out. This stunning winter scene shows what was once Grand Street, the thirty-foot space between the two buildings. Grand Street, like Edwards, was one of the historic streets which were removed by the urban renewal development. George Lane photo

North Mall Today

The 1884 Goodkind Building, on the corner of Sixth and Main, stands in historical isolation on the east side of the gulch, next to a broad parking lot extending to the Arcade Building. On either end of the mall, kiosks are in place, topped with the twin towers of the demolished Novelty Block. Jean Baucus photo

South Mall Looking North

From the statuary which depicts miners washing gold, this view shows the mall curving north towards the Helena Valley and the mountains beyond. The Woman's Mural, the kiosk, and growing trees and plantings add interest to the rows of buildings, old and new, which line Last Chance Gulch. Jean Baucus photo

Helena Bankers and Associates, 1970

This picture, taken at the Montana Club, represents a cross section of Helena banking, business, and agricultural interests in 1970. In the back row, left to right: Clark Pyfer, William Andrews, John J. Baucus, and Michael E. Donovan. In the front row: Jack Luxon, James Dion, J. E. "Eddy" O'Connell, Tom Tobin, Ed Maronick, and Fred Gannon. Courtesy of Northwestern Bank of Helena

Democrats Work Together

Joseph B. Reber and his son, Joseph E., knelt in the foreground in August 1980 when they hosted a get-together of prominent Democratic party leaders, some of whom had been in recent political battles with each other. It was a time for fence-mending and pulling together as the general election approached. The lone woman in the group is Donna Metcalf, widow of U.S. Senator Lee Metcalf. From left to right, others are: Senator Max Baucus, former Governors Tom Judge and Forrest Anderson, Senator John Melcher, Ted Schwinden, who went on to win the governorship, Congressman Pat Williams, and George Turman, who became lieutenant governor in the Schwinden administration. Courtesy of Joseph B. Reber

Pat Donovan, Dallas Cowboy

Helena football fans watch the Dallas Cowboys play with special pride because of Pat Donovan, first string offensive left tackle. Born in Helena in 1953, Donovan is the son of Mr. and Mrs. Michael Donovan and represents a family of outstanding athletes. He played both football and basketball at Cathedral High and later at Helena High, maintaining an A average throughout. He is a graduate of Stanford University, where he was chosen All-American in his junior and senior years. He joined the Cowboys in 1975, and has become, in the words of Coach Tom Landry, "our best offensive lineman in recent years." In 1983, for the fourth consecutive year, Donovan was designated All-Pro in the NFL. Courtesy of Dallas Cowboys

Five and Ten Kilometer Races, 1982

Runners in the Ten Kilometer (6.8 miles) got off to a good start on Cruse Street, just east of the new Federal Building, on June 5, 1982, as they began the run east over Diehl Heights, back down Broadway to the finish line at Broadway and Park. In the skyline are the Placer Hotel, the cathedral spires, and the Masonic Building.

In the lower picture, runners in the Five Kilometer race began their run on Park Avenue, swinging through the west side of Helena, out Flowerree, and back on Stuart to the finish line on Park Avenue. Ellen Ditzler photo; courtesy of Montana Blue Shield

Governor's Cup Marathon, 1982

Winners of the 26-mile, 385-yard Governor's Cup Marathon approached the finish line on Park Avenue, near the City/County Library, after finishing the race which began at Marysville. Seen here are Ann Danzer, winner of the female division, with a time of 2:53:38; Jim Hatcher, who won the male division with 2:20:35; and Senator Max Baucus, whose mark of 3:01:18 established a record for the U.S. Senate. Sponsored by Montana Blue Shield with the help of the volunteer Governor's Cup Committee, the 1982 races marked the ninth anniversary of the events.

Barbara Welter photo

Barbara Welter photo

Mark Meloy photo

Running for Office and Fitness, 1982

Attorney Henry Loble, an avid runner and hiker and member of a pioneer Helena family, ascended to the top of Mount Helena in the 1982 Mount Helena races, with Marcie Scott and Lynn Guay behind him. Loble made another successful run in 1982, for the office of district judge, a position long held by his late father, Lester Loble. John Marcinek and Dan Smith photo; courtesy of Montana Blue Shield

Mount Helena Run Winners

Cheryl Johnson and Jeff Thomas, both of Helena, display the winners' plaque after they won the 1981 run of 5.6 miles up 1,368 feet to the top of Mount Helena. The starting point was the Mountain Fountain on the mall, and the finish line was at the new Federal Building. Jeff's time was 38:45, and Cheryl made it in 46:26. This event, revived in 1975, had its beginnings in 1916, when a professional runner from California challenged local athletes. The first winner that year was the late Ben Burgess of Helena. Bill Schneider photo

Cathedral in Need of Repair

Reverend John Ward of St. Helena Cathedral Parish recently sat in the back of the sanctuary of the great Gothic church, which in recent years has shown signs of decay. Many of the hand-glazed, stained-glass windows were in danger of falling out because of crystallized leading, and the concrete pillars, which rise from a depth of eight feet underground to a height of 150 feet were weakening as the thin shell of scagliola gradually gave way to water action. The red, charcoal, and gold leaf wall and ceiling decor, added during a 1950 renovation, will remain unchanged. Gene Fischer photo

Restoring Stained-Glass Windows

Father Dan Hillen of the Carroll College art department is noted for his work in stained glass and is seen here making a careful inspection of the cathedral's leaded windows. He and his assistants eventually replaced broken leading with carefully baked and matched material. Gordon Warren photo

Repairing a Spire

Reminiscent of the time seventy years ago when courageous workmen posed atop the twin spires of St. Helena Cathedral during construction is this 1982 picture, which shows a modern workman scaling a tiled spire as part of the recent program of cathedral renovation. Gordon Warren photo

Old Drainage Sewer Exposed, 1979

This hand-built, brick drain sewer is part of the original sewer which handled the drains and runoff as well as carrying Last Chance Stream under the city streets. When the Northwestern Bank built its drive-in at the corner of Placer and Fuller, Helena Water Department workmen discovered this old sewer. Courtesy of Helena Water Department

Fish-Eye View of Fire Tower

With a fish-eye lens Gene Fischer was able to capture Mount Helena and some of the mountains to the south as a background to the Fire Tower. Gene Fischer photo

In this dramatic picture, the old Fire Tower is seen through the arch of the Denver Block, which was destroyed by fire in 1981. N. J. Holter purchased the arch in order to save it. Here two workmen, Tom Ulberg, left, and Martin Holt measure the masonry in preparation for taking it down for reconstruction at Women's Park on Neill Avenue. Ulberg is standing on one of the already-removed top slabs which weighed over 6,500 pounds. Gene Fischer photo

Denver Block Arch

Panorama of Helena, 1980
Garry Wunderwald photo

Bibliographical Essay

By far the most complete sequential source of information about any city or town is its press, and in the case of Helena, there have been such sources almost from the beginning. Much information since 1900 has been gleaned from the Helena newspapers on file at the Montana Historical Society, notably the *Independent,* and, in more recent years, the *Independent-Record.*

We would be remiss, however, if we failed to cite the contributions of William C. Campbell, who published his two-volume *From the Quarries of Last Chance Gulch* in 1951 and 1964. In effect, Bill Campbell did our research for us from 1864 through the turn of the century, for his books are based on day-to-day searchings in Helena newspapers, especially Robert Fisk's *Herald.* All newspaper references, whether from our direct research or that published in *Quarries,* are cited parenthetically in the text rather than by footnote.

Books used to support both running text and picture captions include: *The Battle for Butte,* Michael P. Malone, University of Washington Press, 1981; *Comstock Mining and Miners,* Eliot Hood, 1883, republished by Howell-North, San Diego, 1980; *Contributions to the Historical Society of Montana,* Helena, Volume VI, 1907; *Then and Now, or 36 Years in the Rockies,* by Robert Vaughn, Tribune Printing, 1900; *Progressive Men of Montana,* A. W. Bowen and Co., Chicago, 1902; *Montana in the Wars,* compiled by Chester K. Shore, Star Printing, Miles City, Montana, 1977; *Attempts to Start Masonic Lodges in Montana,* by William Ray Kohls, 1964; *Charles M. Russell,* by Ramon F. Adams and Homer E. Britzman, Trails End Publishing, 1948; *Ore Deposits and the Helena Mining Region,* by Adolph Knopf, U.S. Printing Office, 1913; *Montana and the Sky,* by Frank W. Wiley, Montana Aeronautical Assoc., 1966; *Montana Earthquakes: An Illustrated Story of the Earthquakes that Centered Around Helena, Montana, 1935,* by C. R. Anderson and M. P. Martinson, privately published, 1936.

Indexed volumes of *Montana, the Magazine of Western History,* published by the Montana Historical Society, were often consulted, especially the many articles which dealt directly with Helena history. To correlate events here with a larger view of Montana and the region, useful information was found in such histories as *Montana: An Uncommon Land,* by K. Ross Toole, University of Oklahoma Press, 1959; *Montana: A History of Two Centuries,* by Michael P. Malone and Richard B. Roeder, University of Washington Press, 1976; and *Territorial Politics and Government in Montana, 1864-89,* by Clark C. Spence, University of Illinois Press, 1975.

Finally, to add an occasional national and sometimes international dimension to the story of Helena, standard encyclopedias were consulted as well as the large-format *Mid—Century America, 1900-1950,* published in 1950 by Year, Inc., Los Angeles.

Index

A
Aeronautics and flight, 140, 164-166, 178-179
Alder Gulch. *See* Virginia City
Algeria Shrine Temple, 153
Anderson, Carl, 152
Anderson, Forrest, 207, 224
Anderson, Julian, 109, 132, 135, 209
Arcade Building, 106, 218, 223
Archie Bray Foundation, 195
Aronson, J. Hugo, 105, 188, 190, 201
Art and artists, 214-217
Ashby, S. C., 101, 103, 106
Aspen Building, 137, 222
Assay Office, 20, 27, 29, 52, 83
Atlas Block, 136, 206, 218
Ayers, Roy E., 179

B
Babcock, Betty, 64, 104, 208, 209
Babcock, Tim, 64, 104, 208
Bailey Block, 150, 152, 153
Bannack, 10, 11, 76
Barbeau, Eddie, 174, 177, 211
Baucus, Jean Sheriff, 113, 158, 199, 200
Baucus, John J., 190, 210, 224
Baucus, Max, 7, 202, 224, 226
Beidler, John X., 24, 25
Black residents, 109, 110
Blake Block, 27, 29
Bluestone House, 78, 206
Board of Trade, 18, 28, 103
Bonner, John W., 175, 188
Boston Block, 137, 218
Bridge (State) Street, 19, 33, 34, 51, 88
Bristol Hotel, 78, 88
Broadwater, Charles A., 47, 56, 57-58, 60, 80, 85, 106
Broadwater Hotel and Natatorium, 57, 58-59, 124, 132
Broadway Fish Market, 92
Butte, 11, 138, 142

C
Campbell, William C., 56
Camp Rimini, 174, 177
Cannon, Charles W., 56, 85
Cannon, Henry, 111
Canyon Ferry, 41, 42, 43, 85, 86-87, 112, 175, 185, 188, 189
Capital Brewery, 49
Carroll College, 123, 145, 146-147, 162, 167, 178, 191
Carroll, Bishop John Patrick, 145, 146, 147
Carter, Thomas H., 57, 61, 101, 103
Cathedral of the Sacred Hearts of Jesus and Mary, 52, 62
Centennial (1964): train, 206, 207; ball, 208
Chessman Reservoir, 71
Chessman, William A., 60, 96, 105, 133
Chevallier, Phillip, 111
Chinese residents, 29, 108, 109
City/County Building, 34, 82, 94, 206
City/County Library (new), 206
City Hall and Fire Department (old), 89
Civic Center. *See* Algeria Shrine Temple
Clark, Robert "Scratchy", 187
Clark, William A., 11, 57, 80, 81, 118
Clarke, China, 88, 93, 102
Clarke, Malcolm, 20, 35
Colwell Building, 10, 20, 136, 206, 221
Community Concerts, 196, 197
Confederate Gulch. *See* Diamond City
Conrad, John H., 102
Conrad, William G., 34, 93
Cooney, Frank H., 163
Cooper, Gary, 175, 185
Cory, Fanny, 134
Cosmopolitan Hotel, 92, 137
Cougill, Vern, 206
Cowan, John, 10, 16
Crabb, John, 10, 16
Crump, Mr. and Mrs. James, 110
Cruse, Mary (Mamie), 61, 62
Cruse, Thomas, 38, 39, 56, 61-62, 81, 102, 118, 138, 144, 145
Current Topics Club, 148, 181
Custer Battle, 28

D
Daly, Marcus, 11, 57, 81
DeCamp, Ralph, 99, 113, 120
Dempsey, Jack, 179
Denver Block, 68, 230, 231
Depression (economic), 28, 80, 81, 135, 139, 153, 162-164
Dewey, Thomas E., 183
Diamond Block, 73, 206, 220
Diamond City, 11, 38, 40
Diamond R Freight Line, 35, 37, 56
Dixon, Cromwell, 141
Dixon, Joseph M., 120, 152
Donovan, Pat, 225
Drew, Jr. and Co. (merchants), 50

Drum Lummon Mine. *See* Marysville

E
Earhart, Amelia, 162, 165
Earthquakes, 11, 155, 163, 171
Edgerton, Sidney, 10, 24, 76, 81
Edwards Street, 33, 102
Eisenhower, Dwight D., 186, 188
Electric Block, 78, 81, 85, 106
Elkhorn, 38, 41
Erickson, John E., 152, 153, 157, 162

F
Federal Building (new), 82, 171, 206
Federal Building (old). *See* City/County Building
Fergus, James A., 98
Ferguson, Bill, 158
Fires, 11, 28, 29, 30-31, 132, 152, 159, 184
Fire Tower, 32, 217, 221, 230-231
First Special Service Force, 95, 172-176
Fisk, Robert, 18, 28, 29, 46
Fletcher, Robert "Bob," 203
Flowerree, D. A. G., 85, 101, 111
Ford, Nathaniel, 109, 110
Ford, Sam C., 178, 179, 183
Fort Harrison, 58, 81, 95, 138, 143, 163, 172, 175, 176, 204-205, 207
Four Georgians, 10, 11, 17, 46
Frederick, Robert T., 174, 176

G
Gallagher, Larry, 206
Galusha, Hugh, 210
Gans & Klein (merchants), 49, 78, 136
Gates of the Mountains, 99, 100, 113
Gold Block, 73, 132, 150, 159
Golden Canyon Days, 175, 185
Goodkind Building, 218, 223
Governor's Mansion (Original), 77, 96, 103, 105
Grandon Hotel, 206
Granite Block, 150, 152, 153, 159
Great Northern Railway, 57, 80, 81, 123, 145
Gunn, Milton S., 133, 182

H
Hanging Tree, 11, 18, 24, 25
Harrell, Charles "Chuck," 179
Harvey Hotel, 206
Hauser Dam, 64, 188, 189
Hauser Mansion, 104
Hauser, Samuel T., 46, 56, 57, 58, 64-65, 81, 103, 104, 111, 132, 133, 145, 188, 194, 221
Hawthorne School, 78, 94
Haymarket Square, 94, 97
Haynes, F. Jay, 38, 39, 58, 78, 84, 192
Hedges, Cornelius, 66-67, 106
Helena Brewery, 49
Helena High School: in 1876, 192; in 1890, 97, 192; on wheels, 193; football team, 131; orchestra, 129; present building, 188; band, 197
Helena Symphony Society, 196
Hensley, Josephine (Chicago Joe), 90
Hibbard, A. T., 158, 179, 203, 210
Hibbard, Henry, 158, 190
Hibbard, Margaret, 113, 122, 131, 149, 158, 169
Hilger, Judge Nicholas, 99, 100, 113
Hill, James J., 47, 57, 123, 145
Hillen, Rev. Dan, 228
Holter, Anton M., 34, 41, 68-70, 85, 94, 111, 125, 188
Holter Dam, 113, 188
Holter Hardware, 69, 70
Holter, Norman B., 70, 133, 182, 203
Holter, Norman J. "Jeff," 68, 70, 182, 209, 230
Huber, Philip Henry "Shorty," 51
Hunthausen, Bishop Raymond, 75, 191

I
Intermountain Union College, 155, 163
International Hotel, 30, 33, 78, 88
Iron Front Building, 83
Irrigation, 183, 188, 190

J
Jorud, L. H., 160, 171
Judge, Blanche, 199, 200
Judge, Tom, 199, 224

K
Keil, Carrie Drummond, 196, 197
Kessler Brewery and Brickyard, 71, 84, 136, 163
Kessler, Nicholas, 60, 71-72, 221
King and Gillette, 20, 35
Kirkendall, Hugh, 35, 86
Kleinschmidt, Theodore H., 103
Kluge House, 22
Kohrs, Conrad, 21, 111

L
LaLonde Building, 150
Larson, Peter, 97, 105, 145
Lawrence Street, 93, 94
Lee, Darryl, 198, 206
Lewis and Clark County Courthouse, 77, 82
Lewis and Clark Expedition, 10, 68
Lindbergh, Charles A., 152, 156-157, 162
Lissner, Marcus, 33
Lissner School, 51, 88
Little Red School, 53
Loble, Henry, 227
Loble, Lester, 131, 170
Loy, Myrna, 184

M
Mackay Collection, Russell art, 194
McKay, R. H., 126, 127
Maginnis, Martin, 74, 80
Magnolia Hotel, 33
Mansfield, Mike, 188, 202
Marlow Theatre, 171, 220
Marshall, Walter and Doris, 212
Marysville, 36, 56, 61-62, 172
Masonic Lodge and Temples, 17, 33, 66, 67, 78, 206, 225
Meagher, Thomas F., 121
Meloy, Peter, 185, 195
Merchants Bank, 33
Merchants Hotel, 81, 83
Meredith, Claude, 207
Metcalf, Lee, 202, 224
Methodist-Episcopal Church, 18, 52
Miller, D. J., 10
Mimnaugh, Terry, 217
Ming, John, 107; mansion, 102; opera house, 107
Mitchell, Sam H., 178
Montana Central Railroad, 39, 47, 57, 58
Montana Club, 80, 89, 118, 132-135, 181, 182, 188, 203, 210
Montana Company Ltd., 39
Montana Historical Society, 12, 76, 194
Montana National Bank, 57, 184
Montana National Guard, 95, 142, 143, 178
Montana State Fairs, 125-128
Montana Wesleyan College, 53, 155
Montgomery, George, 175
Morgan, Robert F., 207, 215
Morrison, R. E. "Bud," 166, 179
Mount Helena, 101, 129, 131, 175; mall fountain, 222
Mount St. Charles College. *See* Carroll College
Mullan Trail, 35
Mullan Tunnel, 47, 108
Munger, Chub, 156
Murray, James E., 202

N
Neighborhood Center, 206
Nevada City, 11
New York Store, 136, 150, 153, 159
Norris, Edwin L., 125
Northern Pacific Railroad, 28, 46, 47, 50, 76
Novelty Block, 92, 206, 218, 221, 223

O
O'Connell, James E. "Eddy," 154, 203, 224

P
Parades: early, 26; fire department, 33; patriotic, 122, 123; Vigilante, 168
Parchen Block, 78, 102, 132, 206
Parchen, Henry M., 60, 85, 88, 102
Paxson, Edgar S., 120, 215
Paynes Hotel, 34, 94
Pedestrian Mall, 15, 222-223
Pittsburgh Block, 152
Placer Hotel, 135, 218, 222, 225
Police Department: 1891, 89
Population, 28, 46, 139, 174, 188
Potter, John, 20
Potts, Benjamin F., 28, 194
Power Block, 73, 75, 81, 150, 159
Power, Charles Benton, 73, 74, 75, 97, 101, 103, 110, 153, 179
Power Mansion, 75, 79, 94
Power, Thomas C., 61, 73-75, 80, 82, 85, 97, 100, 111
Prickly Pear Canyon. *See* Wolf Creek Canyon
Prohibition, 135, 138, 162-164
Public Library and Auditorium, 97, 106

Q
Quigley, John, 170, 188, 200, 201
Quigley, Kitty Ann, 207, 208

R
Rankin, Jeannette, 118, 120, 138, 217
Rankin, Wellington D., 170, 186
Reber, Joseph B., 224

Reeder's Alley, 48, 79, 217
Reinig, Edward, 145
Rickards, John E., 80
Roosevelt, Franklin D., 106, 162, 188
Roosevelt, Theodore, 106, 118, 123, 132
Russell, Charles M., 111, 113, 122, 135, 155, 182, 188, 202, 215

S
St. Helena Cathedral, 52, 61, 62, 138, 144-145, 163, 170, 191, 228, 229
St. Peter's Hospital, 180
St. Vincent's Academy, 52, 163
Saloons, 90-91
Sanders, Wilbur F., 10, 24, 25, 29, 32, 56, 73, 76-77, 120
Sands Brothers (merchants), 93
Schwinden, Ted, 103, 217, 224
Securities Building, 65, 84, 221
Shafer, Clem L., 89, 123, 196, 198, 199
Sheriff, Court, 42, 43, 86
Sheriff, Fred, 114, 158, 162, 165, 170
Shope, Irvin "Shorty," 215
Shore, Dinah, 175
Sieben, Henry, 11, 113, 114-115, 158; mansion, 104; ranch, 111, 113, 114, 115
Smith, Robert B., 119, 194
Smith, Tucker, 216
Stadler & Kaufman (ranchers), 111
Stanley, Reginald, 10, 16
State Capitol Building, 116, 118, 119-221, 122, 130
Steamboat Block, 73, 94
Steamboats, 74
Steele, Fanny Sperry, 129
Stewart, Sam V., 105, 138, 139
Stinson, Katherine, 141
Street Railroads, 50, 85, 152
Stuart, Granville, 64, 111
Stuart, James E., 56

T
Taft, William Howard, 123, 146
Tatem, B. H., 133, 135, 149
Telephones, 84
Tennis Club, 98
Ten Mile Creek, 18, 68, 71, 183
Theatre: Little Theatre, 185; Calamity Ranch production, 198, 199; home talent, 199, 200; Brewery, 49, 212; Grand Street, 213; Second Story Cinema/Helena Film Society, 214
Thompson, Wanna, 190
Tobin, Jane Power, 73, 101, 103, 110, 217
Tobin, Tom, 73, 101, 103, 110, 182
Toole, Joseph Kemp, 60, 80, 82, 118
Toole, K. Ross, 188, 194
Tour Train, 201
Train, E. H., 48, 108, 109

U
Unionville, 38
Urban Renewal, 11, 204-223

V
Vaughn, Robert, 35
Vigilantes, 24, 25, 76
Virginia City, 10, 11, 28, 38, 68, 76, 98, 149
Von Herbulis, Albert O., 144, 146

W
Walsh, Thomas J., 120, 138, 152, 162-163, 169-170
Walters, Nils P., 89, 123, 155
Ward, Rev. John, 228
Weaver, John B., 202, 214, 222
Weggenman Building. *See* Colwell Building.
Weinstein Brothers (merchants), 160
Weiss cafe, 154
Wheeler, Burton K., 120, 138, 152, 174
Whitlatch-Union Mine, 38
Wickes, 38, 39, 40, 64
Wilder, A. H., 57
Willard, Helen, 178, 180, 185
Willard, John, 209
Wilson, Woodrow, 138, 139
Winestine, Belle, 169, 217
Wolf Creek Canyon, 35
Word-Conrad Mansion, 44, 102, 132
World War I, 138-143
World War II, 172-179

Y
Yaw Yaw Ditch, 18